Cricket Around The World

Cricket Around The World

Anton Rippon

MOORLAND PUBLISHING

Title page: Eighty thousand people pack into the Calcutta stadium for the Fourth Test between India and England in January 1982 (Adrian Murrell)

'For my father, who taught me about cricket.'

ISBN 0 86190 055 3

Printed in the U.K. by Butler and Tanner Ltd, Frome for Moorland Publishing Company Ltd, PO Box 2, 9-11 Station Street, Ashbourne, Derbyshire, DE6 1DZ, England

Picture sources. Illustrations have been provided by: John Grainger Picture Agency: p 10, 11, 17, 19, 20, 29, 30, 37, 41, 59, 61, 66, 70, 73, 77, 88, 95, 98, 110, 112, 128, 138, 140, 141, 152, 161, 177; Adrian Murrell: p 51, 124, 125, 166, 167, 169, 170, 190, 192; Illustrated London News: p 9; Central Press Photos: p 14 (upper and lower), 16 (all three), 42, 45, 49, 50, 67, 131, 145, 147, 164, 178, 182 (left and right), 183; Sporting Pictures: p 83, 121, 144, 188; Patrick Eager: p 84.

Contents

Introduction

The soldiers, sailors, colonial administrators and traders who took cricket from Britain and spread its gospel around the world in the eighteenth century could have had little idea of the immense impact that their game would have on lands as diverse as Australasia, the Indian sub-continent, South Africa and the Caribbean.

Well over a century later, cricket is a world game, struggling against many problems but always, in the final analysis, capturing the hearts of those who play and watch it. The problems of the South African controversy, of slow over-rates, of certain Test captains who have apparently forgotten about the spectators, and of the occasional bouts of loutish behaviour by one or two international players, are all obstacles which cricket has yet to overcome. But in the end, the game will survive all these crises, as it has survived all others.

This book, while having to pay occasional lip service to them, is not primarily concerned with the controversies of the game. Its sole aim is to look at the origins of cricket in each Test-playing country — including South Africa which has been denied a Test now for over a decade, — and chart the progress of each Test team to the present day. The one-day game is largely ignored; and there is, perhaps, less emphasis on the detail of the most recent series which are already well-documented and fresh in everyone's mind. By taking each country individually, there is the danger of repetition, though the author has tried to avoid that wherever possible.

It is essentially the story of the fortunes of Test cricket around the world, with the fortunes of England intertwined throughout.

Author's Note

It had often been said that the cricket book which contains no errors does not exist and it is a fact that records are being constantly updated and revised, particularly as a result of the splendid efforts of the Association of Cricket Statisticians. The author is especially indebted, then to Mr Peter Wynne-Thomas, secretary of that Association, who read the proofs of this book and used his own immense knowledge of cricket facts and figures to correct some errors.

England

Cricket Tour to . . . America

The year 1859 was one of immense significance for the game of cricket. In that year the first-ever overseas cricket tour took place. Mr E. Wilder, of Sussex, and Mr W.P. Pickering of Montreal, spent that summer arranging a visit by a team of English cricketers, captained by George Parr, to North America. The team sailed from Liverpool, en route for Quebec, on 7 September, arriving on 22 September and two days later began their programme with an eight-wicket defeat of XXII* of Lower Canada at Montreal. Parr's team, which included such names as John Lillywhite and John Wisden, as well as Julius Caesar — yes, that was his real name! — went undefeated on this historic tour, following up their inaugural victory with defeats of XXII of the United States in New York, XXII of Philadelphia, XXII of Hamilton, and XXII of the United States and Canada at Rochester. The trip was a resounding financial success — after expenses each player earned himself something like £90 each — and the concept of the overseas tour was born. It was to be a lusty infant, and over 120 years later, the tradition started by George Parr and his men is still one of sport's most enduring.

But who were these cricketers who set the precedent during the first part of Queen Victoria's reign? Their captain, George Parr, was the 'Lion of the North', Nottinghamshire batsman and a mainstay of the great All England XI. Parr was one of the great batsmen of the period. Born in 1826, he became famous for his leg side hitting and on his first appearance for the All England XI he scored a century at Leicester. That, consider, was against a team of odds which fielded far more than the usual eleven fielders. Twelve years later he was boarding the boat at Liverpool as the first overseas touring captain, leading a side of twelve players equally divided between the All England XI and the United England XI, the teams which played almost all the important cricket in England at that time.

The All England XI had been formed in 1846 by another Nottinghamshire man, William Clarke, who was responsible for the laying-out of the cricket ground at Trent Bridge, which became the headquarters of his great team. Clarke's All England XI played its first match against XXII of Sheffield at Hyde Park Ground, Sheffield, in August 1846 and from then until its demise in about 1880, when recognisable county cricket took over, the team travelled the length and breadth of the country, drawing large crowds wherever it played. Following Clarke's death in 1856 — three years before that first overseas tour — George Parr took over the

* Matches 'against odds' were quite common when first-class sides met weaker opposition.

reins. When Parr retired, another Nottinghamshire player, Richard Daft, captained the side and also led a touring team to America in 1879.

But, before all this, there was a split in the ranks of the All England XI when players began to tire of Clarke's blunt manner and apparent unwillingness to part with a realistic match fee. In 1852, John Wisden and Jem Dean broke away to form the United England XI, another professional touring team which played its first match against XX Gentlemen of Hampshire at Southampton in August of that year. Until Clarke's death the relationship between the two teams was not a happy one. But a year after the demise of the All England XI's founder, the two sides met at Lord's for a match to benefit the Cricketers' Fund Friendly Society. The annual fixture was played at Lord's until 1867 when a dispute between the professionals of the North and South saw the match transferred to Manchester. At about this time there were further rumblings in the ranks of England's premier professional cricketers and a United South of England XI was born from the United England team.

So cricket's first overseas touring party was drawn from the first two professional sides which themselves were formed to tour England. John Wisden, original member of Clarke's side until he left to start the United England XI, stood only 5ft 4in tall. The son of a Brighton builder, John Wisden went to live with the Sussex wicketkeeper, Tom Box, after the death of Wisden senior, and it was Box who taught young Wisden his cricket. He first played for Sussex in 1845, the year before he accepted Clarke's invitation, and though short of stature — and weighing only about seven stones — Wisden became a fearsome fast bowler who rejoiced in the nickname of the 'Little Wonder'. John Wisden was a fine cricketer. In 1851 alone he took 455 wickets — 279 of them clean-bowled — and in the four seasons 1848-51 captured 1,307 wickets. In 1850, at Lord's, he clean-bowled all ten South batsman; and when Bramall Lane, Sheffield, was opened in 1855 with a match between Yorkshire and Sussex, Wisden showed his prowess with the bat by scoring 148. Thus, he was one of the finest cricketers of the period, though he is best remembered, not for his cricketing prowess, but for *Wisden Cricketers' Almanack*, which he first brought out in 1864, and which is still the cricketer's 'bible'.

All the other members of Parr's 1859 side were renowned throughout England. John Lillywhite was a fine all-rounder who hit the ball hard, fielded brilliantly, especially at cover point, and whose round-arm bowling — first of fearsome pace and later more cunning 'twisters' — earned him a place in any representative side. The name Lillywhite echoes down cricket's corridor of fame, not only because of the great deeds performed by the Lillywhite family, but also because of their connections with the sports-goods-manufacturing business.

Surrey was well represented in the first touring side with all-rounder, William Caffyn, wicketkeeper Tom Lockyer, the fine batsman and understudy wicketkeeper H.H. Stephenson, who led the first side to Australia in 1861-2, and another great batsman, the splendidly-named Julius Caesar. Caffyn was a batsman who put together many big scores — many of them well into three figures when the scoring of a century was an even greater feat than it is today — and bowled medium pace. Also an accomplished fielder, Caffyn went to Australia with both H.H. Stephenson's team in 1861-2, and with Parr's side of 1863-4, after which he stayed to coach and was a great influence on the early development of Australian

Thomas Hearne, the Middlesex professional who was a member of the first English team to tour Australia in 1861-2

cricket. Julius Caesar was, as his name might imply, a great nineteenth-century cricket character, no doubt having much to live up to with such a famous appelation. John Jackson was another stalwart of the All England XI and he once bowled six batsmen in seven balls playing against XXII of Uppingham.

These, then were some of the men who undertook the historic tour. But why to America? Ask the uninitiated where the first-ever overseas cricket tour was and nine out of ten will probably answer Australia. And the fact that the North American continent was the destination of George Parr's team is greeted with incredulity, for surely, in the United States cricket is treated as some kind of joke? The truth is that at one time, America was one of the world's leading cricket countries. They may never have played a Test Match, but up until World War I, American cricket, led by the redoubtable Philadelphian team, was a match for most sides who cared to visit that continent. As the United States and Canada provided the opposition for the first tourists, it is as well to examine the story of cricket in those two countries.

Not unnaturally, considering the close links between Britain and America, cricket was exported there quite early — certainly no later than its arrival in other outposts of what was then the empire. References to the game are found in America at the beginning of the eighteenth century and the scores of a match between New York and a London XI (presumably based permanently in America and not a touring side) have survived from 1751. By 1760, Boston boasted at least one cricket club and in 1844 the first match took place between the United States and Canada. This makes it the oldest series of matches between two countries and it was revived in 1963 after a break of fifty-one years. Two years after Parr's side toured

America the Civil War broke out and this had a deterimental effect on cricket. More than one cricket historian is of the opinion that the war, which saw baseball become established as a favourite among the troops, cost cricket dearly on the North American continent.

Nevertheless, when the war ended, cricket still had a strong foothold. In 1884 the Gentlemen of Philadelphia became the first team from the United States to visit England where they played eighteen matches against amateur sides, winning eight and drawing five. Philadelphia had boasted a club as early as 1831 and Philadelphia CC was formed in 1854, the Germantown CC a year later. It is still one of the strongholds of American cricket and it was here that America first met an overseas touring side on level terms when they drew with the first full Australian team to make a tour to England. The Australians, besides drawing that one first-class match, played five other games, winning four and drawing the other. In 1889 the Gentlemen of Philadelphia made another tour to England — again all the matches were second-class — and they won four and drew five of their twelve games.

Despite the fast-growing popularity of baseball, American cricket had gained enough ground by 1897 for the Philadelphians to visit Britain once more, this time to play all first-class opposition, including MCC. Captained by G.S. Patterson, the Philadelphians played fifteen matches and won two — against Sussex and Warwickshire — as well as having the upper hand in drawn games against Somerset and Nottinghamshire. Two other matches were drawn and the star of the tour, so far as the Americans were concerned, was the fast bowler J.B. King. King took seven for thirteen against Sussex — including the wicket of the great Ranjitsinhji

The England team which played against Australia at Trent Bridge in 1899 - the first-ever Test to be staged at this famous ground. W.G. Grace, aged 50 years 320 days, was playing his last Test. Only Wilfred Rhodes played Test cricket at a greater age - and he was making his debut in this match. Back, left to right: R.G. Barlow (umpire), Tom Hayward, George Hirst, William Gunn, J.T. Hearne, William Storer, William Brockwell, V.A. Titchmarsh (umpire). Seated: C.B. Fry, K.S. Ranjitsinhji, Dr W.G. Grace, F.S. Jackson. On ground: Wilfred Rhodes, John Tyldesley

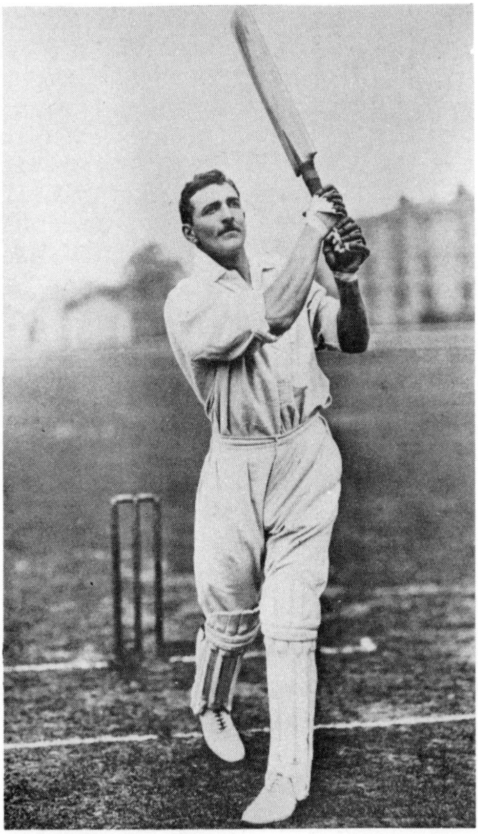

C.B. Fry, legendary English batsman of Edwardian days, was so revered that he was once offered the Kingdom of Albania! Fry played soccer for England and Southampton, for whom he appeared in an FA Cup Final, held the long jump record for 21 years, and played in twenty-six Tests.

who he clean-bowled first ball — and ended the tour with seventy-two wickets at 24.20 each. The Philadelphians made two further visits to Britain. In 1903 they won six out of fourteen first-class matches, and in 1908, four out of ten. In their last tour the Philadelphians were captained by John Barton King who took eighty-seven wickets at 11.01 apiece.

Australia sent several sides to play the Philadelphians and the Americans beat the tourists in 1893, 1896 and 1912, but it was a shift of emphasis by the larger Philadelphia clubs which saw the demise of first-class cricketers from the United States. Conscious of the need to run the clubs more economically and with greater cost-effectiveness, they gradually switched from being solely cricket clubs to country clubs which catered for other more 'instant' sports such as tennis. Of course, cricket was still — and is still — played, but to a much reduced standard. One of the great figures in inter-war American cricket was the legendary Sir C. Aubrey Smith, the former Cambridge, Sussex and England player. Smith became a film actor and started up the famous Hollywood cricket colony. He was president of the South California Cricket Association until his death in 1948. The United States Cricket Association, formed in St Louis in 1961, was elected an associate member of the International Cricket Conference in 1965 and the game is still thriving in California, Chicago, Philadelphia, St Louis, and in New York where West Indian immigrants ensure its survival.

In Canada the game has a strong following today in the Toronto and Montreal areas. Introduced to the country by British Army personnel in the latter half of the eighteenth century, cricket soon spread and in 1840 Toronto played a match against New York. The first overseas tour by Parr's team was sponsored by the Montreal club and in 1868, Edgar Willsher took out another party of English tourists, to be followed, in 1872, by another team captained by R.A. Fitzgerald, then secretary of MCC. Fitzgerald's team included W.G. Grace, the Hon G. (later Lord) Harris, and A.N. Hornby. It was the first all-amateur team from England to tour abroad, thus chalking up another historic first for North American cricket. Several Canadian sides have visited England, though the first tour in 1880 was abandoned due to difficulties, not least of which was the Canadian captain being jailed halfway through the tour as an army deserter.

For two decades, one great figure in Canadian cricket was W.G. Wookey of Toronto. Against the United States he once took eight for 4 and six for 24, and in 1920 claimed 115 wickets at just over four runs each. Though only one first-class match has been played in Canada since the war, when MCC beat Canada on matting at Toronto in September 1951, the game there has been steadily improving and in May 1975 Eastern Canada beat the Australians, who were making their way to England, by five wickets in a one-day match in Toronto. Fourteen years earlier the first Canadian Inter-Provincial Tournament was held at Calgary and won by British Columbia. The Canadian Cricket Association was elected an associate member of the International Cricket Conference in 1968 and Canada has taken part in the World Cup held in England.

So, the hosts of the first tour are still playing the game, though its development has been left far behind that of the Test-playing countries. Cricket is also played in many other countries, and does not belong exclusively to those countries of what became the Commonwealth, though in almost every case it is the British influence which has introduced and largely fostered the game. On the South American continent, for instance, British businessmen see that cricket is played in Argentina, Brazil and Chile. Many African countries play cricket, particularly in East Africa, and the game is alive in Israel, Malaysia, Hong Kong, Singapore, Fiji, and even Papua and New Guinea. In Europe,

Worcester Cathedral provides part of the backdrop for what was at one time the traditional starting point for every Test team which toured England

cricketers can be seen in West Germany, Denmark and Holland. Indeed, the Dutch enjoyed a famous last-over victory against Bobby Simpson's 1964 Australians, and more than one young Dutchman has attracted the attentions of English county sides, though with little or no subsequent success.

The development of the game in the major Test-playing countries, other than England, is discussed in the following chapters and takes us from its early days up to each nation's first Test Match, after which we look at the story of the Test team. In every instance it will be seen that English cricket was the dominating influence in those earliest years, for without the soldiers, sailors, administrators and traders who took cricket to these countries, there would be no Test Matches today. But it is interesting to ponder here on the future of the game, particularly in England. Indeed it is almost ironical, to find that the influence of overseas cricketers on English cricket has had, not only many beneficial effects, but also effects which have probably done the English national side no good at all.

Cricket in England has changed dramatically over the last twenty years. We have seen the end of the distinction between amateur and professional, the introduction of 'instant' one-day cricket, some of the restrictions of which have spilled into the three-day championship, and the introduction of star names from overseas. It has been argued that the ending of 'shamateurism' in English cricket means that the county game is now restricted to a small number of professionals, into which the talented amateur has no chance of breaking. Certainly, counties would be loath to introduce the amateur players of old, often schoolteachers, into the side for the school holidays, which was what used to happen. No doubt the cricketers' own trade union would have something to say if that practice was resumed.

The presenters of the argument hold that this has made cricket that much poorer in that good-class club players cannot now hope to play for their counties, which greatly restricts the possibility of netting all the available talent. They hold up the demise of the Philadelphians as an example. That team played largely undisturbed by new players between 1890 and 1910, so good were the men already in the side. The result was a lack of motivation in up-and-coming young cricketers who saw no possible chance of improving their status. Of course, all sportsmen must have that carrot held before them. But first-class soccer did away with its amateurs long before cricket abandoned them. Soccer is still going strong, even though it too has its difficulties, and it is a fact that in every sport there are talented amateurs who would have made the professional ranks, given the right break. There must be club cricketers, club footballers, and club everybody else who would have made the grade. But the sports are surely none the worse for that. It is like an entrance examination for which there are only a certain number of places. The standard is raised and only the very best go through.

The introduction of one-day cricket has had a much more profound effect on the county game. Without it, it is difficult to imagine just what place in our society cricket might hold today. Lovers of the three-day game — and I include myself in those ranks — were largely appalled at the new, almost vulgar game with its restrictions on the number of overs each bowler could deliver, and its down to earth approach. The quite, sedate calm of English county grounds was replaced by the beery hooting from a section of people who would probably never otherwise have entered a

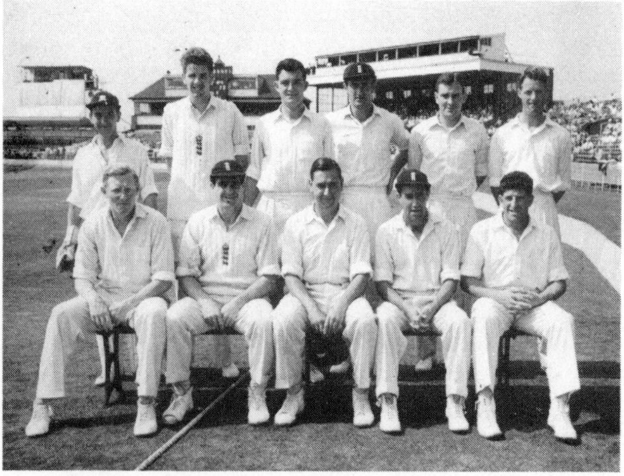

England team which played India at Old Trafford in 1959. Back row left to right: Roy Swetman, Harold Rhodes, Geoff Pullar, Ted Dexter, Ray Illingworth, John Mortimore. Front: Mike Smith, Fred Trueman, Colin Cowdrey (captain), Gilbert Parkhouse, Ken Barrington

cricket ground. It brought the incredible sight of policemen on English county grounds, and on at least one occasion the sad sight of a pitched battle in the stands. But that has more to do with the state of English society rather than the state of cricket. It was at one time possible to enter a football ground with wife and daughter and stand on the terraces undisturbed. Nowadays the average family man palls at that thought.

But even after shifting the blame for that, some people still like to argue that one-day cricket — started with the Gillette Cup in 1963, to be followed by the John Player League, the Benson and Hedges Cup, the NatWest Trophy which replaced the Gillette, and the one-day internationals,

England team which met India at Old Trafford June 1974. Back row left to right: Keith Fletcher, Chris Old, Bob Willis, Tony Greig, Mike Hendrick, Dennis Amiss. Front: Derek Underwood, Geoff Boycott, Mike Denness (captain), John Edrich, Alan Knott

a sort of 'instant Test' — have ruined our game. To them it has to be pointed out that without one-day cricket, it is unlikely that there would be any professional cricket at all. It brought much-needed revenue to the county clubs at a time when the average weekday crowd was the legendary 'two men and a dog'. And not only did it bring cash in its own right, it also recreated new interest in the three-day game. Surely, far more people are now likely to call in on a Schweppes County Championship match in the 1980s, because they were first drawn by one-day cricket, even if the excitement is not so instantaneous.

Once people become interested in their county club through the NatWest, JPL or B & H, it follows that they will follow up that interest in the three-day game whenever they can. I know of many people drawn to cricket by the one-day game and who now take an interest in championship matches which that competition alone could not provoke. One-day cricket has also improved fielding standards beyond the imagination of the cricketers of twenty years ago, some of whom were quite happy to stick out a boot as the ball fizzed past. Close catching has always thrilled; now outfielding has been elevated to an art which brings gasps of admiration and rounds of applause in the same way as does a fine cover drive. Although they are not *first-class* games, let no one try to claim that the winning of the JPL or one of the knockout competitions, is not equally as important to the victors as the winning of the Schweppes County Championship itself.

Of course, one-day cricket has had a deterimental effect on the game in certain ways. The restriction on innings has resulted in young middle-order batsmen never having the luxury of being able to build an innings in the way in which their predecessors did; and the blight has spread over into the three-day game with the same effect. One-day cricket also bred a new species of bowler. Quite naturally, whenever you try to make a game more attacking, you succeed in making it more defensive. When the object is to score as many runs as possible, the object of the other side must be to stop as many runs as possible. Out went the spinners who gave the ball air and could afford to 'buy' their wickets. In came the spinners who pushed the ball through flat. In too came the medium-pace seamers, intent on being economical instead of trying to take wickets. Eight overs for ten runs and no wickets on a Sunday is better than eight overs for thirty runs and two wickets. Also we had the sight of a ring of fielders strung around the boundary as shadows lengthened. Cricket has tampered with its own laws enough, but the introduction of fielding circles in 1982 seems to be working, in that a captain must allow batsmen the chance to find the ropes instead of taking some extraordinarily long singles.

So, cricket is changing all the time. One of the biggest changes in the English game over the past decade has been the introduction of overseas players into the championship. Prior to this, one had to go to the leagues to see the stars of other countries. And the arrival of a Test team from Australia or West Indies was an event of great excitement. Not any more. Today, English cricket fans can see the component parts of the West Indian eleven, for instance, on most county grounds. And the introduction of overseas players has also meant less places for players qualified to play for England. The story is told of the former chairman of the England selectors journeying to watch a particular Derbyshire player, only to spend almost the whole day watching John Wright, a New Zealander, and Peter Kirsten, a South African, dominate the game. A glance at the

English national averages will also reveal the dominance of overseas players when a good seventy-five per cent of the leaders are not qualified to play for England. That can only mean that the England team is the poorer. And yet, how much poorer, too, would be the county game if the overseas players were slowly phased out.

All of these factors have a direct bearing on the future of Test cricket. One can only reflect that if each series played could include at least one match like that between England and Australia at Headingley in 1981, then there would never be any need to fear for the health of international cricket. In the final analysis, after the laws have been changed, the pattern of play altered, the skills and tactics modified to suit the changing face of the game, after all that, it is still the great individual performances of cricketers which will ensure cricket's survival. The deeds of Grace, Hobbs, Jessop and Botham, of Bradman, Miller, Lindwall and Lillee, of Sobers and the rest have always triumphed. One golden moment makes all the darker days worthwhile.

Left: Botham's form suffered when he became England skipper. Once relieved of the burden he became even more devastating as an all-rounder of world class

Centre: Geoff Boycott, yet another who answered the call to give South Africa a taste of international cricket once more

Right: Alan Knott whose decision to play in South Africa with a 'rebel' England team no doubt cost him any further Test appearances

Australia

The Oldest Rivals

On 15 March 1877, the portly, bearded figure of Alfred Shaw, Nottinghamshire slow-medium bowler, propelled a cricket ball towards the Kentish-born batsman, Charles Bannerman, at Melbourne Cricket Ground and what is now regarded as the first-ever Test Match got underway. Shaw, playing for James Lillywhite's professional touring team, and Bannerman, for a combined Melbourne and Sydney team, did not realise that they were the first combatants of what was to become one of the most famous sporting events in the world. Of course, this 'England' team was not the best combination which could represent the country, for almost all their best batsmen of the period were amateurs, and none were in this side. Most conspicuous by his absence was W.G. Grace and after two teams of fifteen players from New South Wales, and one from Victoria, had defeated Lillywhite's side in 1876-7, some of the more confident cricketers in Australia decided that a representative team from their country could beat England at eleven-a-side. The first move was an eleven-a-side match between New South Wales and the touring team. This was drawn and two months later the combined Melbourne and Sydney team met Lillywhite's men.

The great Melbourne Cricket Ground where the first-ever Test Match was played in 1877. It grew to become the biggest cricket stadium in the world

So that is how what we now know as cricket's first Test Match was arranged. History records that Bannerman scored the first runs — he went on to make 165 retired hurt and thus also become cricket's first Test centurion — and Australia won the match by 45 runs after the left-arm spin of Thomas Kendall of Victoria took seven English wickets in their second innings. England levelled the matter when the sides met in a return game at Melbourne towards the end of that month — this time neither Bannerman nor Kendall could reproduce the form which had beaten Lillywhite's team in the first encounter — and so the first Test rubber was squared.

Cricket had been played in Australia since the turn of the century, brought to the country by the British who settled towards the end of the eighteenth century and fostered by soldiers and sailors who played matches against each other and against the authorities who ran the prison colonies. Cricket was played on pitches scraped from rough earth, and the equipment was equally spartan. In the early 1820s the Governor of New South Wales ordered wood from His Majesty's timber yard so that cricket bats might be fashioned for his son — and we can be sure that there was no willow in the batch that was sent along with some garden tools. In 1826, army and navy garrisons formed the first cricket clubs in Australia, though the only suitable ground they could find was a cow paddock in Sydney. Cow paddock or not, the Turnpike became the headquarters of Sydney cricket for some forty years and was only lost when an angry local decided that the cows should take precedence over cricket and burnt down the rough fence which enclosed the ground.

Tasmania, too, was an early centre of cricket, though its much smaller population meant that it eventually lagged far behind the game on the mainland. Hobart Town CC was formed in 1832, changed its name to the Derwent Club in 1837 and played for a while at the railway ground, though here, too, the cricketers found that cows took priority and were forced to move to the Battery Cricket Ground. Here convicts who had been used as road menders were pressed into service as part-time groundsmen after the uneven earth had resisted all attempts by a Government-loaned horse-drawn roller to level it. Even the great Melbourne CC, formed in 1838, started out on a vacant allotment before moving to Batman's Hill. When this second ground found itself right in the middle of the proposed site of Spencer Street railway station, Melbourne CC moved again, only to find that Australia's first railway line was to run through their latest ground. A fourth move took them to Richmond Paddock and what is now the great Melbourne Cricket Ground.

The first match was played on the MCG in November 1854 and the ground grew until it could accommodate what was then the world's biggest cricket match attendance when nearly 91,000 people watched a single day's play in the Fifth Test between Australia and West Indies in February 1961. Inter-colonial matches had started in 1851 with a game at Launceston between Tasmania and Victoria and on Christmas Eve 1861, the first touring team to go out to the Australian continent landed at Melbourne under the captaincy of H.H. Stephenson of Surrey. This was not the first overseas tour — George Parr's team played five games in the United States and Canada in 1859 — but it was Australia's first sight of overseas cricketers and when Stephenson's team played its first match at Melbourne against XVIII of Victoria, over 15,000 people turned up to see them. Stephenson's team won six and drew four of its twelve matches, the defeats coming against XXII of Castlemaine and a combined XXII of Victoria and New South Wales.

In June 1864 a report of the first inter-colonial match played by Queensland — against New South Wales — illustrated the grim conditions which were still endured. The *Brisbane Courier* said: 'In spite of frequent slips and capsizes, of jumpings after the ball into water holes and other mishaps made unavoidable by the appalling conditions, an amount of good play was exhibited.' Eighteen Queensland batsmen made a duck and their highest scorer in the first innings was their number twenty who managed to score 5. Stephenson's team must have experienced these sort of conditions but, nevertheless, the tour was a great success, especially for its sponsors, two gentlemen in the catering trade: C. Pond and F. Spiers, who could afford to pay each player £150 and his expenses and still net a profit in excess of £10,000 for themselves. George Parr, who had declined to join the first tourists to Australia, captained a side there in 1863-4 and in twelve games in Australia and four in New Zealand, steered them through unbeaten. Parr's team included only one amateur, E.M. Grace, and none of its matches were first-class. Neither were any of those on the third English tour to Australia, led by W.G. Grace in 1873-4.

The first English team to tour Australia included Charles Lawrence, the Middlesex and Surrey all-rounder, and it was Lawrence who stayed on to contribute much to the improving standards of Australian cricket. He coached the Sydney team, Albert Club, and engineered the first Australian team to tour England in 1868 when the Aboriginals — who included players with names like Dick-a-Dick, Twopenny, Red Cap and Mosquito. Albert Club also enjoyed the services of another English visitor, William Caffyn, also of Surrey, who toured in 1861-2 and 1863-4. This was a critical time in Australian cricket for their players were in need of experienced professional coaching of the sort which Lawrence and Caffyn could supply and which would add technique and science to their rudimentary skills. The Melbourne Club, meanwhile, produced the first man to make a century in any kind of match in Australia: F.A. Paulett who scored 120 for Married against Singles in 1839 — and the first man to score a hundred in a first-class match in Australia: R.W. Wardill who scored 110 for Victoria against New South Wales in 1867-8.

The first Australian tourists to England were the 1868 Aboriginals. This rare picture shows them playing at Derby against South Derbyshire in September of that year. They sported players with names like Dick-a-Dick, Twopenny, Mosquito, Red Cap and Curzen and after their matches gave displays of boomerang throwing

Inter-colonial rivalry also meant that the standard of cricket was improving and there were — and still are — no greater rivals than New South Wales and Victoria. Overarm bowling — legalised on 10 June 1864 — was another development which favoured Australian cricket, for the advantages of being able to bowl fast *and* derive bounce from banging the ball down with a high arm were never more apparent than on the hard, true pitches of Australia. Parr's team of 1864 brought several fast bowlers, including George Tarrant, who was to have a lasting impression on an eleven-year-old boy from Sydney who saw him bowl several times during that tour. Frederick Robert Spofforth modelled himself on Tarrant and when the Australians played their second Test Match against Lillywhite's team in 1877, Spofforth celebrated his debut with four wickets and was soon to be terrorising English batsmen on their home soil. Years later, he wrote 'I never failed in my allegiance to Tarrant and I found my constancy rewarded. The boys of my age were absolutely terrified by my deliveries.'

The first white Australian team to tour England arrived in the summer of 1878. The Australian tourists, captained by Dave Gregory, the bearded New South Wales batsman who led the side in their first two Tests, played fifteen first-class matches, winning seven and drawing four, and thirty-seven games altogether, with eighteen wins and twelve draws. Spofforth, in particular, revelled in English conditions, taking ninety-seven wickets for only 11 runs each and taking six for 4 and four for 16 at

W.L. Murdoch who played in eighteen Tests for Australia, captained them in six rubbers against England including the 1880 first Test to be played in England - and then played for England against South Africa in 1891-2 after settling in Sussex and captaining that county

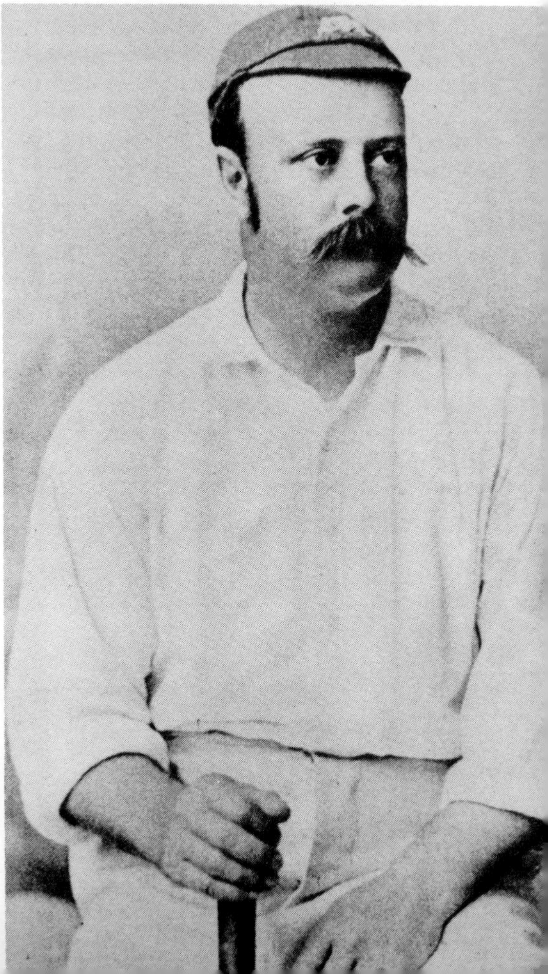

Lord's when the Australians beat MCC in one day after skittling them for 33 and 19. Spofforth ended the entire trip, which pulled in visits to New Zealand and America, with the astonishing haul of 764 wickets at less than 7 runs each.

The Australians played one Test in 1879, in January at Melbourne, at least it is now regarded as the third Test Match of all time. It was originally billed as the Gentlemen of England (with Ulyett and Emmett) versus The Australian XI.

The 'Demon', as Spofforth became known, continued his form against Lord Harris's team. He was probably the most accurate of all fast-bowlers, standing 6ft 3in and hurling the ball down with great speed and uncanny accuracy. Thirteen wickets, including the first Test Match hat-trick, saw Australia to a ten-wickets win in this third Test.

No Tests had been arranged in England in 1878, and when Australia paid another visit there in 1880, there was still no prospect of a Test. In fact, the tour was badly organised and at one stage the Australians — now captained by Billy Murdoch of New South Wales who replaced the original choice, Harry Boyle, on the boat — were reduced to advertising for matches. MCC told them that the season's fixtures had been arranged and could not be altered, and advertisements in the *Sporting Life* failed to produce any opponents. Lord Harris said he would try to arrange some matches, providing the Australian visit was not a 'commercial' undertaking, but this was unacceptable to the tourists who went north to play against odds in the Midlands and Yorkshire. Spofforth broke a finger batting against a team of eighteen players at Scarborough at the beginning of August and missed almost all the rest of the tour, whereupon Lord Harris decided at the end of August to arrange a Test after all.

So the first Test Match on English soil took place at Surrey's Kennington Oval on 6, 7, 8 September 1880. The Australians were due to play Sussex over that period, but £100 compensation from Surrey eased Sussex's disappointment. By this time in an English summer, all the self-respecting amateur players were shooting grouse on the moors. However, when the team assembled at The Oval, it was just about the best that England could field. W.G. Grace and his brother, E.M. Grace, opened the innings, with the younger G.F. Grace (to die from a chill within one month of this game) batting down the order in a team captained by Lord Harris. Australia, minus Spofforth, were completely outplayed in the first innings, W.G. Grace scoring England's first Test century with 152, and with his brother putting on 91 for the first wicket, before the Nottinghamshire left-arm fast bowler, Fred Morley, took five wickets and Australia trailed by 271 runs. But Grace was not to be the top scorer of the match. That honour fell to Murdoch who scored 153 not out to give Australia some dignity after they had followed-on. Murdoch batted number 3 in Australia's 327, but that still left England needing only 57 to win. They got the runs, but not before Boyle and George Palmer had five England wickets down for 31.

Murdoch's great innings had rescued a side which had at one time been 14 for three. From Murdoch's first ball of that second innings Morley felt he had him caught, though the umpire, H.H. Stephenson, leader of the first visit to Australia and now almost fifty years old, failed to hear the snick which would have confirmed Morley's suspicions. So England had won the first Test on her own soil. Alfred Shaw took a team to Australia in 1881-2 and lost two of the four Tests against Murdoch's team, drawing the other two which were the last undecided Tests in Australia until 1946-7 when it was decided not to play to a finish, but to limit play to a five-day duration. Spofforth played in only the last Test and took just one wicket. But when Australia sailed for England in the *Assam* in March 1882, Spofforth was aboard and ready to play a major part in the only Test of that summer — the Test which was to give birth to the legend of the Ashes.

Though Australia were toppled for only 63 in their first innings of the Oval Test in August 1882, thanks to some fine bowling from Dick Barlow and Ted Peate, England were to fare even worse at the hands of Spofforth. 'The Demon' took seven for 46 in England's first innings, yorking W.G. Grace for only 4 and generally causing havoc in the England ranks. Yet England had a lead of 38, and after Australia managed only 122 in their second innings — and had young Sammy Jones controversially run out by W.G. Grace after the youngster had gone up to prod the pitch — this still left England to score only 85 for victory. It looked a foregone conclusion and yet absolutely nothing is certain in cricket. Spofforth struck with the score at 15 by bowling Hornby; and with his very next ball sent Barlow's wicket flying. Grace, and to a lesser extent, Ulyett and the Hon Alfred Lyttelton, took England nearer their target but with 15 runs still needed, England were six wickets down. Spofforth had five of them and two balls later he claimed his sixth victim when he bowled Read. At 75 Lucas, who had spent twenty overs making five runs, played on to Spofforth. With the score unaltered, Murdoch caught Barnes off Boyle and it was 75 for nine, the last seven wickets having fallen for only 24 runs. Out came Peate with three balls to face and perhaps dwelling on the fact that he had already scored 20 off this same Australian attack earlier in the season. Whatever his feelings, Peate decided to attack. From the first ball he swung out and while the ball dropped perilously close to a fielder down at long leg, he and Charles Studd ran two. Heartened by this apparently successful tactic, Peate decided to repeat the stroke. This time Boyle saw him coming. The ball was dropped a little shorter and Peate's swinging bat missed it altogether. There was the 'death rattle' as the stumps went over and Australia had won their first Test in England by just 7 runs. Spofforth finished the match with fourteen for 90 and the following day the *Sporting Times* carried its now legendary obituary notice.

The following winter, England went to Australia under the captaincy of the Hon Ivo Bligh, later the eighth Earl of Darnley, and lost the First Test at Melbourne by nine wickets. England, however, won the next two and secured the rubber, their first victory bringing about the first innings victory in Tests and England's first hat trick when Billy Bates, the Yorkshire round-arm spinner, dismissed McDonnell, Giffen and Bonnor. After the second victory at Sydney, where England won despite another eleven-wicket haul for Spofforth, some local ladies burnt a bail — some say it was a stump — and sealed the ashes in an urn before presenting it to Ivo Bligh. It remained his private property until, upon his death in 1927, he bequeathed it to MCC and it now stays in the Lord's cricket museum, irrespective of whether England or Australia 'hold' this almost mystical sporting trophy.

Australia and England met with great regularity throughout the next thirty years; indeed by the start of World War I, no less than twenty-one rubbers had been played since the concept of the Ashes was begun in 1882. England started that period as holders of the Ashes, though strictly speaking the 1882-3 rubber had been squared when the teams played a fourth match at Sydney which Australia won by four wickets. That match had been arranged after the Ashes were deemed to have been won, however, and as an experiment each side batted on a separate pitch. England held on to the Ashes until 1891-2, though for the first half of that period Australia probably had a better side with their bowlers, Spofforth, Garrett, Boyle and Palmer, who would have held the balance, but for Australia's wayward batting which cost them several matches. Thereafter, Australian cricket went into decline and England won ten out of eleven Tests between 1886 and 1890, Australia claiming only one. Even the emergence of two more great bowlers did nothing to help Australia, so unreliable was her batting. C.T.B. 'Terror' Turner, fast-medium right-armer from New South Wales, and Jack Ferris, left-arm medium-fast, also from New South Wales, terrorised English batsmen from the moment they made their debut at Sydney in 1887. Bowling unchanged they shot England out for 45, yet so woeful was Australia's batting reply that England still won by 13 runs. In the next Test they took eighteen wickets between them — and still England won after Australia were themselves bowled out for 84 and 150.

England, too, had her bowlers and George Lohmann, the Surrey fast-medium who became the first bowler to take eight wickets in one innings of a Test — at Sydney in 1887 — and the left-arm spinners Johnny Briggs of Lancashire and Bobby Peel of Yorkshire were often the cause of the Australian collapses which set the tone for the period. The difference between the two sides never being more graphically illustrated than in the only Test played in Australia in 1887-8 when Turner took twelve wickets, and Ferris six, and England were bowled out for 113 and 137 at Sydney. Even the skills of Turner and Ferris could not save Australia who fell for 42 and 82 in the face of Lohmann (nine for 52) and Peel (ten for 58). The one Test won by Australia during this trough in their affairs, came in 1888 when Turner and Ferris did find their efforts rewarded. At Lord's, a wet pitch contrived to bring about the lowest aggregate of runs ever recorded in a completed England-Australia Test. Lohmann and Peel were again among the wickets when Australia made only 116 and 60; but this time Turner (ten for 63) and Ferris (eight for 45) were the winners with England making only 53 and 62. Australia were soon back in the doldrums, however, and in the last two Tests, though Turner took eleven wickets in two England innings, Australia lost both matches by an innings.

Throughout the period, Melbourne Cricket Club had taken the lead as the influential power in Australian cricket, pressing ahead of the Sydney clubs, Albert and Maitland. Australia's MCC became *the* authority, financing early England tours and ensuring that the seat of cricket government rested safely in their city. In the 1890s, the Sydney cricket authorities took on the responsibility of inviting England teams to Australia and rivalry between the two centres was intense, only being resolved in 1905 with the formation of the Australian Board of Control with New South Wales and Victoria as the founder-members, soon to be joined by South Australia and Queensland, with Tasmania joining in 1908 and Western Australia, whose cricket association had been formed in 1885, some ten years later. In 1892-3, Australia's premier domestic competition, the Sheffield Shield, got underway.

In 1891, Lord Sheffield, a patron of Sussex CCC, financed an England team to Australia, captained by W.G. Grace. It was this tour which saw an upturn in the fortunes of both domestic and international cricket in Australia. Grace's team, though a strong one, lost the first two Tests and therefore the rubber, failing to combat the skills of Turner and his new partner, George Giffen, the South Australian all-rounder who bowled accurate slow-medium. With Turner and Giffen in charge of their attack, Australia had now come to terms with the need for more cautious batting at Test level and England could find no way around Alec Bannerman, the great stonewaller from New South Wales who had now perfected the art of crease occupation. In the first match, which Australia won by 54 runs, Bannerman batted seven and a quarter hours for his aggregate of 86; his 91 in the next Test, at Sydney, took seven and a half hours, and painful though it was, Bannerman's blockade was just what the Australian innings wanted. It enabled the side to score steady if unspectacular runs and gave Turner and Giffen reasonable totals at which to bowl. When Bannerman did fall early in the final Test — scoring only 12 and 1 — England enjoyed her biggest-ever win by an innings and 230 runs.

So Australia had the Ashes — and they also had a new domestic competition. Lord Sheffield presented money for the benefit of Australian cricket and the authorities decided to purchase a shield for competition between New South Wales, South Australia and Victoria. The Sheffield Shield got underway, other states joined later, and Australia had her competition which is similar to the English county championship, though, of course, affording Australians far less first-class cricket with only a comparative handful of teams taking part. Victoria were the first winners, to be followed in 1893-4 by South Australia, before they regained the trophy in 1894-5. In 1895-6, New South Wales, with an emergent Victor Trumper, took the Sheffield Shield for the first time. Since then they have been the dominant power in the competition.

Australian cricket had turned the corner in 1891-2, though England won the next three series, in 1893, 1894-5, and 1896. England's great batsmen of this period, Stoddart, Shrewsbury, Grace, F.S. Jackson, Ranjitsinhji, were complemented by the fast bowling of Tom Richardson, the 'Surrey catapult' who took sixty-six wickets in his first nine Tests. In the First Test of 1894-5, England became the first team to win a Test after following-on, thanks to 117 by Albert Ward in the second innings at Sydney, followed by six for 67 from Peel. By the final Test, at Melbourne, the Australians had drawn level at two games each with two huge wins in the Third and Fourth Tests. England took the series after Jack Brown's whirlwind century (his fifty came in twenty-eight minutes; his hundred in ninety-five minutes) enabled them to score 298 in 215 minutes for victory.

Australia were to finish the 1890s by winning the last two series with players like Victor Trumper — scorer of 135 not out at the age of twenty-one in only his second Test Match — Monty Noble, Joe Darling, Clem Hill and Hugh Trumble now emerging to take Australian cricket into a new century and on the crest of success. Their first rubber of the twentieth century saw them beat England 4-1 in Australia. England's sensation was S.F. Barnes who was taken from league cricket and, with only limited first-class experience, took nineteen wickets in the first two Tests, each side winning one. Archie MacLaren, the England skipper who had been impressed by Barnes at the Old Trafford nets and who had personally seen to it that the league bowler was included in the party, overbowled Barnes and he broke down in the next Test, Australia winning the remaining three matches. Their batting star was Clem Hill, the South Australian left-hander who scored over 500 runs in the rubber; Australia's bowling was again in good shape and the medium pacers Noble and Trumble took sixty wickets between them.

When the 1902 Australians arrived in England they found the weather pretty awful. In the First Test at Edgbaston, they faced a strong England batting side — all eleven had made centuries in first-class cricket — and after England made 376, Australia were bowled out for their lowest Test score — just 36 — in the face of some fine bowling from George Hirst and Wilfred Rhodes. Rhodes was in particularly fine form with seven for 17 and Australia were 46 for two in the second innings at the close of a rain-ruined match. Rain was the victor at Lord's where there were only 105 minutes play, but Noble's eleven wickets at Sheffield — the only Test ever played there — earned Australia a win by 143 runs. The stage was now set for two remarkable Tests, the like of which would not be seen again in England until 1982. At Old Trafford, Victor Trumper became the first man to score a century before lunch on the first day of a Test. Nevertheless, England needed only 124 to win and failed by just four runs to get them in what was one of the most thrilling of all Test Matches. Hugh Trumble, with six wickets, and John Saunders, with four, pipped England with the crowd hardly daring to watch this nail-biting finish.

Though Australia had now won the series, the Test at The Oval was equally thrilling when Australia set England 263 to win, and had them at 48 for five and seemingly poised for another defeat. Gilbert Jessop of Gloucestershire then arrived and scored the fastest century in Test cricket — it came in just eighty-five minutes — leaving England's last pair to score 15. That pair was Rhodes and Hirst and together they applied canny Yorkshire grit in steering their side home for the first one-wicket victory in Test cricket. A summer which had started out so appallingly had ended in brilliant fashion with two of the greatest Test Matches ever played. Australia, the Ashes secure, stopped off at Cape Town and Johannesburg en route for home to play their first Tests against South Africa. The tour was designed to help South African cricket back on to its feet after the Boer War, and to remove any bad feelings which might still linger over the use of Australian soldiers against the Boers.

Trumper continued his brilliant form with 218 against Transvaal and Australia won the Tests 2-0 with Hill averaging almost 82 for the three-match series. England went to Australia in 1903-4 where the googlies of B.J.T. Bosanquet proved the Australians' undoing at Sydney where they lost by 157 runs. That defeat meant that Australia had lost the Ashes, though they won the final Test, and they failed to regain them in England in 1905 where Joe Darling's team were beaten 2-0 in five Tests. Darling, the versatile left-hander from South Australia, had now skippered Australia in four rubbers — in England in 1899 and 1902, in South Africa in 1902-3, and now again in England in 1905, missing the 1903-4 series against Plum Warner's team. His career in Test cricket had an inauspicious start — bowled for a duck by Tom Richardson at Sydney in 1894 — but by the time he played in his final Test in 1905, when he made 57 and 12 not out, he had scored 1,657 runs in thirty-four Tests, and led Australia with great tactical skill.

Up to World War I, Australia played another four series against England, together with two against the South Africans, the second of those rubbers against the Springboks taking place as part of the failed

Triangular Tournament of 1912 when the vagaries of an English summer thwarted what might otherwise have been a good idea. Noble's side won the 1907-8 series against a poor England batting side, made weaker by the failure of any agreement over money which resulted in several players not touring. Australia's 4-1 win was the third time in four successive tours that Australia had trounced England by that margin. Noble led another victorious side to England in 1909 and in 1910-11, P.W. Sherwell's South African's paid their first visit to Australia and were also beaten 4-1, the googly battery of Faulkner, Schwarz and Vogler finding the turf pitches rather less to their liking than the matting of the Union. In 1911-12, England made their last visit to Australia before World War I and the result was again 4-1, only this time England were the victors. J.W.H.T. Douglas's side — he took over from Warner who was taken ill after scoring in the opening match against South Australia and took no further part in the tour — had the bowling of Frank Foster and Sydney Barnes to thank for their success.

Australia won the First Test at Sydney but after that England took complete control. The pattern for the rest of the series was set when Barnes opened the Second Test at Melbourne by dismissing Kellaway with his first ball, and then followed up with Bardsley, Hill and Armstrong for just one run in five overs, by which time Australia were 11 for four. England won that Test by eight wickets, the next by seven wickets after Jack Hobbs scored his second hundred in successive Test innings, and then triumphed by an innings and 225 runs in the next after Hobbs (178) and Rhodes (179) gave them a wonderful start with an opening stand of 323. Australia went down by 70 runs in the final Test and then got themselves ready for the 1912 Triangular Tournament in England. Australia opened the tournament with a match against South Africa and won it by an innings and 88 runs after Victoria's leg-spinner, Jimmy Matthews, became the only man to take a hat trick in each innings of a Test. Australia's record at the end of the tournament was six matches, two wins, one defeat — by 244 runs in the last match against England in a 'Timeless Test' — and three drawn games which left them in second place behind England. That was the Australians' last Test for eight years. By the time they played their next, the world would have changed for ever.

The forerunner of Australia's post-war Test side was the Australian Imperial Forces team which toured England in 1919, under the captaincy of Herbert Collins, a professional bookmaker and right-handed batsman from New South Wales. In April of that year, Australian officers were ordered to send the best cricketers still stationed in England to The Oval where, after lengthy net sessions, the side was selected, among them Jack Gregory, a left-handed batsman and right-arm fast bowler who admitted to playing 'a bit' for North Sydney Fourth team. One of Australia's most dynamic all-rounders was about to be unleashed on English batsmen. Gregory scored 942 runs and took 131 wickets in that first peacetime summer for five years. The AIF side played twenty-eight first-class matches, won twelve and lost only four to give due warning that when Test cricket started up again, Australia would be a powerful force.

Test cricket got underway when Johnny Douglas took MCC to Australia in 1920-1. The Englishmen were completely outplayed by Australia, captained by Warwick Armstong, the Victorian batsman who first played for Australia in 1901-2. 'The Big Ship', as Armstrong was known, had a fine side under his guidance while Douglas was short of batsmen and bowlers, only Hobbs being of real Test class on this tour, though Woolley, Hendren and Rhodes were in the side. Australia won all five Tests by big margins — 377 runs; an innings and 91 runs; 119 runs; eight wickets; and nine wickets — with their batsmen scoring so many runs that Gregory and Arthur Mailey had almost a free hand to achieve their aims. Mailey, the great leg break bowler from New South Wales and one of cricket's most colourful characters, took thirty-six wickets to establish a new record for the series, and with Gregory by far the most penetrative fast-bowler on show, Australia were never flattered by the margins of their wins.

In England in 1921, the slaughter continued. Australia won the rubber 3-0 and by winning the first three Tests extended their winning sequence against England to eight Tests. Gregory achieved the double with 1,135 runs and 116 wickets during that English summer as Australian cricket marched on to new heights. A 1-0 win in the South African tour of 1921-2 carried this great Australian team into their series against the English tourists in 1924-5 which they won 4-1. For English cricket followers there seemed no end to Australia's dominance, though they had now managed to win a Test and might have triumphed in another when an injury to

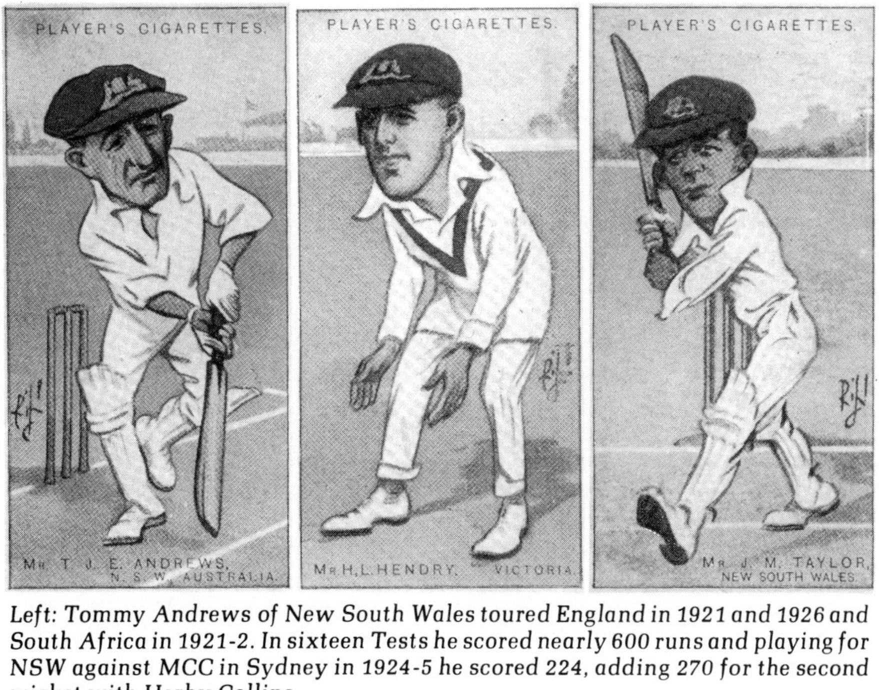

Left: Tommy Andrews of New South Wales toured England in 1921 and 1926 and South Africa in 1921-2. In sixteen Tests he scored nearly 600 runs and playing for NSW against MCC in Sydney in 1924-5 he scored 224, adding 270 for the second wicket with Herby Collins

Centre: 'Stork' Hendry of New South Wales and Victoria played in eleven Tests, touring England in 1921 and 1926, South Africa in 1921-2 and India in 1935-6, as well as playing against England in 1928-9 when he scored 112 at Sydney. A fast-medium seamer, he took sixteen Test wickets. In 1925 he scored 325 not out for Victoria against the New Zealanders

Right: Johnny Taylor also of New South Wales, was a member of the 1919 Australian Imperial Forces team which toured England. He played in twenty Tests and missed 1,000 runs for his country by just three. He was a small batsman, but one who dealt the ball a savage blow

Left: Bill Oldfield, another great New South Welshman, the small, wiry wicketkeeper who also made his mark with the 1919 AIF side. He played in fifty-four Tests throughout the inter-war period and was awarded the MBE. He made 130 Test dismissals and scored 1,427 Test runs

Right: Clarrie Grimmett of Victoria, South Australia and Wellington whose leg-spinners took 216 Test wickets in the 20s and 30s

Maurice Tate probably cost them victory in the Third Test when the margin was only 11 runs. In the last Test of the series, Australia introduced a new bowler to Test cricket, Clarrie Grimmett, a New Zealander by birth, who bowled uncannily accurate leg-spinners and took eleven wickets in his first Test Match to speed Australia to victory by 307 runs. Australian cricket had never been at a greater peak and they looked towards their 1926 tour to England and wondered just who could stop them now.

The answer to that question came somewhat sooner than the Australians had hoped. After four drawn Tests the teams reached the final Test at The Oval with everything to play for, the destination of the Ashes now resting on what had taken on all the meaning of a cup final. England dropped their skipper, Arthur Carr, and brought in Percy Chapman of Kent to lead the side. Harold Larwood, the Notts fast bowler, was recalled, and so was Wilfred Rhodes, now forty-eight years of age. This was a splendid match from the first ball that was bowled. Hobbs and Sutcliffe gave England a start of 53 runs before they were parted, whereupon the middle and late order contributed vital runs to see England close at 280. Australia's later batting was responsible for their ability to lead England by 22 runs. But then England took charge of the match. Hobbs and Sutcliffe put on 172 runs for the first England wicket in what was probably the best opening stand in any Test Match, taking into account the unpredictable pitch. Both men reached hundreds and England's final total of 436 meant that Australia needed 415 to win.

It was out of the question. Rhodes and Larwood led the way and Australia were bowled out for 125 to give England the Ashes which they had lost as far back as 1921. The crowds spilled onto The Oval in delight. Australia had fallen at last and though the pitch was a bad one, it has to be said that Hobbs and Sutcliffe mastered the 'sticky dog' with greater skill and application. The match brought to an end the incredible run which this remarkable Australian side had enjoyed since the end of World War I. With batsmen of the calibre of Woodfull, Bardsley, Macartney, Ponsford and Collins; and bowlers like Gregory, Grimmett and Mailey, they were one of the greatest Test teams of the twentieth century. But their day was over. In 1928-9, Chapman took a team to Australia and retained the Ashes by winning the series 4-1, thanks to some remarkable batting by Wally Hammond who made two double centuries, two single centuries, and finished only 95 short of 1,000 runs in the series. Australia had her centurions — Woodfull, Hendry, Kippax, Ryder, the brilliant and tragic Archie Jackson, and a young man named Donald Bradman from New South Wales. But Hammond, together with Hobbs and Sutcliffe, tipped the balance of power.

Australia's next encounter with England was in the summer of 1930 when English crowds had their first sight of Don Bradman. The son of a Sydney carpenter, Bradman's second Test appearance, at the age of barely twenty, brought him the first of his record twenty-nine Test centuries. Now he stood poised to dominate the 1930 series, just as Wally Hammond had dominated the one before. Though England won the First Test at Trent Bridge by 93 runs — Stan McCabe made his debut there — Bradman signalled his intentions with 131 in Australia's second innings. The Lord's Test found Duleepsinhji, nephew of the great Ranji, in brilliant form. Duleep scored 173 — and then was allegedly scolded by his uncle for getting himself out with an injudicious shot! England's 425 looked to be a useful score — but that was reckoning without Donald Bradman. This small, insignificant-looking man with the immense power of concentration batted for 339 minutes to score 254 runs. With Woodfull (155) he added 231 for the second wicket as Australia marched to 729 for six, at which point Woodfull declared. Though England, led by Chapman with a hundred, made a brave fight of it in their second innings, Australia needed only 72 to win, though in scoring them, they lost Bradman — out for a single — Ponsford and Kippax.

The Headingley Test was drawn, but will be remembered for ever by those who saw the first day's play when Bradman scored 105 before lunch, 115 between lunch and tea, and 89 in the final session to become the only man to score over 300 on the first day of a Test. His double-century in 214 minutes remains the fastest in Test cricket and he passed 1,000 Test runs in only thirteen innings. Bradman's batting was quite extraordinary.

Play during the 1930 Oval Test when England scored 405 in their first innings, but Bradman replied with 232, helping Australia to 695 and an eventual innings victory

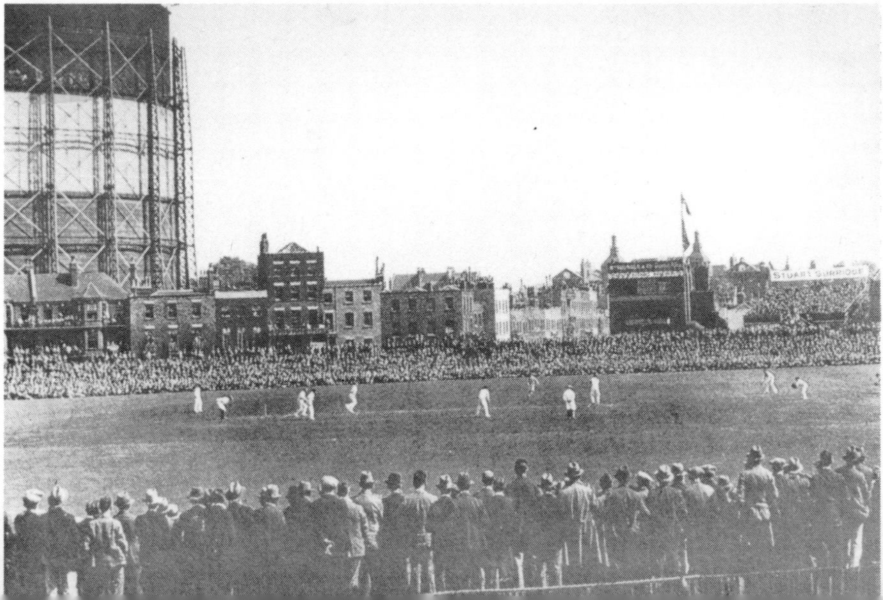

Rain robbed the Old Trafford Test of a day's play and the sides went into the last match at The Oval which would settle the destiny of the Ashes. Woodfull lost the toss and England batted first, making 405 with Sutcliffe taking the lion's share of that with 161. That might normally have been a match-winning score — but not when the opposition had Bradman. This run-machine scored yet another double-century — 232 — and with Ponsford also making a hundred and all the other Australians adding useful scores, the tourists amassed 695 runs. England had no answer to this. The left-arm slow-medium bowler from Queensland, Percy Hornibrook, took seven wickets, England were all out to give Australia victory by an innings and 39 runs, and Bradman finished the series with the incredible aggregate of 974 runs at an average of 139.14.

While not repeating that amazing performance, Bradman still found a double-century and a century when Australia met the West Indies for the first time. They won the 1930-1 rubber 4-1 — West Indies triumphed on a sticky Sydney pitch in the last Test — and Bradman scored 223 at Brisbane and 152 at Melbourne. Ponsford had successive scores of 92 not out, 183 and 109, and though West Indies pinned great hopes on their fast bowlers, Francis and Griffith, and the all-round skills of Constantine, it was the leg-spin of Clarrie Grimmett which determined the series. Grimmett took thirty-three wickets, including eleven in the First Test, and he and the great Australian batsmen in Woodfull's side made sure that West Indies left Australia empty-handed, save for that crumb of comfort in the final Test. South Africa's visit in 1931-2 served only to confirm Australia's superiority, though the Springboks also had difficulty in making the transition from matting to turf. Australia won all five Tests by big margins — three by an innings — and Bradman's average for the rubber was 201.50 with scores of 226, 112, 2, 167 and 299 not out, being unable to bat in the last Test through injury.

The 1932-3 visit to England was one of the most controversial sporting contests ever staged. Mindful of the need to tame Bradman and company, England's captain, Douglas Jardine, wheeled out his 'bodyline' plan, designed to thwart Australian attempts by bowling fast on or just outside the leg stump with a ring of close leg side catchers. Jardine had just the bowlers in Harold Larwood and Bill Voce and the tactic worked superbly, though Woodfull and Oldfield were both hit fearful blows, ironically by balls which were not really 'leg-theory'. After three Tests, England led 2-1 and the controversy reached a crisis when cables were exchanged between Australia and London and for a while it seemed that the remainder of the tour might

Donald Bradman pictured on his last tour of England in 1948

be cancelled. Happily, common sense prevailed and cricket went ahead. It was not a happy series, however, and it is sad that 'bodyline' has always overshadowed the feat of Lancashire's Eddie Paynter who, though suffering from tonsilitis, left a hospital bed and made 83 in the Fourth Test, going on to win back the Ashes for England with a 6.

So Australia lost the Ashes. On the same day that Paynter struck Bill O'Reilly into the crowd to defeat Australia, Archie Jackson died at the age of twenty-three. Illness struck down this great batsman when he still had so much to achieve. In only twenty-three Sheffield Shield matches for New South Wales he scored 1,858 runs and averaged 54.64; in only eight Tests he made 474 runs, including that brilliant century at Adelaide in 1928-9, and averaged 47.40. His first-class career had lasted only five short seasons. His death was a grievous blow to Australian cricket.

The 'bodyline' controversy contributed to England being without Jardine, Voce and Larwood when Australia went there in 1934. The Australians won a thrilling First Test at Trent Bridge with only ten minutes to spare — and it was the only time between 1928 and 1938 that they beat England without the help of a Bradman century. Arthur Chipperfield might have made a century on his debut for Australia. He was 99 not out at lunch and fell to the third ball after the interval when Ames caught him off Ken Farnes. Australia's hero, though, was Bill O'Reilly who took seven for 54 in England's second innings. O'Reilly was now in the middle of a run which made him an essential part of Australia's attack. O'Reilly leapt to the fore in 1931-2 when a brilliant spell with New South Wales in the Sheffield Shield earned him a place in the last two Tests against the touring South Africans. In the final Test his leg breaks and googlies had helped bowl out the Springboks at Melbourne. O'Reilly's eleven wicket haul at Trent Bridge in 1934 helped Australia to victory by 238 runs. Verity took fourteen wickets at Lord's to see England level in the Second Test by an innings and 38 runs. Under an untypically scorching sun at Old Trafford, Australia were left to toil in the field as England amassed 627 and when McCabe's century took Australia to almost 500, the game was doomed to a draw.

It was rain which robbed Australia at Headingley. They bowled out England for only 200, and then watched as Bradman and Ponsford rescued them from potential disaster at 39 for three and took them to 427 before they were parted. Bradman was in incredible form again. He was finally out, bowled by Bowes, after he had scored 304 in 430 minutes. It was his second triple century in successive Tests at Leeds and his partnership of 388 with Ponsford (181) was a record for any wicket in Anglo-Australian Tests. Australia led by 384 and had England on the verge of defeat at 229 for six when rain came down at lunch on the last day and washed out any hopes Australia might have had of success. The sides went to The Oval with the series all-square. It was the Test in which Bradman and Ponsford excelled even that previous record. Brown was bowled by Clark for 10; when Australia's second wicket fell, Bradman and Ponsford had taken them to 472! Their stand of 451 in 316 minutes was an epic. Bradman (244) and Ponsford (266) had put the game beyond England's reach. From that unbeatable springboard they reached 701 and a stunning victory by an innings and 562 runs to regain the Ashes at the first opportunity.

The Australians' 1935-6 visit to South Africa brought a similar story. The rubber was won by four games to one, three of them by an innings.

The Australian spinners O'Reilly (twenty-seven wickets) and Grimmett (forty-four) dominated the Springbok batsmen; their batsman led by McCabe (with an average of 84) and Jack Fingleton (79), also revelled in South African conditions and the Australians continued their march through the Thirties. The first two Tests of the 1936-7 series against England resulted in Australian defeats and for a time it appeared that the great Australian run might be at an end. The First Test, played on a rain-affected Brisbane pitch, saw Australia shot out for their lowest home total this century of 58. At Sydney, England made 426 with a double-century from Hammond, and then Australia fell foul of another rain-affected pitch and were all out for 80. Though they made 334 in their second innings, the damage was done and England won by an innings.

The margin of defeat suffered by Bradman's side — The Don was now leading his country into battle — in those first two Tests was great. The weather had compounded England's advantages and there was, as yet, no big scoring from Bradman who had made two ducks in the opening matches. At Melbourne, the scales tipped firmly in Australia's favour — and, not unnaturally, this coincided with a return to top form by Don Bradman. Yet by mid-afternoon on the first day, England seemed to have the Ashes firmly in their grasp. Australia were struggling at 130 for six and finished the day at 181 for nine, of which Bradman's contribution was just 13 before he gave Robins a simple catch at short leg off the bowling of Verity. Rain ended play just before five o'clock and did not start again until the following afternoon when Bradman declared after Australia had reached 200. Modest score though that was, on this pitch — 'spiteful and eccentric' according to Neville Cardus — it was good enough.

When England batted, only Hammond stood firm and made 32 before Morris Seivers, the Victorian giant of a seamer, got one to come back wickedly and Darling took a brilliant, tumbling catch. Seivers was virtually unplayable on this 'sticky'. He took three wickets in an over and when England had limped to 76 with one wicket to fall, Allen declared, anxious to let Australia taste some of the horrors of this pitch. Bradman responded by sending out O'Reilly and Fleetwood-Smith, his numbers nine and eleven batsmen, and before a run had been scored, O'Reilly was back in the pavilion, caught by Voce off his own bowling. Frank Ward, the South Australian leg-spinner who had replaced Grimmett in the Australian team, came out and this number ten batsman saw Australia to the close at 3 for one. Without a run added, Fleetwood-Smith became the first victim of a new day and before long half the Australian side was back in the pavilion with the scoreboard registering three runs short of the hundred. It was a finely-balanced position. Australia were 221 ahead with five wickets left on a pitch that would become more predictable. Bradman came in and knew that his side's fortunes now rested largely with their captain.

Rain again came down and interrupted play; when it was resumed the England bowlers found themselves inconvenienced by the wet ball and Voce was hit for 13 off five deliveries, Bradman taking the fullest advantage of the conditions. Between the showers Bradman advanced to 56 and Australia to 194 for five at the close with Fingleton on 39, having helped his captain to restore Australia's fortunes to the tune of another 97 runs. From that springboard, Australia marched on towards victory. The fourth day brought runs, runs and more runs. The pitch which had been so spiteful for so long was now a rich vein from which Bradman and

Fingleton extracted a score to put their country beyond defeat and poised on the brink of triumph. Their stand realised 346 — they took Australia from 97 for five to 443 for six, at which point Fingleton, after making 136, was caught behind off the spin of Sims. Their stand was the highest sixth-wicket partnership in Test cricket and Australia's close of play score was 500 for six, of which Don Bradman had scored 248, towards the end, helping himself with impunity from England's weary attack.

Voce was unable to open the attack on the fifth day and Sims began with Allen. Allen trapped McCabe leg before, and the next ball bowled Darling. Australia were 511 for eight. They reached 564 before their last wicket fell, Bradman having taken his score to 270 before apparently wearying of it all and skying Verity — who had bowled brilliantly throughout — into the field where Allen took a well-judged catch, running back to face the crowd as the ball came over his head. England needed 689 to win with a day and half left to save the match. The task was, of course, beyond them, though they battled valiantly for much of the time. The match was won by Australia when Seivers bowled Hammond after tea. The Gloucestershire man had scored 51 and with him went England's last hope. Leyland was not out 69, but only four wickets were left to fall and England were still 453 runs short of victory. The mathematics of the situation were ludicrous. For a while on the last day, Leyland and Robins treated the Australian attack with contempt. Leyland reached his century with two 4s off Fleetwood-Smith, and Robins reached 69 before he fell. The pair had added 111 and restored some pride to England's cause. Leyland was 111 not out when the last wicket fell for 323 and Australia were home by 365 runs.

Australia were now back in the hunt, trailing by two matches to one. The Melbourne Test had been watched by a record 350,534 spectators with 87,798 paying on the fourth day alone. The series had turned on this Test and at Adelaide, Bradman confirmed that his form was the critical factor. After his magnificent double-century at Melbourne, Australia's captain scored another at Adelaide Oval, his second-innings 212 putting the match once more beyond England's reach. This was the third time that Bradman had scored successive double-centuries against England. The tourists needed 392 to win; six wickets from Fleetwood-Smith broke their innings and Australia won by 148 runs to square the series. With all to play for at Melbourne in the final Test, Australia's batsmen again did their country proud. Bradman was there once more — 169 before he was bowled by Farnes — and McCabe and Badcock were also centurions, Australia reaching 604. Bill O'Reilly, with five for 51, and Laurie Nash, with four for 70, saw to it that England were never in a position to mount a tangible response. Nash, a fast bowler who had first made his name with Tasmania and had played only one game for Victoria when he was chosen for his second — and final — Test at Melbourne. England followed-on, 365 behind, and this time O'Reilly, with three more wickets, and Fleetwood-Smith, also with three, broke their back a second time. Australia retained the Ashes, winning the Test by an innings and 200 runs. The seemingly superhuman powers of Bradman, together with a change of luck over the weather, had seen Australia become the first side to win a Test rubber after losing the first two matches.

Australia ended the Thirties as they had started the decade with a tour of England. The pitches for this summer's Tests were largely over-prepared and the first two matches were drawn. At Trent Bridge, McCabe was a double-centurion in Australia's first innings after Paynter had earlier made 216 for England, who with centuries from Barnett, Hutton and Compton had totalled 658. Though McCabe's 232 could not prevent Australia following-on, centuries from Bradman and Brown easily saved the match. Five centuries and two double-centuries tell the story of this pitch only too graphically. At Lord's the run-making continued — a double-century from Brown (206 not out) and one from Hammond (240) meant another inconclusive match, while at Old Trafford, rain meant that not a ball could be bowled. The Australians now moved to Headingley and Don Bradman's favourite ground. The pitch was dusty but Bradman made his third century in successive Test innings at Leeds. His 103 was once more enough to swing the balance of the game. O'Reilly and Fleetwood-Smith spun out England twice, taking seventeen wickets between them, and Australia moved ahead in the series with victory by five wickets.

Australia could not now lose the Ashes and even a mammoth score by England in the final Test at The Oval did nothing more than square the series, though it did give Len Hutton a record Test score. Hutton's 364, scored in thirteen hours and seventeen minutes — the longest innings by an England batsman — was over one third of England's score. The Australians toiled for hour after hour as he and Leyland (who was run out for 187) added a record 382 for the second wicket. Joe Hardstaff was 169 not out when Hammond declared at a Test record of 903 for seven. Poor Fleetwood-Smith also had a record — one wicket for 298 runs — and Australia were doomed in the face of this massive score which was compounded by injuries to both Bradman and Fingleton, neither of whom could bat in the match. Without these two, Australia's cause was hopeless. They lost by an innings and 579 runs, a record margin in any Test. It was an ironic curtain call for this great Australian side of the thirties, for they were a fine side, but circumstance had overtaken them and left them on the receiving end of a hatful of records on their last appearance before war left Test cricket in limbo until a new decade was well under way.

A twenty-five-year-old batsman had made his debut for Australia in the 1938 Trent Bridge Test. Lindsay Hassett, the tiny right-handed batsman from Victoria, played throughout the series. His start was inauspicious — 1 and 2 — and he did not make a great impression on the series, though he scored a half-century in his third Test innings. But those who knew a class batsman when they saw one, also knew that Hassett would make good. It is a tragedy that the war took six years out of his career at Test level, for he went on to become one of Australia's greatest post-war batsman. Hassett was in the side when Australia played the first Test Match to be staged anywhere after the end of the war. In the absence of Bradman, Brown led a side to New Zealand and in March 1946, the two countries met at full Test level for the first time (though the ICC did not grant the match full Test status until two years later). New Zealand were shot out for 42 and 54 and Australia won by an innings and 103 runs on a poor pitch.

Hassett was joined in that side by several players making their debuts for Australia, including Keith Miller, Ray Lindwall, Ian Johnson and Don Tallon. Miller was already a great all-rounder. He had toured with the Australian Services side in 1945 and the Lord's crowd had been thrilled by his 185 in 165 minutes, playing for the Dominions team. His Victory

Test performances were nothing short of brilliant and he walked into the first official Australian team of the post-war era. Tall, dark and handsome, a wartime pilot, aggressive batsman and natural fast bowler, Miller was everything one expects of a sporting hero. Lindwall, Miller's opening partner for much of their career together, was a great fast bowler. He was genuinely quick, possessed the ability to swing the ball about with great variety, and was accurate — all qualities which, combined with that indefinable edge that marks all great fast bowlers, made him a ready candidate for cricket's all-time Hall of Fame. Victoria's Ian Johnson, in his twenty-eighth year, was one of the few top-class off-spinners to be produced by Australia, and a more than useful batsman into the bargain. He, too, was embarking on a fine Test career. Queensland's wicketkeeper, Don Tallon, already shared a world record. In the 1938-9 Sheffield Shield, this brilliant stumper had twelve victims in the match against New South Wales at Sydney. He too was an automatic Australian choice.

Together with Don Bradman, still on the Test Match scene at the age of thirty-eight despite doubts about his fitness, these players formed the backbone of Australia's team which met England in 1946-7. The previous Test between the two countries had resulted in a record win for England. This match gave Australia their biggest-ever victory. Bradman, who was given not out when Ikin appeared to have caught him at second slip off Bill Voce when he had made 28, rejoiced at his let-off and went on to make 187. With Hassett (128) he took Australia from 46 for two to 322 for three. Australia totalled 645 and then Miller (with seven for 60 in the first innings) and New South Wales left-arm seamer Ernie Toshack (six for 82 in the second) shot Australia to victory by an innings and 332 runs. Bradman's apparent slice of luck had brought him back to form with a vengeance. At Sydney he scored 234 and with Barnes, who also scored 234, added 405 for the fifth wicket. Australia declared at 659 for eight — 404 ahead of England — and won by an innings and 33 runs to confirm their status. Johnson had been the first innings destroyer with six wickets; Colin McCool took five wickets in the second innings, bringing his match haul to eight for 182. Barnes's double-century had taken 570 minutes, the slowest recorded in first-class cricket, and even a brave century by Bill Edrich when England batted again could not prevent Australia from going two games ahead. Arthur Morris, the New South Wales batsman who scored 148 and 111 on his first-class debut against Queensland in 1940-1, played his first Test in the mammoth Australian win at Brisbane and contributed only two runs out of Australia's 645.

In the Third Test at Melbourne, Hassett, along with McCool, Lindwall and, for England, Washbrook, scored a hundred in what was the first drawn Test in Australia since 1881-2. The elegant left-handed stroke play of Morris was to grace forty-six Tests for Australia in amassing over 3,500 runs. This Melbourne Test century was the first of twelve. In the Fourth Test at Adelaide, Morris scored a century in each innings — so did Compton for England — and the Test was drawn. The Ashes now retained, Australia moved to Sydney for the final Test. Here it was Lindwall's turn with seven for 63 in England's first inning. There were some fine individual performances from each side — Hutton's century, Doug Wright's seven wickets, McCool's five — and Australia took the last match by five wickets to underline the fact that England would have a hard task on their hands in recapturing the Ashes. One great Australian side had gone; another was in the making.

Australia's first official Test series against India, in Australia in 1947-8, resulted in a 4-0 win for the Australians who again could rely on plenty of runs from Bradman — his scores were 185, 13, 132, 127, 201 and 57 retired hurt. In England in 1948, where Australia romped home 4-0, thanks to the fact that Miller and Lindwall were now nearing their peak, Bradman was again amongst the runs, scoring two centuries in the Tests and being well supported — if that is the right word — by Arthur Morris who had now blossomed into one of the world's great left-handers. Australia won the First Test by eight wickets; the Second by 409 runs; drew the Third; and won the Fourth by seven wickets.

That took them to The Oval where Arthur Morris was run out just 4 runs short of 200 and where Australia, after Lindwall (six for 20) had bowled out England for 52, won by an innings and 149 runs. But all these statistics are largely forgotten beside the fate which befell Don Bradman in his last Test Match. Bradman came out to bat needing only 4 runs to bring his Test Match aggregate to 7,000 runs and his average to exactly 100. Sensing that this would be the last time that they would see him in a Test, the crowd applauded Don Bradman all the way to the wicket. What happened next is a sporting legend. Eric Hollies the Warwickshire leg-spinner, bowled Bradman for a duck. The aggregate and the average were missed, the crowd stunned, and even poor Hollies perhaps a shade red. No one on that ground, not even the bowler, would have begrudged Bradman those four miserable runs. But that was not to be; the scorer of hundreds, double-hundreds, and triple-hundreds could not have those four singles. Bradman's great Test career was over, though he had much still to offer Australian cricket. It was a sad end, and yet, perhaps, it served only to enhance the legend of this great man, this fine cricketer, who stands alongside — and probably head and shoulders above — the greatest of all time. They talk of Bradman in the same breath as Grace. For almost two decades, Donald Bradman, later Sir Don, *was* Australian cricket.

Lindsay Hassett assumed the captaincy of Australia and took a fine side to South Africa in 1949-50 where the Springboks were no match for the Australian batsmen led by Hassett, Morris and Neil Harvey, the man in the middle of a remarkable run in the Australian team and one of the greatest left-handers that cricket has ever seen. Harvey's debut against the Indians brought him a century in only his second Test; his first appearance in England as the youngest member of the 1948 touring side was marked by another century; and runs galore in South Africa were a contributory factor in Australia winning the series 4-0 against a weak Springboks bowling side.

In 1950-1, England went to Australia and faced a side still led by Hassett and which included Jack Iverson, the 'mystery bowler' from Victoria. During the war, Iverson had spent some of his time in the army serving in the jungles of New Guinea and there he had developed a curious method of spinning the ball between thumb and bent middle finger. He made his Test debut against England at Brisbane in the first match of the 1950-1 rubber and took three wickets, though being overshadowed by the left-arm fast-medium of Bill Johnston who grabbed seven victims in Australia's 70-runs victory. In the Second Test at Melbourne, Ken Archer, the Queensland opener, made his debut. Australia set England 179 in just over three days, but in the context of a low-scoring match, that would have been quite an achievement Hutton top-scored with 40 and

Ray Lindwall bowls to Len Hutton with a 'Carmody' field. Lindwall and Keith Miller were ideal bowlers for this kind of close catching ring

Australia got home by 29 runs in a nail-biting finish. Iverson had six wickets in that match; in the next Test, at Sydney where Australia clinched the series. Iverson's second-innings six for 27 was largely instrumental in England being bowled out for 123, Australia winning by an innings and 13 runs against an England team weakened by the loss of Bailey and Wright through injuries. Australia went 4-0 ahead at Adelaide where Arthur Morris hit a magnificent 206. Jim Burke, playing in his first Test at the age of twenty, scored a century in the Australian innings and Hutton, with 156, carried his bat through the England first innings as the rest of his batsmen fell far short of the skills needed to combat Lindwall, Iverson and Johnston. At Melbourne, Australia lost their first Test Match since 1938 when England won by eight wickets, thanks largely to Reg Simpson (156 not out), Hutton (79 and 60 not out) and Alec Bedser (ten wickets for 105 runs in the match).

Fresh from their latest triumph over England, Australia met West Indies. It was twenty-one years since their last meeting — the first between the two countries — and although West Indian cricket had made great strides, Australia were still too strong for them and won the rubber 4-1, losing only the Third Test at Adelaide. When the Springboks came in 1952-3, they won their first victory over Australia since 1910-11 and drew the rubber 2-2. In the last Test, at Melbourne, Ian Craig, the New South Wales youngster who was the youngest player ever to play Sheffield Shield cricket — aged sixteen and a half — made his debut to chalk up another record, that of being Australia's youngest Test cricketer at only seventeen years of age. Ron Archer, younger brother of Ken, also made his debut, Craig scored 53 and 47; Archer did rather less well — 18 and 0. Australian cricket had a different look. Colin McDonald, the Victorian right-hander who was so strong on the back foot, opened the innings with Morris. Gil Langley, the burly South Australian, kept wicket; and Richie Benaud, leg-spinner, batsman and brilliant close fielder from New South Wales, was a regular fixture. Benaud made his debut in the last Test against the 1951-2 West Indians. He was destined to become one of the great Test captains.

These were the players, along with Hassett, Miller, Harvey, Lindwall and Johnston, who formed the basis of the 1953 Australian party to England. Four Tests were drawn and the Australians arrived at The Oval facing the stark realisation that they were but one game away from losing the Ashes they had held since 1934. They had kept them for a record period of almost nineteen years when Edrich and Compton coasted England to an eight-wickets win, thus wresting back the coveted urn. Australia's greatest enemies were the Surrey spinners, Jim Laker and Tony Lock. Laker and Lock took nine second-innings wickets between them and in Coronation Year — and the year in which Everest was finally conquered — England climbed to a crowning glory against their oldest rivals. Australia had no answer to the spinners who operated on a pitch typical of their home ground at The Oval. Perhaps Australia might have already been a match ahead, however. Only some dubious tactics at Headingley, where Bailey bowled off a long run and fired wide of the leg stump, denied Australia the chance to score 177 runs in 115 minutes.

When England went back to Australia for the 1954-5 rubber, an Australian victory in the First Test at Brisbane seemed to signal an Australian revival and the return of the Ashes at the earliest opportunity. Australia won the match by an innings and 154 runs, thanks mainly to centuries from Harvey (162) and Morris (153) which helped them to a total of over 600 before Ian Johnson declared with eight men out. But an Australian victory in the rubber was not to be. With Frank Tyson, the Northants typhoon, the main destroyer, and with brilliant support from Brian Statham, England won the next three Tests. Australia might also have lost the final Test at Sydney where play could not start until the fourth day due to rain, whereupon Australia found themselves following-on before time ran out. Later that month, Australia were in the Caribbean where they won their first Test in the West Indies. They went on to win the rubber 3-0, Miller and Harvey each making three Test centuries, and in the final Test, where they won by an innings and 82 runs, Australia topped 750 with five centurions — Harvey (204), Archer (128), McDonald (127), Benaud (121) and Miller (109). Benaud's hundred came up in only seventy-eight minutes.

Australia were still too good for most sides. Now they had to prove once more that they were too good for England. In 1956, Ian Johnson led the Australians to England as they bid to recapture the Ashes lost on their previous tour in 1953. At Trent Bridge they faced an England side much reorganised through injuries. Much of the match was lost to rain and even two declarations could not force a result. At Lord's, Australia went ahead, beating Peter May's side by 185 runs after Miller claimed five wickets in each innings. But when the sides met at Headingley, it was Australia's turn to bow in the face of some fine spin bowling from Laker (eleven for 113) and Lock (seven for 81). These two, Surrey's mainstay in the days when the southerners were monopolising the County Championship, earned England victory by an innings and 42 runs. Laker had already taken all ten wickets in an innings for Surrey against the Australians that summer. When the Ashes show moved on to Old Trafford for the Fourth Test in July 1956, the Australians were set to become the hapless victims of cricket's greatest bowling feat.

England batted first at Old Trafford and reached 459 in very quick time, thanks to hundreds from Peter Richardson and the Rev David Sheppard. The runs had come in just a day and a half and at just after half past two on the second afternoon, Australia began their reply. McDonald and Burke took them to 48 without loss and up to that point Jim Laker had nought for 21. Then May switched his spinner to the Stretford End and Laker responded immediately with two wickets. McDonald was caught by Lock for 32 and with the score still on 48, Harvey was caught in two minds and bowled. Burke and Craig prevented any immediate further disasters but they were only postponing the denouement. Lock picked up his only wicket of the match and then Laker assumed complete control. When Australia's last wicket fell at 84, Laker had nine of them for 37; when they followed-on, Australia were tormented still further by the Surrey off-spinner. Ten more wickets gave him the world-record match haul in any first-class cricket. Australia were beaten by an innings and 170 runs and the Ashes remained in England. Laker's match analysis of nineteen for 90 will surely never be bettered. There were dark whispers that the pitch had been specially prepared for Laker, and Arthur Morris, writing in the *Daily Express*, claimed that it was not fit for a Test Match. Thousands of words have been written since about Laker's feat. It is sufficient to say here that he was the difference between the two sides. Whatever the conditions — 'prepared' or not — Australia had no bowler capable of utilising the pitch. England had Jim Laker. On their way home Australia played one Test in Pakistan — the first meeting between the two countries — and lost by nine wickets on the matting at Karachi where they and Pakistan contrived to produce what was then the slowest day's play in Test history. Three Tests in India followed and Australia won the rubber 2-1, Benaud in particular finding the turf pitches more to his liking.

The series in South Africa in 1957-8 brought several new faces into the Australian side. Bobby Simpson, Wally Grout, Ian Meckiff and Lindsay Kline all made their debuts in the first match at Johannesburg. Simpson, who developed into one of Australia's finest all-rounders, started his Test career with 60 off the Springboks' bowling, though he achieved little else during the tour. Grout, the popular Queensland wicketkeeper, set a world record in his first Test by holding six catches in an innings, and Meckiff, Victoria's left-arm paceman, whose doubtful action cost him his career, helped himself to eight wickets. Australia won the rubber 3-0 and extended their unbeaten run in South Africa to twenty-one Tests. A new generation of Australian Test players was coming through and when England toured in 1958-9, the peaks reached by Alan Davidson, the great New South Wales left-handed all-rounder, by Richie Benaud, and by Colin McDonald, were the main reasons why Australia recaptured the Ashes. They won four Tests and McDonald's application earned him over 500 runs in the series. With Burke, Harvey, and the new boy, Norman O'Neill, in fine form, May's bowlers never mastered the Australian batting. O'Neill made an immediate impact. A brilliant right-hander from New South Wales, he averaged over 56 in the Tests that Australian summer, and gave a glimpse of the sort of form which would earn him the title of the 'new Don Bradman'. A tour to the Indian sub-continent in 1959-60, where Australia won both series against India and Pakistan, brought O'Neill three Test centuries and he now stood on the verge of one of his greatest triumphs, achieved in one of Test cricket's most remarkable — and certainly unique — matches.

When Frank Worrell brought the West Indians to Australia in 1960-1, no one rated the tourists' chances. While Australia, under the captaincy of Richie Benaud, were riding high, the West Indians were still smarting from their defeats by England in 1957 and 1959-60. Into the bargain, they lost two state matches — against Western Australia and New South Wales (who won by an innings) — and when the First Test at Brisbane began it would have been difficult to imagine a more demoralised team. For all that, West Indies started the Test in fine style. Sobers made 132 and the tourists reached the wholly respectable total of 453. Australia replied with a lead of 52 after Norman O'Neill had scored a magnificent 181. This fine Australian batsman's powerful driving and nimble footwork delighted the Woolloongabba crowd and gave the home team a fine edge as the second innings began. Alan Davidson, at the peak of his all-round powers, bowled brilliantly as West Indies strived to set Australia a reasonable target. Davidson's return was six wickets for 87, West Indies all out for 284, and Australia needing 233 to win at a rate of some 45 an hour. They started disasterously, losing the first two wickets for seven runs and folding to 92 for six before Davidson (80) and Benaud (52) put on 134 and took them to within just seven runs of victory with four wickets still standing. This had been an epic stand and the result now seemed a foregone conclusion. People even started to leave the ground and the Australians were poised to go one match up in the series.

Then the sensational ending to this Test Match began. Benaud called Davidson for a sharp single and the Australian skipper saw his fellow all-rounder run out; suddenly, time was critical for there was now room for only one more over in which Australia had to score six more runs. Hall came in to bowl and Wally Grout scrambled through for a leg-bye; off the second, Benaud was caught at the wicket for a fine half-century; off the third there was no run and off the fourth, Meckiff and Grout ran a bye to the wicketkeeper; Grout survived a chance off the fifth and picked up a run instead; and off the sixth Meckiff and Grout turned for a third run as Hunte's throw sped from the boundary to beat Grout by inches; Two balls to go and the last man, Kline, at the wicket. Hall came steaming in and Kline swung his bat hard, the ball arrowing away towards square leg. The batsman set off for what was surely the winning run with Meckiff pumping hard towards him. They crossed and kept going. Solomon, who had earlier run out Davidson, picked up the ball and threw it at the end to which Meckiff, who had been backing up fast, was running,Meckiff had his bat down, scraping along the turf towards the crease. Solomon's throw hurtled towards the single stump at which he was forced to aim. It hit, the wicket was shattered, and Meckiff was run out. The match went into the history books as the first Test ever to be tied.

With that kind of build up, what had looked like being an ordinary sort of Test rubber, took on much greater importance. It had, after all, started with arguably the greatest Test Match in history. The rest of the series did not let the spectators down. Australia won the Second Test by seven wickets against a strangely subdued West Indian side. Then the West Indians squared the rubber in the next Test, winning by 222 runs at Sydney, where centuries from Sobers and Alexander and the spin of Gibbs and Valentine decided the match. Australia survived a Gibbs hat trick at Adelaide where the last-wicket pair, Kline and Mackay, earned Australia a nail-biting draw by batting out the final 100 minutes of the match when defeat looked certain. West Indies had missed their chance and at Melbourne, Australia took the rubber with victory by two wickets, triumphing late on the last day when Mackay and Martin scrambled a bye in a situation very like the thrilling finale in the First Test. This had been a fine series, providing exciting, enterprising cricket with great individual feats and some close finishes. Australia had the edge in the end but they had been made to fight every inch of the way.

From that remarkable series they went to England and the 1961 tour. When they arrived at Old Trafford for the Fourth Test, the sides stood

Richie Benaud, one of Australia's greatest captains, introduces another great Aussie, Test batsman Neil Harvey, to Queen Elizabeth II at Lord's in 1961. Benaud was unable to play in this Test and Colin McDonald (extreme right) took over the captaincy

level at one game each and it was here that a remarkable piece of bowling — and captaincy — by Richie Benaud won them the rubber. Benaud went round the wicket, dropped his leg-spinners in the rough, and took six for 70 to take his side to victory by 54 runs with twenty minutes to spare after England, led by Dexter, had threatened to score 256 for victory. Benaud's spell for five for 12 in twenty-five balls was one of the finest pieces of bowling seen in any Test.

Benaud was a great leg-spinner and a great captain who must rank alongside the finest to have led Australia. He drove the side hard, was a totally committed leader, a great tactician — and, most important, a man who loved his cricket and played the game to enjoy it, an approach which mirrored itself in his matches, much to the profit of all those who watched. After the successes of 1961, Benaud led Australia against England in 1962-3 and with Alan Davidson — in his last series — finding top form with twenty-four wickets, Australia drew the rubber and retained the Ashes once more. Dropped catches aided England's demise, but although Ted Dexter's side could have done better, the fact remained that Australia were still too good for them. Neil Hawke, the powerful fast-medium bowler who started his first-class career with Western Australia, made his debut in the final Test and impressed sufficiently to be selected against the South Africans in 1963-4. Hawke's chance came again when Ian Meckiff was no-balled for throwing in the First Test at Brisbane and promptly announced his retirement. Hawke played in the last four Tests and took fourteen wickets against a Springbok side which surprised everyone by drawing the series.

More Australian debutants appeared in this rubber — Alan Connolly, Tommy Veivers and Ian Redpath, all of whom were to serve Australia well in the ensuing years. The trio were selected for England in 1964 when Australia, now captained by Bobby Simpson, won the rubber by taking the Third Test at Leeds by seven wickets. The other Tests were drawn, due largely to the weather, and in the first encounter at Trent Bridge, a young bespectacled opening batsman from Yorkshire named Geoffrey Boycott made his debut for England, scoring 48 and 17. After Peter Burge's 160 was followed up by some fine bowling from Hawke and Graham McKenzie, the Western Australian with the classic pace bowler's action, Australia took the Headingley Test and from that moment on it was obvious that Simpson had no intention of losing the rubber. When he took strike in the Old Trafford Test, Simpson had one thing in mind — to stay at the wicket as long as possible. He and Bill Lawry put on 201 before Lawry was out for 106. Simpson batted on until

Saturday morning, scoring 311 in 762 minutes, the third-longest innings in all first-class cricket. Australia declared at 656 for eight, Barrington scored 256 and with Dexter (174) saw England to 611 and an inevitable draw.

With the Ashes safe once more, Australia played Tests in India and Pakistan on the way home. India's first win over Australia ensured that the rubber there was drawn, and then followed two drawn Tests against Pakistan, one in Karachi and one in Melbourne a few weeks later where Ian Chappell made his debut. Defeat in the Caribbean in early 1965 meant that Australia lost their first rubber to West Indies, despite Lawry and Simpson becoming the first Test openers each to score a double-hundred in the same innings.

When Australia entertained England less than a year later, Simpson and Lawry were still in run-making form with another fine stand in the Fourth Test at Adelaide in January 1966. After two drawn matches, England had gone ahead at Sydney where centuries by John Edrich and Bob Barber set them up for an innings win. At Adelaide, 'Garth' McKenzie ripped through England to take six wickets as they were dismissed for 241. Then Simpson and Lawry got to work. They were three runs past England's total before they were parted. Lawry went for 119, Simpson stayed to make 225 and their stand was worth 243, the highest opening partnership by Australia on their own soil. They were all out for 516 and Hawke, with five wickets, started another England slide. Australia won by an innings and 9 runs. Bob Cowper came in for the final Test at Melbourne and made Australia's only triple century in a home Test. He reached 307 before he was bowled by Barry Knight, and with England already having made 485, and Australia finding another centurion in Lawry, the match was drawn and the Ashes once more safe in Australian hands. But other sides had less difficulty in beating them. West Indies had

Ashley Mallett feels the pressure as England close in for victory during the final Test of 1968

won their first rubber over Australia and in 1966-7 it was the turn of South Africa when the Springboks won a splendid series 3-1. The writing was on the wall for Australia when, before the Tests started, Transvaal became the first team to score a win over the Australians in South Africa. Once van der Merwe's team got on top of Simpson's side, they never released their grip.

A 4-0 whitewash of the Indians in 1967-8 was followed by another visit to England. Again the rubber was drawn and Australia kept those precious Ashes. They went ahead, winning the First Test at Old Trafford by 159 runs before being shot out for 78 at Lord's, but managing to save the match. Rain meant another draw at Edgbaston and at Headingley the Ashes were safe when England failed to score 326 for victory in 295 minutes. The rubber now beyond England's reach, Australia nevertheless found themselves on the receiving end of a thrilling finish at The Oval where Derek Underwood took seven for 50 — the last man, Invararity, inexplicably padding up to 'Deadly Derek' with only five minutes to play and being adjudged lbw for 56 after earlier threatening to carry his bat and save Australia. The West Indians were beaten 3-1 in Australia in 1968-9, the Australians taking the final Test by 382 runs after Doug Walters led the way with a stunning innings of 242 and then followed up that in the second innings with another hundred. Walters was brilliant on hard pitches, though England never saw his best and South Africa, too, missed much of the Walters magic. His brilliance was there for Australia to see during the 1965-6 visit by England when he scored 155 and 115 in his first two Tests.

A 3-1 win over India in the sub-continent in 1969-70, was followed immediately by a visit to South Africa where Australia lost all four Tests to a brilliant Springbok side, the last of these at Port Elizabeth being the last official Test Match played by South Africa to date. Connolly took his 100th Test wicket in the match, but Australia had been thoroughly outplayed throughout the rubber and could only confirm just what great strides South African cricket had made immediately prior to the Springboks' exclusion from the world arena. But defeat by the Springboks did not detract from the fact that Australia had now held the Ashes since 1958-9. England captains had come and gone, players had started their Test careers and ended them in the period of Australia's dominance over their oldest rivals. The Australians looked forward to England's visit in 1970-1 and saw no special reason to fear Ray Illingworth's side.

The series opened at Brisbane where Keith Stackpole got Australia away to a commanding start to the rubber. Stackpole scored 207 — he was given the benefit of the doubt over an appeal for run out when he was 18 — and Walters 112 before the Australians' last seven wickets fell for 15 runs in less than fifty minutes, thanks mainly to John Snow who took six for 114. Solid batting throughout England's rank left them with a lead of 31 and it was left to a dour 84 from Bill Lawry to save Australia after they had been bowled into early trouble at 64 for three. Lawry was again in the thick of the inaction at Perth where Australia were asked to score 245 in 145 minutes and Lawry responded by scoring only six runs in the next thirty-eight minutes, though the second of them gave the Australian captain his 5,000th Test run, the third his 2,000th against England. At Melbourne, the Third Test was abandoned without a ball being bowled which took the sides to Sydney still level, though an additional Test, at Melbourne, had been arranged.

Australia were about to fall behind. On a wicket of uncertain bounce, England gained a first innings lead of 96 before Boycott consolidated that with 142 not out and Illingworth was able to declare at 319 for five, leaving Australia 416 for victory. They were never given a chance. John Snow roared in, took seven for 40, and Australia lost by 299 runs, their heaviest defeat by a run margin against England since 1936-7. The re-arranged Melbourne Test produced three centuries — Ian Chappell 111, Luckhurst 109, D'Oliveira 117 — and another drawn match. Another draw at Adelaide, where Boycott showed his petulance when run out and further fanned the flames by allegedly refusing to apologise to the umpires, meant that the series would now be decided in what had become the Seventh Test. The showdown threatened to produce some fine cricket — which it did — but it was also marred by incidents on and off the field which cricket could well have done without.

Boycott missed England's latest attempt to regain the Ashes after all those years. Yorkshire's run machine, who had an average in the 90s, injured an arm in a minor match and took no further part in England's Ashes bid. Greg Chappell won the toss and put England in to bat in his first Test at Australia's captain. The rest is well-known. England tumbled to 184 all out and Australia took command with a first innings lead of 80. When England batted again, almost everyone got useful scores and they totalled 302, leaving Australia 223 to retain the Ashes once more. Australia could not manage that. Though Snow, the bowler who took thirty-one wickets in the series, fractured his finger after taking the first wicket, the Australians collapsed to 160 all out and defeat by 62 runs. After holding the Ashes throughout the previous decade and before, they lost them in one display of poor batting against some good English bowling. But England's victory had been marred by incidents earlier in the game. Jenner was hit by a Snow bouncer who was warned by the umpire for intimidation and not for the first time. A long-threatened confrontation between Illingworth and the umpires took place and when Snow went down to field on the boundary he was manhandled by a drunk, whereupon Illingworth led his team off the field until tempers had cooled. Technically he was wrong, but common sense prevailed and the cricket got underway again. From England's point of view it was sad that when the last wicket fell, Snow was not there to share in their triumph.

In 1972 a new bowler burst upon the Test scene when Western Australia's medium-pacer, Bob Massie, enjoyed a sensational debut at Lord's. England took the First Test by 89 runs, but their superiority was short-lived as Massie took eight first innings wickets, followed that up with eight in the second to give himself a match analysis of sixteen for 137. No other player has made such an immediate impact on Test cricket. Massie's swing and swerve in the humid Lord's conditions completely bemused England's batsmen and Greg Chappell's first innings century turned the final screw as Australia won by eight wickets. Massie was never as successful again and played only six Tests for Australia, over half his total wickets coming in that first match. The Third Test was drawn before freak weather conditions at Leeds helped Derek Underwood to bowl Australia to defeat with over two days to spare. The Ashes were now beyond Australia's reach, though they squared the series in the last Test. But Dennis Lillee, who took a record thirty-one wickets in this rubber, would soon be partnering a new opening bowler — and Australia would be back.

New South Wales paceman, Jeff Thomson, had an unsuccessful start to his Test career, making his debut in the Second Test against Pakistan at Melbourne in 1972-3. Australia won the rubber 3-0 but Thomson's contribution was nought for 100 and nought for 10 before it was discovered that he had played with a broken bone in his foot. Thomson did not play in Australia's five-Test rubber in the Caribbean in 1973 when Australia won the series 2-0, despite losing Lillee with a bad back injury. Lillee's loss with stress fractures was a severe blow to Australia. Since he had burst to prominence with Western Australia in 1969-70, taking thirty-two wickets in eight Sheffield Shield matches, Lillee had seldom been out of the headlines. The absence of one of Australia's greatest post-war fast bowlers was a blot on the first Test ever to be played between Australia and New Zealand in Australia in 1973-4. It was, of course, only the second time that the countries had met anywhere at official level and Australia won the rubber 2-0, both by an innings. When the sides moved to New Zealand, the Kiwis enjoyed their first success over their nearest opponents.

Max Walker has Tony Greig caught by Rodney Marsh in the 1975 Edgbaston Test

England's visit to Australia in 1974-5 marked the real beginning of the Lillee-Thomson partnership and how they terrorised the English batsmen. They bowled like men possessed, Australia won four of the Tests, and only in the last Test, when both Thomson and Lillee were unfit, did England manage to score their lone success of this tour. Thomson grabbed thirty-three wickets, signalling his intentions in the very first match when he got the ball to lift just short of a length on an unprepared Gabba pitch to capture nine wickets. The gamble which the selectors had made in selecting Thomson, now playing for Queensland, was an extraordinary success. Against him and Lillee, who had twenty-five wickets in the series, the England batsmen prodded and pushed themselves to defeat, the most favourite dismissal shot being a wave of the bat outside the off stump to steer the ball into the hungry slip corden. The Ashes returned to Australia after a comparatively short break and England's batsmen went home to look again at their game in an effort to come to terms with this incredible opening pair.

It was Lillee and Thomson who saw to it that Australia held on tight to the Ashes in 1975 when they bowled their country to an innings win in the First Test at Edgbaston. The series was of four matches, starting after the World Cup, and after Lillee's five for 15 was followed up by five for 38 from Thomson, Australia took the lead, bowling out England for 101 and 173. Thereafter, the remaining Tests were drawn, though England brought in their most unlikely hero in the shape of the Northants batsman David Steele. Greying and bespectacled, Steele produced scores of 50, 45, 73, 92, 39 and 66 to show that guts and application could combat the threat posed by Lillee and Thomson, though it must be said that they were less effective on the slow English pitches. The West Indies conditions were a different prospect, however, and in 1975-6 Lillee and Thomson outbowled the fearsome West Indian pace attack and helped their country to win the rubber 5-1. Thomson revelled in the Caribbean, taking twenty-nine wickets, Lillee had twenty-seven, and their partnership prospered still further. Lillee passed 100 Test wickets in the series and Greg Chappell's team were just too good for the West Indians. Thomson, however, was soon to be sidelined. In the First Test against Pakistan at Adelaide in December 1976, he collided with Alan Turner, broke his collar bone and took no further part in a rubber which Australia drew 1-1. Lillee again had plenty of victims and when Australia went to New Zealand in 1977 he was once more amongst the wickets, taking eleven for 123 at Auckland where Australia won by ten wickets to take the two-match rubber. Later that March, England visited Australia for the Centenary Test. The Ashes were not at stake in this one match which celebrated the 100th anniversary of the first Test. Australia repeated the outcome — winning by 45 runs in a fine match which saw England's Derek Randall score 174 as England chased 463 runs. The match at Melbourne attracted what was then the largest gathering of international cricketers in the history of the game. It was a fine way to celebrate a century of Test cricket. The bowling of Dennis Lillee had resolved the outcome.

Lillee had taken eleven wickets in the Centenary Test but when Australia went to England in 1977 they had to make do without him. For the Australians the tour was a disaster. After a drawn First Test — the Jubilee Test at Lord's which commemorated twenty-five years of the reign of Queen Elizabeth II — Australia lost the next three Tests and so too the Ashes. After a nine-wicket defeat at Old Trafford, Australia saw the return of Geoff Boycott, back from a self-imposed exile which kept him out of Test cricket for thirty matches, marked with the Yorkshireman's ninety-eighth first-class century at Trent Bridge. That, and some fine bowling from Bob Willis, set up a seven-wickets win for England who now needed to take one of the remaining two Tests. They did not pause in their winning drive.

At Headingley, Boycott became the first batsman to make his 100th century in a Test Match. Mike Hendrick (with nine wickets) and Ian Botham (five for 21 in only his second Test) followed up Boycott's 191 and at almost 4.40pm on 15 August, Rodney Marsh skied Hendrick to cover, Randall completed the catch before performing a somersault, and Australia had lost the Ashes. Marsh's knock of 63 had been typical of the gutsy Western Australian who had kept wicket for Australia so brilliantly since he made his debut in 1970-1. As wicketkeeper-batsmen go, Marsh is one of the greatest to play for Australia. His very first match for Western Australia saw him score 106 against the West Indians. That was how he continued, a powerful, lusty batsman and a safe, reliable wicketkeeper.

By the time another Australian side took the field, Marsh would not be in it. Neither would another eleven players who appeared in England in 1977. They had defected to World Series Cricket and Kerry Packer. That part of cricket's story is already well-documented. When Australia's 'second team' took on Australia in 1977-8, the selectors recalled Bobby Simpson to lead the side. It was Simpson's first Test since 1967-8 but he managed to steer them to a 3-2 victory in a rubber better supported by the Australian public than the rival WSC matches going on at the same time. The 'Packer Affair' did allow faces like Craig Serjeant, Gary Cosier, Peter Toohey, Bruce Yardley, Graeme Wood, Rick Darling and Alan Hurst a chance to establish themselves as Australia's future hopes.

Jeff Thomson had rejected an initial offer to join his team mates with Kerry Packer and took twenty-two wickets against India. Simpson's return to the Test scene after a ten-year absence saw him score 176 at Perth and after a successful return to the top, he was happy to lead Australia to the Caribbean in early 1978. Here, however, this greatly weakened Australian team found themselves outclassed by a West Indies team which had no qualms about including all their WSC cricketers until a dispute saw them drop out. The series was lost 3-1 and Australia slumped to 90 all out in the First Test, and 94 in the Fourth.

The Australian selectors now looked towards the visit of England in 1978-9. There seemed little prospect of the Ashes being regained. In 1977, Greg Chappell's full-strength team had lost three Tests in England. Now Australia was shorn of her best players through the Packer Affair. Australian pessimism was not misplaced, for Brearley's team won five Tests out of six. In twenty months Australia had now lost eight out of eleven Tests against England and their team can hardly have been weaker since Test cricket began over a century earlier. Graham Yallop was pressed into the captaincy well before he was ready, and Brearley's tactical cunning and experience only added to England's already overwhelming advantage. Only at Melbourne did Australia triumph, and that was due almost entirely to Yallop winning the toss on a pitch of unpredictable bounce. If Brearley's luck had been in when the coin hit the ground, then Australia would almost certainly have lost and Brearley would have extended his record of being the first captain to win five Tests in Australia. Yet for Australia there was one bright flame amid all this gloom: the form of Rodney Hogg, the twenty-seven-year-old pace bowler from South Australia, who marked his first Test series with a record forty-one wickets at the amazingly low average of 12.85 each. It was the best performance by any Australian bowler against England, though Hogg had one more Test than Arthur Mailey, the previous record holder who took thirty-six in 1920-1. Alan Hurst supported him well with twenty-five wickets, but Australia's batsmen were totally inconsistent and only Border and Yallop managed to average over 30. The selectors chopped and changed while England fielded an unchanged team for the last four Tests. With their bowlers Miller, Hendrick, Emburey, Willis and Botham (in that order in the final averages) in total charge, England could afford to have only two centurions — Gower and Randall — in the Tests.

One month after losing the Sixth Test against England, Australia played Pakistan who had just ended a longer tour of New Zealand. Only two Tests were played, both littered with unpleasant incidents, and in the first, at Melbourne, Australia needed only 77 runs for victory with seven wickets in hand at half past four on the final afternoon. They stood at 305 for three. Sixty-five balls later they were all out for 310, skittled to a 71-runs defeat by Sarfraz who took an amazing seven wickets for one run in thirty-three deliveries. Australia levelled the two-match rubber at Perth, Pakistan never recovering from 90 for five in their first innings. Australia had the brilliance of Darling, supported well by Border, to thank for their victory and Kim Hughes, called up when Yallop was injured, celebrated his being the first Western Australian to captain his country with a seven-wickets victory. For the selectors looking for a winning combination for the forthcoming World Cup in England, the leadership of Hughes, the fine batting of Darling and Border, and the bowling of Hogg and Hurst, who between them collected twenty-five of the thirty-five Pakistan wickets to fall, gave cheer. So, eleven of the twelve on duty at Perth made the trip, though they finished third out of four in their group behind England and Pakistan and did not qualify for the semi-finals.

In September 1979, Australia began a six-Test rubber in India. The Indians were just back from a strenuous tour of England, but Australia faced them with a team vastly inexperienced in the art of touring — and India is hardly the place to begin — with ten of their fifteen players never having toured before. Though Hughes and Border both developed markedly through the tour — the final series played by Australia before agreement was reached over WSC and the defection of the top players — it was India who triumphed 2-0. The Australian batting was inconsistent once more, and apart from Hughes, Border and Yallop, there was little sign of anyone playing a major innings. Hogg disappointed and it was the veteran Geoff Dymock, and the debutant leg-spinner Jim Higgs, with seven for 143 in his first Test, who gave Australia most hope of breaking through a powerful Indian batting side.

The agreement reached between the Australian Cricket Board and World Series Cricket resulted in a complicated triangular tour by both England and the West Indies in 1979-80. Each played three alternate Tests in Australia, together with the one-day Benson and Hedges World Series Cup. It was a whirlwind and arduous programme and it affected Australia almost as much as the visiting sides. It resulted in Australia beating England 3-0 in a 'non-Ashes' mini-series, and losing to the West Indians 2-0. In between all this, West Indies and England reached the final

Denis Lillee, a world record holder

of the one-day competition which West Indies won 2-0. Australia's first full Test was against the West Indies and we should consider that short series first, though the Tests were played against alternate countries. The First Test at Brisbane was drawn, the last two, at Melbourne and Adelaide, lost heavily. Viv Richards dominated an Australian team now back to full strength. Injuries to Thomson and Hogg meant that Lillee did not have the support he might have reasonably expected; Australia lacked an all-rounder of Test class; and though Greg Chappell, reinstated as captain, and Hughes both showed the occasional flash of their old selves, only Bruce Laird, the little Western Australian, showed any consistency.

For England it was an unhappy tour. Brearley was constantly and cruelly baited by the Australian spectators and there was the boring 'Lillee and his aluminium bat' affair at Perth. How sad it is that this truly great fast bowler has so often stooped to such behaviour. Australia won by 138 runs at Perth, by six wickets — and with a day to spare — at Sydney, and by eight wickets at Melbourne. For the first time in three years Australia had Lillee and Thomson available, plus the bowling of Hogg, which should have tipped the scales firmly their way. It happened that with Hogg and Thomson injured, it was the left-arm pace of Dymock which supported Lillee so well that Dymock finished top of the averages. With Greg Chappell's return, the re-appearance of brother Ian, despite some trouble while leading South Australia, and Border, Hughes and

Kim Hughes, Australian captain who found Ian Botham the difference between his side and England in the epic 1981 series

Laird, Australia won the day, though perhaps they were not so far ahead of England as the 3-0 margin suggested.

A three-Test tour of Pakistan followed immediately on the heels of the hectic visits of England and West Indies, and here Australia lost the First Test at Karachi, mainly to the Pakistan spin attack, before drawing in Faisalabad and Lahore. For Border it was a memorable tour. In the Third Test he scored 150 and 153, bringing him five Test centuries in twenty matches, and not surprisingly topped the averages with 674 runs at 112.33 per innings. Greg Chappell averaged over 76 and scored his 5,000th Test run at Karachi; and the left-arm spin of Ray Bright brought him most wickets — fifteen — and left him way above his nearest rivals, Chappell and Lillee, who had only three each.

Chappell's side flew into London in August 1980 for a handful of county games prior to their Centenary Test against England at The Oval, scheduled to mark a century of Test cricket between the two sides in England. Some 200 former England and Australia Test stars assembled for the big occasion, but the weather was determined to dampen the celebrations. In the first three days almost ten hours were lost to rain and the match ended in a tame draw. The match was regrettably marred by some MCC members who jostled umpire David Constant following the fifth pitch inspection on the Saturday. MCC issued a statement apologising for the incident and the match continued under this shadow. Wood and Hughes, each with a century, moved Australia to 385 for five declared before Lennie Pascoe and Dennis Lillee (five and four wickets respectively) bowled out England for 205. Another fine innings by Hughes (84) in a stand with Chappell (59) led Australia to declare at 189 for four, leaving England 370 at almost a run a minute. With two wickets down for 43 — those of Gooch and Athey — Botham's team did not attempt the target and they survived to 244 for three with Boycott making an undefeated 128. The crowd did not like it one little bit, and the only man to enjoy this celebratory match was Boycott who passed the Test aggregates of both Hutton and Bradman. Hughes took £500 for the Man of the Match award.

The pace of Lillee largely defeated New Zealand by 2-0 in the three-match series in Australia in the last few weeks of 1980; in the New Year, India shared a series with the Australians after bowling them out for 83 in the final Test at Melbourne. Earlier in the rubber Australia could boast of double centuries from Greg Chappell and Kim Hughes. But against Kapil Dev they floundered and fell along with the other Australian batsmen.

Kim Hughes, it was, who brought the Australians to England for their 1981 tour. Of course, millions of words have been written about this incredible series which started off so triumphantly for Australia, and ended in such sensational manner for England. Hughes's team won the First Test at Trent Bridge. Their victory came at fifty minutes after tea on the fourth day of a low scoring match where even on this unpredictable pitch, the 132 which England left them to score was an easy target which the Australians reached with four wickets to spare. At Lord's everyone waited to see if Boycott could score a hundred in his 100th Test but he made 17 and 60, Botham bagged a 'pair', and a largely unmemorable match was drawn. At about three o'clock on the fourth afternoon of the Headingley Test, it seemed that Australia would soon be two games ahead. Bob Taylor had just been caught off his glove by Ray Bright at short leg and England were 135 for seven — still 92 runs away from avoiding an innings defeat. What happened next is already legendary. Graham Dilley joined Ian Botham, now happy to serve under the recalled Brearley, and between them they added 117 runs for the next wicket. Botham went on to a brilliant 149 not out on the last morning and astonishingly England led Australia by 129. Then Bob Willis set to work. The Warwickshire war horse, so often written off by the media, claimed eight for 43 and England had won one of the most astonishing Test

How our forefathers would have shuddered! A rock concert for Sydney's famous Hill during a one-day international

Matches in history by 18 runs. There was more to follow at Edgbaston where Botham won the game for England, this time with the ball, taking five for one in twenty-eight balls in a match where not one batsman scored even a half-century despite the ordinary nature of the pitch. From being one ahead, Australia were now two down. At Old Trafford another incredible innings by Botham — 118 lusty runs — seemed to have won the game for England.

Indeed it did, but not before centuries from Yallop and Border steered Australia to a worthy second innings 402. Though they still lost by 103 runs the Australians had made a great fight of it. The Ashes were now beyond Australia's grasp and the final Test at The Oval, which was drawn, was of interest only to the statisticians who recorded, amongst other things, that Lillee, rather surprisingly, took seven wickets in a Test innings for the first time. Dirk Wellham, who scored a century on his debut for New South Wales not long before, completed a nice double with a century in his first Test. Australia had taken part in one of the most memorable of Test series and although they failed to regain the Ashes, they were not so far short of England. Hughes summed up the difference between the two sides: 'Ian Botham'.

From the series in England, Australia went home to prepare for the visit of Pakistan. The first two Tests were won quite easily, the bowling of Alderman, Lillee and Yardley, and the batting of Greg Chappell, who scored 201 at Brisbane, seeing to that, before Pakistan came back with a shock innings victory at Melbourne on a pitch criticised by Australia's captain even before the start. But the series was marred by the disgraceful Lillee-Miandad incident (see the Pakistan chapter of this book). The players decided to fine Lillee 200 Australian dollars (about £120), but the authorities quashed that and imposed a two-match ban on their star fast bowler. The matches concerned were two one-day internationals and the 'crime' perpetrated by the fast bowling MBE, even allowing for Miandad's reputation as something of a 'niggler' was not really met by an appropriate punishment. The series with the West Indies which followed immediately after the Pakistan rubber was drawn, one game each, West Indies winning an exciting last Test at Adelaide to square the rubber. It was in the first match, at Melbourne, that Dennis Lillee reached a new Test wicket-taking record. When he took the wicket of Gomes, Lillee passed Lance Gibbs's record of 309 victims. He went on to take ten in the match and sixteen in the series to maintain his incredible run as the world's greatest fast bowler of the present day.

Lillee was still taking wickets when Australia drew a three-match series in New Zealand in 1982. Yet again the old firm of Thomson and Lillee was together, though sadly, Lillee was forced to drop out of the last Test with a knee injury. Australian cricket owes him a great debt, notwithstanding his occasional outbursts, and he, and all the other great cricketers who have worn the famous green cap, have earned Australia many famous victories, many golden moments, all of which have enriched greatly the fabric of cricket around the world.

South Africa

Cricket with the Springboks

Cricket was introduced around the world by British servicemen and traders who spread the game wherever they pitched camp or set up a trading post during the nineteenth century, and the fact that the first recorded match in South Africa was played between Officers of Artillery Mess and Officers of the Colony, at Cape Town on 5 January 1808 (for a stake of one thousand dollars a side, incidentally), shows that the origin of cricket in this part of the world was no exception. Almost certainly cricket was played in South Africa before that Cape Town match — the British Army may have played the game there from the time they captured the Cape of Good Hope in 1795 — but it was really the settlers from England who established cricket during the middle of the nineteenth century. In the 1840s and 1850s, clubs were started in Pietermaritzburg, Port Elizabeth and Bloemfontein, and so the spread of the game can be readily traced. By 1876 there were enough cricket clubs in the Cape of Good Hope for the townsfolk of Port Elizabeth to present a trophy, called the Championship Bat, and the first cricket competition in South Africa got underway. Ten years earlier, the Western Province Cricket Club had been formed and now challenge matches between army teams and people born in South Africa became the forerunners of the international clashes that were not far distant.

In 1888-9 South African cricket took its most significant step forward. An English touring team, possibly the joint enterprise of one Major Warton and Sir Donald Currie, founder of the Castle Line which later became the Union Castle, landed in South Africa for the first Test Matches to be played outside the England-Australia series. Just as important, Sir Donald presented a cup to the team which put up the best performance against the tourists. It was won by Kimberley, later to be absorbed into Griqualand West; when Transvaal successfully challenged them at Kimberley on 5-8 April 1890 the Currie Cup, South Africa's major domestic trophy, played for by the major provinces, was born.

The first-ever Test Match played by South Africa thus began at St George's Park, Port Elizabeth, on 12 March 1889. The match was played on matting and the novice Test team of South Africa faced an England side led by C. Aubrey Smith of Cambridge University and Sussex. This was in his only Test appearance and he later went to Hollywood, became a famous film actor, and started the legendary Hollywood cricket 'colony'. He was knighted for services to Anglo-American friendship, but before all this, he remained in South Africa after the England tour of 1889. He became a stockbroker in Johannesburg and in 1890 played for Transvaal, his right-arm slow-medium bowling helping them to the first Currie Cup win in matches between the provinces. His touring side included such experienced English county players as Bobby Abel of Surrey, George Ulyett of Yorkshire, Johnny Briggs of Lancashire, John Read of Surrey, and Frank Hearne of Kent. Hearne, too, was to find South Africa to his liking and played, not only with Western Province, but also had the rare distinction of playing Test cricket for two countries when he played for South Africa against England in subsequent series.

South Africa's team for this inaugural Test Match was, in batting order, Albert Innes (Transvaal), Bernard Tancred (Griqualand West), Philip Hutchinson (Natal), Charles Vintcent (Griqualand West), Arthur Ochse (Transvaal), William Milton (Western Province), Owen Dunell (Eastern Province), Major Robert Stewart (Eastern Province), Frederick Smith (Transvaal), Charles Finlason (Griqualand West), Gustav Kempis (Natal). Owen Dunell was South Africa's first Test captain. An Old Etonian who went on to Oxford (he was neither in the Eton eleven, nor an Oxford blue), Dunell, South African-born, blossomed into a useful batsman with Eastern Province. The Test side's wicketkeeper in that historic match was Frederick Smith who was also a good middle-order batsman, playing his initial first-class cricket with Kimberley, a side he captained successfully.

Dunell won the toss and South Africa took strike on their Test debut. They endured a disastrous start. Two wickets fell without a run on the board, Innes and Hutchinson falling to the left-arm slows of Johnny Briggs. Indeed, there were only two South African batsmen who came to terms with the England bowling. When the last wicket fell at 84, only Tancred and Dunell had reached double figures, Bernard Tancred, the elder of five famous South African cricketing brothers, made 29 before he was bowled by Smith; Dunell hit 26 not out. Tancred was perhaps the greatest of early South African batsmen, averaging nearly 75 over the first two Currie Cup competitions of 1889-91. Briggs ended his first bowl against South Africa with four for 39; C.A. Smith rattled through the later order with five for 19. When England batted, they too were soon in trouble and lost their first two wickets for 14. But careful batting by Abel (46) and Hearne (27) restored some order and, although there was a middle-order collapse against the bowling of Innes, lusty hitting by the tail, during which last man Arnold Fothergill of Somerset made 32, saw England to 148.

For South Africa, Innes had five wickets for 43, Kempis three for 53. Just as Briggs slow-left arm had puzzled South Africa's batsmen, so Innes's similar style had charmed out people like Bobby Abel. One year later he was to make 55 and take five for 98 for Kimberley against Transvaal in the first Currie Cup tournament. Gus Kempis was also a left-armer, though he sent the ball down at a much greater pace and with immaculate length and the ability to move the ball either way off the seam, he was one of South Africa's best bowlers, ranking with any down the ages. When South Africa batted again, Tancred again made 29, and again it was the top score. More players got into double figures this time and the innings closed at 129, leaving England 66 to win. They got the runs for the loss of two wickets, the game ending just before half past three on the second day.

The Second Test, played at Newlands, Cape Town, also ended in an English victory, and this one was by even bigger proportions. Abel raced to 120 in an England total of 292, though the slow-medium left-armer, Bill

Ashley, playing in his only Test, took seven for 95. South Africa's reply was disastrous. They were all out for 47, Briggs taking seven for 17 and Tancred, with 26, becoming the first Test batsman to carry his bat through a completed innings. Following-on, South Africa fared even worse. Briggs took eight for 11, all of them clean bowled, and South Africa were all out for 43 to lose by an innings and 202 runs. Briggs's fifteen wickets for 28 in the match set a record for being the most wickets taken by one bowler in a single day of a Test Match. During the entire tour, Briggs took nearly 300 wickets in all games — all of which were played on matting wickets, for there were no first-class turf pitches in South Africa until 1926-7.

South Africa's introduction to Test cricket had taught them that there were no easy pickings in the arena of international cricket, even in those early days. The first eight Test Matches played between South Africa and England — all in South Africa — were all won by England. In 1891-2, just one Test was played, at Newlands, where England triumphed by an innings and 189 runs. Captained by the aggressive Surrey batsman, Walter Read, England's team was streets ahead of the South Africans. Left-arm medium-pace bowler Jack Ferris, who had played eight Tests for Australia before settling in England and playing for Gloucestershire, played in his only Test for England and took six for 54 as South Africa crumbled to 97 all out. England stormed into a big lead, making 369 with 134 not out from wicketkeeper Henry Wood, who served Surrey so well. South Africa's second innings realised only 83 — Ferris having seven for 37 this time — and the match was over well within three days. The match was the second time that three brothers had played in the same Test when Frank Hearne appeared for South Africa and brothers Alec and George turning out for England. Their cousin, J.T. Hearne of Middlesex, also played in the match for England.

In 1894 the first South African team visited England but no Tests were played and the tourists were not accorded first-class status, although they did enjoy victory over an MCC team — captained by W.G. Grace — at Lord's. In 1895-6, however, Tests were played when an England team arrived in South Africa. The First Test, at Port Elizabeth, began in February 1896 with eight Englishmen and seven South Africans making their debuts, the English team also including the Somerset captain, Sammy Woods, who had played three games for his native Australia in 1888 before settling in Taunton. South Africa's wicketkeeper-captain, 'Barberton' Halliwell of Transvaal, won the toss and put England into bat. It seemed the correct decision, for England lost their first wicket, that of George Lohmann of Surrey, without a run scored, and went on to make 185 in the face of some wily left-arm spin bowling from James Middleton. Middleton, born in Durham but serving in the army in South Africa when Cape Town CC thought enough of his skills to buy him out, had been a big success on the first tour to England, taking eighty-three wickets, including twelve for 83 against MCC. Middleton had five for 64 as the England team faltered in Port Elizabeth.

But when the South Africans batted they found George Lohmann in splendid form. The man who was to settle in South Africa and play for Western Province before dying of tuberculosis in 1901, shot through the home side's frail batting, taking seven for 38 — all clean bowled — as South Africa made just 93. England made 226 in their second innings before Lohmann once more ripped the heart out of South Africa's batting.

In only ninety-four deliveries the South Africans were all out for 30. Lohmann had ended the match in two days with eight for seven, finishing off with a hat trick. It was the lowest score by a Test side until 1954-5 and, thanks to Lohmann's medium-pacers, England were home by 288 runs.

For the South Africans there was worse to follow in the Second Test on the Old Wanderers ground, Johannesburg, where Lohmann struck once more. As soon as Lord Hawke's team began to pile on the runs in their first innings it was evident that another huge defeat for the South Africans was on the cards. They had their early successes though, the slow left-arm of George Rowe of Western Province bowling Sir Timothy O'Brien before England had scored, and Jimmy Sinclair's rocket-like delivery accounting for Lohmann with 8 scored. Rowe went on to take five wickets on his Test debut; Sinclair, who was soon to make his mark as one of South Africa's leading all-rounders, took four. But by the time the last of those had fallen, England had a commanding position. Surrey's Tom Hayward had rescued them with 122, and several other English batsmen weighed in with big scores. Bromley-Davenport (84), Lord Hawke (71), Arthur Hill (65) and C.B. Fry (64) all led the way to 482.

South Africa stood little chance of saving the match. There was a little resistance, notably from Sinclair who scored 40, but Lohmann was again on top form. He took nine wickets — only Jim Laker's legendary feat in 1956 bettered that — and South Africa were all out for 151. When they followed-on, they lost a wicket before scoring and went down by an innings and 197 runs. Lohmann had not finished with South Africa. In the final Test, played at Newlands, he took seven more wickets as South Africa tumbled to 115 Hill's century gave England the springboard for a lead of 150. Batting again, South Africa were 33 runs short of avoiding an innings defeat while another wicket for Lohmann gave him thirty-five in the three-match rubber at a cost of only 5.8 runs apiece.

Lord Hawke brought another team to South Africa in 1898-9, and again South Africa failed to win a Test, losing in Johannesburg and Cape Town. The rubber had its compensations for the Springboks, however. At the Old Wanderers ground in the First Test they were up against 'Plum' Warner who scored a century in his first Test and failed by just 32 runs to win after Albert Trott, yet another Australian Test player to appear for England, took five wickets to help them out for 99.

In the Second Test, though South Africa lost by 210 runs, after a second innings disaster of 35 all out against Trott (four for 19) and Yorkshire's Schofield Haigh (six for 11), they did reach a landmark when Jimmy Sinclair, having scored South Africa's first Test fifty in the previous match, hit their first Test century with 106 in their first innings 177. Sinclair had a fine match in Cape Town, for in addition to his century, he tok nine wickets in the match to establish himself as a South African who could rank high in the lists of Test cricketers at that time — and Springbok cricket had little to cheer at international level during these formative years. Sinclair was a colourful character. Captured by the Boers during the war, he escaped and made his way through enemy lines to safety; and on a subsequent tour to England he hit the great Wilfred Rhodes clean out of the Harrogate ground and knocked a cabby from his vehicle. But the Test at Cape Town in April 1899 still found South Africa wanting and after eight Tests they had suffered eight defeats. Visits to England in 1901 and 1904 followed, but no Tests were played.

The outbreak of war in 1899 obviously held back South African cricket.

But cricket administrators in the country showed great courage and foresight in 1902 when they invited Joe Darling's Australians to visit South Africa en route from their recent tour of England where they had won the series by two games to one in what had turned out to be one of the greatest rubbers in Test history. Within hours of landing at the Cape, Darling's team was in action in the first-ever Test between South Africa and Australia. The historic match began in Johannesburg on 11 October 1902 and after Henry Taberer — emulating C.A. Smith by captaining his country in his only Test — put his side into bat, South African cricket took on a completely new identity. They made 454, with 90s from Louis Tancred and Charles Llewellyn, and an eighth-wicket stand of 124 between A.W. 'Dave' Nourse, the man who was on the threshold of becoming one of South Africa's greatest cricketers, and 'Barberton' Halliwell.

Australia transferred from the turf pitches of England to the matting of South Africa and made 296. Llewellyn's left-arm mixture of slow and medium-pace accounting for six wickets, Sinclair capturing the other four. South Africa now had the wholly unfamiliar task of asking the opposition to follow-on, though Australia this time had no difficulty in saving the match with 142 from Clem Hill. Nevertheless, South Africa had stopped their dreadful run of defeats. It was to be resumed in the next two Tests when Australia twice bowled out South Africa for 85 — at Old Wanderers again, and at Newlands — to win by 159 runs and ten wickets respectively. Their final victory was delayed, however, by a whirlwind innings from Jimmy Sinclair whose 104 in eighty minutes including six 6s. The Australians continued on their way, but by agreeing to play Tests in the Cape they had made a great contribution to South African cricket. For the Springboks, success at Test level was now not far away.

South Africa's first Test victory came in their very next match, although they did have to wait another three years for the historic event. After defeat by Australia in November 1902, the Springboks next Test was against 'Plum' Warner's England team in Johannesburg starting on 2 January 1906. Warner's team, though including players like himself and Colin Blythe, the great Kent slow left-arm bowler, was perhaps more of an England second eleven. Indeed, England had never sent their best team to South Africa, for they had never had to do so in order to win resounding victories. But cricket in the Union had progressed immensely and Warner's team were in for a shock. South Africa blooded six new players for the Johannesburg Test — Faulkner, Schwarz, Sherwell, Snooke, Vogler and White — and South African Test cricket was about to establish itself alongside England and Australia. With only six runs on the board England had lost two wickets. Fifteen was the total when the third wicket fell — and only some determined hitting by the middle and late order saw the tourists to the barely adequate total of 184.

The damage had been done by South Africa's new men. Leading the wicket-takers with three victims was Reggie Schwarz, the man who had a modest career with Middlesex before emigrating to South Africa. Schwarz returned to England with the 1904 Springboks and learned the art of googly bowling. On his return to the Union, Schwarz imparted his knowledge to other South African bowlers, though he himself bowled only googlies. His colleagues, Aubrey Faulkner, Bert Vogler and Gordon White, all bowled leg breaks and googlies and all took wickets that day. The only exception was Jimmy Sinclair who claimed his two wickets with good old-fashioned fast bowling. South Africa, however, failed miserably when they began their reply and the bowling of Walter Lees (five wickets), Colin Blythe (three) and John Crawford (two) toppled them out for 91. But on this matting wicket, googlies were to win the day and England could do no better than 190 in their second innings, Faulkner and Vogler again leading the way, though this time the medium-pace of another debutant, 'Tip' Snooke weighed in with two wickets. Nourse, too, found success with two for 7 off six overs.

South Africa thus needed 284 runs to win and by the close of this second day they had progressed to 68 for two. The wickets to fall were those of Louis Tancred — caught by Warner off Blythe for 10 — and Transvaal's Maitland Hathorn, an unspectacular right-hand bat who was caught by Crawford off Lees for 4. On the third morning England began in splendid style. William Shalders, always an impetuous player, was run out; Snooke leg before to Lees; Sinclair brilliantly caught at long on by Fane; and Faulkner also run out when Gloucestershire wicketkeeper, Jack Board, broke the stumps at the far end in brilliant fashion. South Africa were 105 for six and yet another Test against England looked on the brink of defeat. Then Nourse and White came together. White had stayed calm while wickets fell about him. Now he cut loose with Nourse keeping pace with him. Together, they raised 121 runs for the seventh wicket, scoring them in 145 minutes, before White was bowled by Relf for 81. The stand had seen some of the finest cricket ever played on the Old Wanderers ground — exciting batting, good bowling in the face of the onslaught, and excellent fielding. Nourse had given a sharp chance to the slips when he had made only 11 and it was going to prove a costly miss. The score was 226 when White departed and just four runs later, Vogler was bowled by Hayes. The tea interval was one of high drama in anticipation of events to come. Yet immediately after the break it seemed that South Africa's cause was lost when a ball from Relf kicked up off the matting and Schwarz could only pop it back to the bowler. Nine South African wickets were now down for 239 — still 45 short of victory. The odds were obviously heaped in England's favour. Yet the number eleven batsman making his way to the wicket was no rabbit. Percy Sherwell was the Springboks wicketkeeper and captain and a batsman good enough to score three Test centuries in ensuing years.

The first ball received by Sherwell was smacked firmly to the ropes for 4, and with Nourse still carving runs, Warner began to switch his bowlers, but to no avail. South Africa's last pair eased along until they were just eight runs away from an incredible victory. Crawford sent down a fast ball, but Sherwell got his bat to it and edged it through the slips to the boundary — a lucky escape but now only four runs were needed. Nourse clipped Relf through the leg side and the batsmen ran — one, two, three — the game was now tied! Warner brought his fielders in round the bat and Sherwell played the first two balls from Relf with great circumspection before letting the third pass harmlessly by. The fourth ball of the over was the slowest full-pitcher down the leg side and Sherwell needed no second chance. It fizzed past where square leg would have been and thundered into the boundary fence — South Africa had won their first Test Match!

The scenes on the Old Wanderers ground were incredible as the crowd spilled onto the field. Hats and walking sticks flew into the air, people laughed, people cried. For Nourse it was a special triumph for he had

South Africa 1907. Standing: A.W. Nourse, H.E. Smith, W.A. Shalders, M. Hathorn, G.A. Faulkner, G. Allsop (manager). Front: J.H. Sinclair, R.O. Schwarz, Rev C.D. Robinson, P.W. Sherwell (captain), L.J. Tancred, A.E. Vogler, J.J. Kotze. On ground: S.J. Snooke, G.C. White, S.D. Snooke

batted three and a half hours for an unbeaten 93, scored with exceptional strength off the back foot, beautiful cuts behind point, and delicate clips through the leg side field. Sherwell's innings had been a classic captain's knock of 22 priceless runs and the skipper and his left-hander had added 48 seemingly impossible runs for victory. It was a classic cricket match and one fitting of South Africa's first win. South Africa were now riding high and they relied on the same eleven players to see them through the series, hammering Warner's side in all but the Fourth Test. In the Second Test, also at Johannesburg, they won by nine wickets, following that with a 243-runs victory, again at Old Wanderers, and success by an innings and 16 runs in the last Test at Newlands, England winning the previous match by four wickets on the same ground. The googly bowling of Faulkner, Schwarz, Vogler and White had proved almost unplayable at times on the matting wickets; Snooke who took eight for 70 in the Third Test had blossomed into a fine opening bowler; 'Dave' Nourse, who came to South Africa as a teenage army trumpeter, was to appear in forty-five consecutive Tests from 1902 until 1924.

The South African's triumph over Warner's touring side saw them accorded full Test status in England when they embarked on their 1907 tour. The England side which faced the Springboks was now a full-strength combination — most of the England players had been in the side which had beaten Australia 2-0 two years earlier — and only Blythe and Crawford had played against the South Africans before the First Test at Lord's in July 1907. Yet South Africa, despite their new-found status abroad, were still short of beating their hosts. After Gilbert Jessop (93) and Len Braund (104) had scored 145 for the sixth wicket in seventy-five minutes, England were all out for 428. When South Africa batted there was a Springbok collapse in the face of Worcestershire's fast-medium bowler, Ted Arnold. After three wickets had fallen for 18 runs, Nourse and Faulkner guided South Africa to 116 before their fourth wicket fell. Half the side were out for 134 and South Africa actually lost their last six wickets in only twenty-four balls in reaching a meagre 140. They followed-on and this time their captain, Percy Sherwell, who opened the innings in this match after being promoted from the tail-end of the batting, carved 115. When the rains came to save South Africa they had climbed to a more respectable second innings total of 185 for three.

In the Second Test, at Leeds, South Africa might well have scored their first Test victory in England, had it not been for Colin Blythe. When England started the match they were caught on a rain-affected wicket and Faulkner's six for 17 was largely responsible for an England collapse. They reached only 76 and even when Blythe took eight South African wickets, the tourists still looked in command with a lead of 34 runs. England made a better fist of it second time around, but still South Africa needed only 129 to win. They failed by 53 runs, thanks to Colin Blythe who claimed a further seven wickets to finish with a match analysis of fifteen for 99. The last match of the three-Test series was drawn with honours even and on balance South Africa emerged from their first Test series abroad with an enhanced reputation.

South African cricket now had a world-wide reputation and when England toured the Union in 1909-10, Leveson-Gower's team opened its batting with Hobbs, Rhodes, Denton, Fane and Woolley. But though the batting was strong, England lacked the bowlers to penetrate a fine South African batting side and in the First Test, in Johannesburg, they failed by 19 runs to prevent a South African victory. It was a remarkable match which saw Worcestershire's George Simpson-Hayward make his Test debut and take six for 43 on the matting with his lobs — the last bowler of such quaint style to play for England. But the match belonged to Aubrey Faulkner, the Transvaal player who was now one of cricket's greatest all-rounders. On the 1907 tour Faulkner had taken sixty-four wickets in all games and scored over 1,000 runs. Now, in Johannesburg in January 1910, he became the only player to score 200 runs and take eight wickets in the same Test Match. He made 78 and 123 in South African totals of 208 and 345, and took five for 120 and three for 40 as England fell just short of victory.

South Africa went 2-0 ahead at Durban where Faulkner's second innings six for 87 sent England reeling to a 95-runs defeat after Gordon White's second-innings 118 for the Springboks. Although Yorkshire's David Denton cut, pulled and hooked his way to 104 in 100 minutes as England won the Third Test in Johannesburg by three wickets, South Africa clinched the rubber in the Fourth Test at Newlands. In a low-scoring match dominated by their spinners, South Africa scored 175 in their last innings to win by four wickets. South Africa were now victors, though England took the last Test by nine wickets — a prospect always in view after Jack Hobbs first-innings 187. Even then South Africa enjoyed further records, albeit surrounding a batting collapse, when Transvaal's Billy Zulch became only the second South African to carry his bat through a completed Test innings. This talented opener, who never played with South Africa in England, made 43 not out when Blythe ran through the Springboks first innings, taking seven wickets as they fell to 103 all out.

This was becoming a golden age of South African cricket and when Sherwell took the first Springbok team to Australia in 1910-11, he did so comforted by the knowledge that the battery of leg-spin and googly bowlers produced by the Union had brought great success to his county. Alas, they were not as effective on Australian turf, which was far

South Africa versus Australia at Old Trafford during the 1912 ill-fated Triangular Tournament

removed from the matting of the Union. Coupled with the fact that they had no genuine fast bowler, South Africa found that their less-effective spinners enabled Australia to pile on the runs. Australia won the Test at Sydney by an innings and 114 runs, Bardsley and Hill moving them from 52 for one to 276 for two in a day when Australia scored 494 for six — the highest total for the first day of any Test Match. In the Second Test at Melbourne, though Faulkner scored South Africa's first double-century, almost bizarre scores of 506 and 80 saw them fall by 89 runs. Australia won the Fourth and Fifth Tests — the Fourth, at Melbourne, by an incredible 530 runs — but in the Third Test played at Adelaide, South Africa did taste their first win over Australia in a match which produced a record runs aggregate in Test cricket to that time — 1,646 runs for forty wickets. Zulch and 'Tip' Snooke, whose brother Stanley, with whom he is often confused, made his sole Test appearance in England in 1907, made centuries; Victor Trumper scored 214 not out to set a new record for Australia; Faulkner hammered 115 in South Africa's second innings; and four wickets from Schwarz enabled the Springboks to bowl out Australia to win by 38 runs.

South Africa's next Test series was in the ill-advised and ill-fated Triangular Tournament between England. South Africa and Australia in England in the wet summer of 1912. South African cricket, after riding on a comparatively high note for so long, was about to thud to earth. They lost all three Tests to England and the first two played against Australia. The first match at Old Trafford set the pattern for the rest of the tour when South Africa were on the receiving end of a unique performance by Australia's Jimmy Matthews who took a hat trick in each innings of the Test as South Africa — for whom former England Test player Frank Mitchell was making his debut — lost by an innings and 88 runs. Mitchell had played two Tests in the Union for England in 1899 and then captained the Springbok teams to England in the non-Test 1904 tour, and now in this ill-starred visit.

In the very next match South Africa again lost by an innings, Sydney Barnes — who was to be a great thorn in their side throughout this tournament — and Frank Foster taking five apiece as they collapsed to 58 all out on the first day of the match. Even the medium-pace leg-spin of

Transvaal's Sid Pegler, who had seven for 65 in this match and finished the tournament with twenty-nine wickets, could not help them. They lost their third match, to England by 174 runs, and their fourth, against Australia, by ten wickets. Only in their fifth game did South Africa reclaim any dignity when they took a first innings lead of 110 runs over Australia at Trent Bridge before rain washed out the last day. The last match of the tournament, so far as South Africa were concerned, was against England at The Oval. England had it won by lunch on the second day. Barnes, with five for 28 and eight for 29, bowled them out for 95 and 93 to end the three-match mini-rubber against South Africa with thirty-four wickets. South Africa lost the match by ten wickets to finish bottom of the table which was topped by England.

It was the start of a serious decline in the fortunes of South African Test cricket. Sydney Barnes, the medium-pace bowler who could cut and swing the ball either way to make himself one of the greatest bowlers that cricket has ever seen, had a big hand in that demise. Barnes, who made an astonishing leap to fame during England's visit to Australia in 1901 and who had spells with Warwickshire and Lancashire before settling down to league and Minor Counties cricket with Staffordshire, from where he continued to play for England, had wrecked South Africa in 1912. When he visited the Union with MCC in 1913-14, Barnes took forty-nine wickets in the first four Tests and South Africa lost the series 0-4 with one match drawn. South Africa had in their skipper Herbie Taylor of Natal and later Transvaal, a great Test batsman, probably the best ever seen on matting wickets. With lightning footwork and a whole range of cultured strokes, Taylor was the one hope which South Africa had of doing well in this series. But England had Hobbs, Rhodes, Mead and Woolley to make their runs; and, of course, Barnes to take their wickets. The first two Tests were lost by an innings — Barnes taking seventeen wickets in the latter to establish a record not beaten until Jim Laker's feat in 1956 — and the gap between the two sides was enormous.

England won the Third Test at Johannesburg by 91 runs, though South Africa made 304 in their second innings, and even the drawn Fourth Test at Durban found Barnes in tremendous form. It was his last Test appearance and he marked it with fourteen wickets to bring his total against South Africa in seven Tests to an amazing eighty-three at only 9.85 each. Six times he had taken ten or more in a match; on twelve occasions he had five in an innings. Even without Barnes England won the last Test at Port Elizabeth by ten wickets. Philip Mead, the unspectacular left-hander who was the iron rod of Hampshire's order for three decades, made 117 before Jimmy Blanckenberg had him caught and bowled, and although 'Bill' Lundie bowled steadily into the wind to take four wickets in his only Test appearance, South Africa still trailed by over 200 runs on the first innings. The deficit was too great, and when South African Test cricket closed down for World War I it was at its lowest point since those formative years of the previous century.

Just as an Australian side visited South Africa after the Boer War, they were also the first visitors to the Union after 1918. Herbie Collins's Australian Imperial Forces team came first, though the matches were not of Test status despite the Test-strength Australian team, and in 1921-2, Collins took over the reins of the side which was returning from England. Warwick Armstrong who had led the Australians in England in 1921, was injured during the voyage and Collins marked his elevation by scoring

203 in the Second Test at Johannesburg. The first two Tests were drawn. In the second match South Africa had followed-on and been rescued by Nourse and Charlie Frank. South Africa were 207 behind when they began their second innings and were 149 for three when the two saviours came together. They took South Africa to 355 before they were parted. Nourse made 111 and Frank, the little right-hander who had been badly gassed during the war, stayed for eight hours and thirty-eight minutes to resist the might of Jack Gregory, Ted McDonald and Arthur Mailey with 152, one of the slowest of all Test innings. But it was Mailey, together with Charlie Macartney, who broke through in the final Test at Cape Town. There were no South African heroics this time as they went down by ten wickets.

Thus, South African cricket was still in the doldrums and though they ran England close when Freddie Mann took a team to the Union in 1922-3, the difference between the two sides was still firmly in England's favour. There were bright spots for South Africa, however, and in the First Test at Johannesburg, Herbie Taylor underlined his Test-class batsmanship with a brilliant 176 in a second innings total of 420 — South Africa's then highest against England. It left England too much to do to obtain victory and when the one-eyed Norwegian 'Buster' Nupen began to bowl his fast-medium cutters round the wicket, England's batsmen, lacking the skills of Jack Hobbs who missed the tour through illness, fell 168 runs short.

The Second Test played at Newlands was a real thriller. England began their second innings needing 173 to win but when the left-arm medium-pace of Lancastrian, Alf Hall, captured seven wickets — on his Test debut at that — England found themselves a handful of runs short with their last pair at the wicket. George Macaulay of Yorkshire was playing in his first Test and had already taken seven wickets — including that of Hearne with his first ball. Now the versatile Yorkshireman joined Alec Kennedy of Hampshire and won the match by clipping Hall for a single. The Third Test — the first to be played on the new Kingsmead ground in Durban — was drawn when rain washed out the third day after Phil Mead had scored 181 for England; and with the Fourth Test at Old Wanderers also failing to produce a result, all now rested on the final match back in Durban. It was England's game all the way. Jack Russell of Essex became the first Englishman to score a century in each innings of the same Test in what proved to be his final match, thus ending his Test career with scores of 96, 140 and 111. Though Herbie Taylor made 102 — his runs for the series being 582 — and batted for 270 minutes for his third century of the rubber, England bowled South Africa out to win by 109 runs. South Africa had lost yet another rubber.

South Africa's next series, against England in 1924, brought about one of the most sensational matches ever played by a Springboks team. The South Africans began the tour in unconvincing form and by the time the First Test was due to start at Edgbaston, Herbie Taylor realised that his side's bowling needed strengthening. He called up George Parker, Cape Town-born but who was playing professional cricket in the Bradford League. On 14 June 1924, Parker made his Test debut with just one first-class match under his belt. Parker, a steady and unspectacular seamer, opened the bowling and in the face of some fierce hitting by the England batsmen — the first six were Hobbs, Sutcliffe, Woolley, Hendren, Chapman and Fender — bowled like a hero, plugging away for thirty-seven overs to take six for 152 in England's 438 all out.

But England also had a debutant playing in this match — Sussex seamer Maurice Tate — and with his first ball in Test cricket Tate had Manfred Susskind caught by Kilner. Tate's Sussex colleague, Arthur Gilligan, had already bowled Bob Catterall and within seventy-five minutes South Africa were all out for 30 to equal the lowest Test score set by the Springboks themselves in 1895-6. Gilligan had six for 7, Tate four for 12, and although the South African early order, led by Catterall with 120, made a much harder fight of it when they followed on, England were triumphant by an innings and 18 runs. Strangely, Catterall made another 120 in the next Test, played at Lord's and again England won by an innings and 18 runs, powering to 531 for two declared thanks to Hobbs (211), Sutcliffe (122) and Woolley (134 not out). At Leeds, Tate again wrecked South Africa and England went 3-0 up. It was a disastrous tour for South Africa and after rain restricted play to less than three hours at Old Trafford, more bad weather ensured that the Fifth Test at The Oval was also drawn, though Catterall scored 95. Catterall had been South Africa's one bright star, his brilliant driving and leg side shots piling up 471 runs at an average of more than 67.

Cricket in South Africa was now entering a new era and in 1926-7 the first Currie Cup match was played on a turf pitch at Durban, although the first Test Match to be played on turf in South Africa would not take place until Percy Chapman's team played in Cape Town in 1930-1. Natal had pioneered the development of the 'natural' pitch in the Union, although it would be 1935 before a Currie Cup match on turf would be played in Transvaal when the home side established what was then a record 609 runs against the Orange Free State at the Wanderers.

So, just one year after the introduction of turf by Natal, the MCC team which toured South Africa still found itself playing Tests on the old matting wickets. Captain Stanyforth who played three games for Yorkshire in 1928, an amateur wicketkeeper, led the MCC side after the original skipper, Captain G.R. Jackson of Derbyshire, was forced to stand down through ill health. South Africa, too, had a new captain with Taylor standing down at the age of thirty-eight — though he would play in several more Tests — and 'Nummy' Deane of Natal and later Transvaal, an aggressive batsman and brilliant fielder, led the side. South Africa also included a promising young wicketkeeper, Horace Cameron, who played with Transvaal and Western Province, and looked set to give England a rare battle.

In the First Test it was England who took all the honours, centuries from Sutcliffe and Tyldesley and twelve wickets from George Geary, setting them up for a victory by ten wickets; and although George Bissett of Griqualand West, on his Test debut, took five wickets with his fast bowling, England won the Second Test by 87 runs. Two games down after three Tests — the third match at Kingsmead was drawn, Cyril Vincent's left-arm spinners accounting for six wickets in England's first innings — South Africa came back 'from the dead' to level the series. The pace bowling of Bissett and Hall took seventeen wickets at Johannesburg as the Springboks triumphed by four wickets; and at Kingsmead, Taylor — who made 101 in the previous Test — saw Catterall score 119 as South Africa declared 50 runs ahead. Now Bissett let loose. In nineteen overs he had seven for 29 and South Africa needed only 69 to win, which they got for the loss of two wickets.

 So South Africa had fought back to halve the series. Yet when they came back to England in 1929 they still failed to win a Test outside the Union. The difference obviously lay in the matting wickets — on which they had won ten Tests by this stage — and the turf pitches on which they had won none. The 1929 tour was no exception and England won by 2-0 with three Tests drawn, although on four occasions South Africa led on the first innings. The First Test, played at Edgbaston, saw the debut of a young batsman from Transvaal, Bruce Mitchell. Mitchell had originally played Currie Cup cricket on the strength of his bowling and at the age of seventeen had taken eleven for 95 against Border in East London. Now aged twenty, Mitchell went into the South African Test side and scored 88 and 61 not out, sharing in opening stands of 119 and 171 with Bob Catterall. It was the start of a fine career which saw him play forty-two Tests in all — thirty-seven in succession — and although his 149 runs in that debut game took him 575 minutes, he showed that he was very much at home in the electrified atmosphere of a Test Match.

Bad light saved South Africa on the final day of the Second Test at Lord's; but at Leeds there was to be no such reprieve and Woolley and Tate scored 76 in forty-five minutes to take England to a wholly-deserved five-wickets win. Yet South Africa had enjoyed her fling and the last-wicket partnership between 'Tuppy' Owen-Smith (129) and 'Sandy' Bell (26 not out), raised 103 in just sixty-five minutes, still a South African record for the tenth wicket. Owen-Smith, a doctor of medicine and brilliant all-rounder with Western Province, Oxford University and Middlesex, a triple blue at rugby, cricket and boxing, and England's rugby captain, was one of the great sporting personalities of the pre-war era, going on to 1950 before his first-class cricket career finally ended.

The Fourth Test of 1929 was England's by an innings and 32 runs. Centuries from Wyatt and Woolley, followed by twelve wickets from Kent's great leg-spinner 'Tich' Freeman, earned them a resounding victory and in South Africa's first innings of 130, only Denys Morkel of Western Province prospered with 63 runs. Morkel was the best all-rounder on this tour. In the final Test at The Oval he scored 81 to take his runs for the summer on towards a final total of 1,443, with sixty-nine wickets. In Tests alone, Morkel scored 321 runs (45.85) and took fourteen wickets at 32.71, more Test runs and wickets than any other player. In that final game at The Oval, South Africa's batsmen found their form at last. They made 492 before declaring with eight wickets down. Taylor led the way with 121 and besides Morkel, Dean, Cameron and McMillan all weighed in with fifties or more.

On Christmas Eve 1930, the first Test played on a grass pitch in South Africa began at Old Wanderers against Percy Chapman's touring side. The England team was a strong combination, one of the strongest to visit the Union. Nevertheless, South Africa showed that they had made the transition from matting to turf successfully and although they made only 126 when batting first, the Springboks bowled out England in their second innings for 211 to win by 28 runs. Nupens had five wickets in the first innings and he added six more as South Africa powered on. At Cape Town England only just avoided an innings defeat. Mitchell (123) and Ivan 'Jack' Siedle of Natal, who made 141, got South Africa off to a wonderful start with an opening stand of 260 — still a South African Test record. Taylor made 117 and South Africa declared at 513 for eight. England made 350 and 252 (Duckworth was absent hurt in the second innings) but there was no time for South Africa to score the runs needed to go 2-0 ahead. Draws in the last three Tests meant that South Africa had won the rubber against an England side which included Hammond, Leyland, Wyatt, Sandham, Hendren, Voce, Tate and 'Farmer' White.

It was a different story when the Springboks, now skippered by Jock Cameron, went to Australia in 1931-2 and met a side which contained Don Bradman at his best. All five Tests were lost — all by large margins, three by an innings — and Bradman made 226 in the First Test, 112 in the Second, 167 in the Third, 299 in the Fourth when he was not out, and was not needed in the Fifth. In fact, Bradman was absent hurt, but that mattered little for South Africa had been bowled out for 36 and 45 to lose by an innings and 72 runs on a vicious Melbourne 'sticky' which yielded up only 234 runs, still the lowest aggregate for a completed Test Match. The slow left-arm of Bert Ironmonger took eleven for 24 and Bradman finished with an average of 201.50 against the Springboks. On the way home, a demoralised South African team stopped off in New Zealand to play the first official Tests between the two countries. Here there were easier pickings and Mitchell (113) and Jim Christy (103) put on 196 for the first wicket. South Africa won by an innings and it also marked the last Test Match by Herbie Taylor. In forty-two Tests he had scored 2,936 runs, including seven centuries, and of the pre-1914 Test players, only England's Frank Woolley played later. After this historic Test at Christchurch, the sides played a second match at the Basin Reserve, Wellington, which South Africa won by eight wickets to redeem just a little honour from an otherwise disastrous tour.

Yet South Africa's first victory in England was not far off. In 1935 they came to England and in the First Test at Trent Bridge, Dudley Nourse, son of the great 'Dave' Nourse, made his debut. His bold and aggressive batting with Natal had won him a place and he was about to embark on a career which would more than equal that of his illustrious father, whose own Test career had ended at The Oval eleven years earlier after forty-

South African players are presented to King George V during the Lord's Test of 1935

five Tests, 2,234 runs and forty-one wickets. Also playing his first game in that Trent Bridge Test of 1935 — the Springboks' first appearance in a Test on that famous old ground — was Eric Rowan of Transvaal who, with younger brother Athol, would contribute much to Springbok cricket.

The Trent Bridge match lost a day to rain and was drawn. But at Lord's, South Africa were victorious for the first time in England. They batted first and made a modest 228. When England replied they were bemused by the leg-spin, and occasional googly, of Xenophon Balaskas. Fewer less-likely sounding players can have appeared in Test cricket, but 'Bally', a short, thickset Greek who bowled uncommonly fast for his type, took five for 49 and England were all out for 198. South Africa's first innings total had been largely due to Jock Cameron, who hit 90 out of 126 in 105 minutes; in the second innings it was Bruce Mitchell with 164 in five and a half hours, aided by Rowan, who scored his second 40 of the match, and Arthur Langton — tallest and youngest of the tourists — who steered them to 278 for seven declared, leaving England to score 309 to win in 315 minutes. They were dismissed with ease, Balaskas taking another four wickets, and South Africa were home by 157 runs for an historic victory. Thereafter, the remaining three Tests were drawn and South Africa never looked in difficulty in any of them. Another great hurdle had been safely negotiated.

Sadly, Jock Cameron was to die within a few weeks of the end of this marvellously uplifting tour. When Vic Richardson's Australians came to the Union towards the end of 1935, they found their opponents in sombre mood, quite in contrast to the jubilant party which had sailed from England some weeks earlier. Australia won four of the five Tests, and would have won the Second Test at Johannesburg had not a storm intervened when they were 125 runs short of victory with eight wickets in

'Tuppy' Owen-Smith played only five Tests for South Africa, but in one of them he emerged almost a national hero. In the Headingley Test of 1929 he scored 129 and with last man, 'Sandy' Bell added 103 in 65 minutes for what is still a Springbok record for the last wicket. They almost redeemed a hopeless situation but in the end, England still won the match

hand. Even a brilliant 231 from Dudley Nourse — a Springbok Test record until 1951 — could not detract from the fact that Australia were by far the better side. During the series, Clarrie Grimmett established a new Test wicket-taking record, becoming the first bowler to take 200 wickets, and Jack Fingleton scored three successive centuries. Although Australia had done much to foster South African cricket, especially after two wars, it was certain that they still had a stranglehold over the Union.

Wally Hammond took the last England team to visit South Africa before World War II and it was by now clear that, despite the pasting the Springboks had received at the hands of the Australians, he would need his best possible combination. The 1938-9 series was won by Hammond's team 1-0 with four drawn matches. But although other Tests all had their highlights — Eddie Paynter's two separate centuries and Tom Goddard's hat trick at Johannesburg, Paynter's 243 in England's win by an innings and 13 runs at Durban included — it was the last Test started at Durban on 3 March 1939 which is always recalled from this tour.

This was the 'Timeless Test' which lasted for ten days — the longest first-class match ever played — and which ended only when England, set to get 696 to win, had to give up the chase just 42 runs short of a remarkable victory when they had to leave to catch the boat home. It was an amazing match. South Africa made 530 with centuries from Nourse and Pieter van de Bijl, and England replied with 316. South Africa batted a second time and a century from their captain, Alan Melville, the stylish right-hander who played first-class cricket with Natal, Transvaal, Oxford University and Sussex and who later served as a Test selector for many years, set them on the road to 481 and all the time in the world, so it seemed, to bowl England out. England began cautiously and their batsmen steered the side towards the runs. The eighth day was lost to rain, Paul Gibb and Wally Hammond made centuries, Bill Edrich carved 219. The tenth day dawned with England needing 200 further runs, but rain again ate into play and just a handful of runs short of their target, England were forced to give up and begin a two-day trip back to their boat in Cape Town. The match, the last 'Timeless Test' realised 1,981 runs and England's 654 for five remains the highest fourth innings score in first-class cricket.

For the second time this century South African cricket suffered from a world war which claimed the lives of many young Springboks. Indeed, a whole generation which would have provided some of the new talent needed to sustain South African cricket were too busy to play much cricket. So the 1947 touring team to England had a rather mature look about it, with skipper Alan Melville, Bruce Mitchell, and Dudley Nourse among those who had seen it all before. These Springboks arrived in England at the start of the glorious summer which followed the equally cold winter from which Northern Europe had just emerged. They had the misfortune to arrive also, just at the time when the Middlesex players, Denis Compton and Bill Edrich, were about to rewrite the record books, partly at South Africa's expense. Compton took six centuries off the tourists, four in Tests, while Edrich played in four Tests and scored over 500 runs, averaging over 110. Compton made over 750 runs in the series at an average of 94, and although the Springboks contributed to a great rubber which was a fine advertisement for cricket, they were well and truly on the receiving end.

 England won three Tests with the other two drawn. Yet in the First

Test, played at Trent Bridge, South Africa had a big lead on first innings and forced England to follow-on. Melville and Nourse were the early heroes. Melville scored 189, Nourse 149, and the pair took South Africa from 44 for two to 363 for three. They were all out for 533 and then Lindsay Tuckett of the Orange Free State and Vivian Smith of Natal bowled out England for only 208. The medium-pace of Tuckett claimed five wickets, including those of Washbrook, Compton and Yardley, while Smith's leg-spin dismissed Edrich, Evans and Bedser. Led by Compton with 163, England fought back to 551 all out, leaving South Africa to score 227 to win in 138 minutes. They reached 166 for one and Melville's unbeaten 104 made him the first South African to score a century in each innings of a Test. After this, Compton and Edrich took sole charge and England won the next three Tests. Only in the last Test did South Africa come back in any force when Mitchell emulated Melville's feat with 120 and 189 not out and, at 423 for seven, South Africa were just 28 runs short of an epic win.

South Africa's main weakness in their first post-war tour had been a lack of front-line bowling; and in the face of the onslaught by the Middlesex pair that was fatal. Eighteen months later, England, under the captaincy of Freddie Mann, returned to the Union with a strong side. They won the series there by two games to nil with three drawn after starting off with a famous victory at Durban. Worcestershire leg-spinner 'Roley' Jenkins took Eric Rowan's wicket with his third ball in Test cricket, Alec Bedser and Cliff Gladwin wrecked the Springboks and their all out score of 161 was just not enough. England replied with 253, thanks mainly to Hutton (83) and Compton (72), as Norman Mann, known to all as 'Tufty', trundled down his left-arm spin to take six for 59. When South Africa batted again they could manage but 219, setting England only 128 to win.

Yet this seemingly paltry score was not so easy as it first appeared, taking into account the unpredictable pitch. This time South Africa's unlikely hero was the erratic pace bowler from Natal, Cuan McCarthy. McCarthy ripped out six England batsman and by the time the tourists had drawn level with South Africa, eight wickets had fallen. As the big Derbyshire seamer, Cliff Gladwin, strode to the wicket — coining the immortal phrase 'Cometh the hour, cometh the man!' — England needed twelve runs to win; the Springboks needed two wickets to record their victory. Gladwin and Alec Bedser edged England nearer until they needed eight runs off the last eight-ball over. Seven were scored to level the aggregate, and off the last ball of the match, Gladwin felt the ball brush his pads, Bedser was charging down the wicket, and England were home.

The next three Tests were drawn, Hutton and Washbrook scoring an opening partnership of 359 in 310 minutes in the Second Test at Ellis Park, Johannesburg. It was — and still is — England's first wicket record in any Test. Eric Rowan saved this game for South Africa by batting throughout the last day to score an unbeaten 156, having already learned that he had been dropped from the side. At Newlands South Africa were set 229 to win in 125 minutes — and made 142 of them for the loss of four wickets — and back at Ellis Park, Mann set them 376 in 270 minutes, an invitation they not unnaturally declined.

So to the last Test which England won, but in unusual circumstances. Mitchell had made 99 and wicketkeeper Walter Wade of Natal 125 in a South African first innings total of 379. Mann led England with an unbeaten 136 and they took a small lead. But when South Africa reached

187 for three in their second innings, Dudley Nourse declared. One match down in the series, he really had to try to obtain a result. England were set 172 runs in about ninety-five minutes. They certainly meant to have a go and Hutton and Washbrook hit their first balls for 4 and 6 respectively, going on to add 58 in less than half an hour. With the last over to be bowled by Mann, England had lost seven wickets to justify Nourse's declaration — there were those who felt he would never have time to bowl out England — and Gloucestershire's Jack Crapp hit ten runs off three consecutive balls to win a thrilling match for England with just one minute to spare. It had been a marvellous series for the game of cricket and showed just what enterprising captaincy might achieve. Overall this had been a successful tour and had done so much to restore interest in top-level cricket in the Union.

The last Australian team to visit South Africa before the war — in 1935-6 — had enjoyed an easy ride. The first post-war tourists also won four of the five Tests with South Africa's bowling now desperately short of penetration. With Linday Hassett, Neil Harvey and Arthur Morris in fine form for the Australians, the Springboks had little to cheer them. The Second Test, played at Newlands, was one of the brighter spots when Norman Mann (46) and the young off-spinner Hugh Tayfield (75) put on 100 for the eighth wicket in the second innings in just under an hour. Australia still won by eight wickets but Tayfield, who played with Natal, Rhodesia and Transvaal before his distinguished career was over, had signalled his promise, though it was with the ball that 'Toey' Tayfield — so named because of his habit of stubbing his toe into the ground before each delivery — made his name. Two games ahead — they had taken the First Test by an innings — Australia gained a remarkable third victory at Kingsmead. After Tayfield had taken seven for 23 in only his third Test,

 Bird's eye view of the Wanderers ground, Johannesburg, packed for a Test Match

and the tourists had been skittled for 75 (which was their lowest total in Australia-South Africa rubbers), Neil Harvey scored a brilliant 151 not out as his side made 336 for victory in 410 minutes. In their first innings of this astonishing match, South Africa had reached 311 with Eric Rowan scoring 143. Then Dudley Nourse decided against the follow-on, though his side was 236 runs ahead, and when South Africa batted again it was the combined efforts of Bill Johnston and Ian Johnson which shot them out for 99. After a draw at Ellis Park, Johannesburg, Australia went right back to the top at Port Elizabeth, scoring 549 for seven declared — centuries from Morris, Harvey and Hassett — before bowling out the Springboks for 158 and 132. It merely underlined the fact that, in the face of a batting assault from some of the world's greatest players, South Africa just did not possess the attack to come to terms with it.

By the time that Nourse brought the 1951 Springboks to England, several younger players had made the side, notably a tough little opening batsman from Natal, Jackie McGlew; Eastern Province wicketkeeper-batsman John Waite, who later played with Transvaal; and the elegant young batsman from Natal, Roy McLean whose great attacking fervour broke the mould of the many more defensively-minded batsmen produced by the Union after the war. Nourse and Eric Rowan were still there, so too was Athol Rowan, though Tayfield, who was not in this Test side, would soon stake a regular place. Before the end of the tour, Russell Endean, a batsman good enough to open the innings and a solid wicketkeeper, though never reaching the heights of Waite, also played his first game. So too did the bespectacled Rhodesian all-rounder Percy Mansell — excellent bat, inexpensive leg-spinner and totally reliable slip fielder; Clive van Ryneveld another all-rounder of the batting and leg-spin variety; and Geoff Chubb, also a wearer of spectacles, who bowled medium-pace, for Transvaal. Chubb's Test career started at the age of forty years, the oldest South African debutant, and during the tour his ability to move the ball through the air and off the pitch brought him seventy-six wickets. Van Ryneveld was a completely different character. An Oxford blue, van Ryneveld played rugby football for England and during the 1951 tour he scored 983 runs and compiled a chance-free 150 at Bramall Lane for his highest-ever score. These then were the Springboks of 1951.

Alas, they failed to win a series once more and England took the rubber 3-1. Yet in the First Test at Trent Bridge, South Africa won their first Test since 1935 when Nourse made 208, despite a broken thumb. He batted a painful 550 minutes and then took no further part in the match. Athol Rowan (five for 68) and Norman Mann (four for 24) bowled South Africa to victory by 71 runs to end of run of twenty-eight Tests without success. That was the last such success that South Africa would taste in this summer however, and rain at Lord's helped Roy Tattersall to take twelve wickets in England's ten wickets win.

At Old Trafford, England won by nine wickets when it was Alec Bedser's turn to profit from the rain with twelve wickets, though Geoff Chubb, who later had two spells as president of the South African Cricket Association, also enjoyed himself with six for 21 to become the Springboks' leading wicket-taker. At Headingley the Fourth Test was drawn, though it was remarkable for Eric Rowan's 236, the highest by a Springbok in games between the two countries. His giant score helped South Africa to a first innings 538. But when England batted they were more than ready for the task. Surrey's Peter May became another Englishman to make a century on his Test debut, Len Hutton made exactly one hundred and England were only 33 runs behind.

It was the final Test at The Oval, however, which took the 1951 series into the record books. The pitch took spin from the start and South Africa's modest 202 was met by just 194 from England. Jim Laker, who had four wickets in the first innings, took six for 55 when South Africa batted again and England now needed 163 to win. The score was 53 for no wicket and Len Hutton was 27 when a ball from Athol Rowan ballooned up from Hutton's gloves or bat. In trying to protect his wicket, Hutton fended the ball out of the reach of the debutant wicketkeeper Russell Endean. He was given out *obstructing the field,* an 'offence' which had been recorded only four times in first-class cricket anywhere in the world, and which had not been 'committed' for half a century. But England still got home by four wickets and South African cricket still found itself short of the required 'bite' to make it a world force.

From the depths of England in 1951, South Africa went to Australia in 1952-3 and, under the captaincy of Western Province's cheery Jack Cheetham, won two Tests to square the rubber and give their cricket a mighty fillip. Cheetham had scored 271 against Orange Free State at Bloemfontein in 1950-1 — a highest-ever Currie Cup score at that time. With his enthusiastic leadership, and his insistance that first-rate fielding was all important, he turned what had left the Union as an ordinary team into a thoroughbred Test side.

South Africa had not won a state match, and had actually lost to New South Wales, when they met Australia for the First Test. Not surprisingly, South Africa lost this match too, Ray Lindwall bowling the Australians to victory by 96 runs. Then South Africa shocked the cricket world with their first win over Australia for forty-two years. A brilliant 162 not out from Russell Endean and thirteen wickets from Hugh Tayfield gave them victory by 82 runs. Within two weeks, Australia were ahead again, Harvey's 190 — the third of his four centuries in this series — setting up an innings win. When South Africa had much the worse of the drawn Fourth Test at Adelaide — where McDonald and Hassett put on a record 275 for the second Australian wicket — there was a grave temptation to write off South Africa's win as a flash in the pan. When Australia, led by Harvey with 205, started the Fifth Test with 520, that view looked completely justified. But every South African reached double figures as the tourists were all out for 435. Then Western Province seamer, Eddie Fuller, and Hugh Tayfield set to work. Fuller took five for 66, giving him eight for 140 in the match, Tayfield took three for 73, and with Mansell weighing in with two wickets, South Africa needed 295 to win.

They started steadily and at 191 for four, the match was still finely-balanced. Then in came Roy McLean. Cutting and hooking with immense power, McLean hammered 76 out of 106 in eighty minutes and the Springboks became the first Test side to win after facing a 500-plus total in the first innings. For Australia, a young batsman called Ian Craig became the youngest man to play for the Aussies — at seventeen years of age — and scored 53 and 47. But it was the Springboks who took all the honours. Tayfield, in particular, had performed magnificently, despite breaking a thumb. He had thirty wickets in the Tests, eighty-four in all first-class matches; and when the South Africans played two Tests in New Zealand at the end of the tour, he took a further ten. In the First Test,

The Springboks party which toured New Zealand in 1952-3. Back row left to right: H.J. Tayfield, J.C. Watkins, A.R.A. Murray, M.G. Mele. Middle: W. Ferguson (scorer), K.J. Funston, H.J. Keith, E.B. Norton, G.A. Innes, E.R. Fuller. Front: J.H.B. Waite, P.N.F. Marshall, J.E. Cheetham (captain), K.G. Viljoen (manager), D.J. McGlew, W.R. Endean, R.A. McLean

at Wellington, Jackie McGlew made South Africa's highest Test score — an unbeaten 255 — and became only the second man to be on the field throughout a Test as the Springboks bowled themselves to victory by an innings and 180 runs. With Eastern Province's Anton Murray (109), McGlew added a record 246 for the seventh wicket, the best in any Test at that time. Endean made a century in the Second Test at Eden Park, Auckland, but this ended in a dull draw.

There was nothing dull about the 1955 tour of England, however, when South Africa contributed greatly to what most people thought was the best post-war Test series up until then. England won the first two Tests — by an innings and 5 runs at Trent Bridge and by 71 runs at Lord's where Tayfield overhauled Vincent's South African Test record of 84 wickets — and South Africa took the next two matches, by three wickets at Old Trafford and by 224 runs at Leeds. The Old Trafford match found South Africa needing 145 runs to win in 135 minutes. They got them with nine balls to spare to inflict upon England their first defeat at Old Trafford since 1902. South Africa had three first innings century-makers, McGlew, Waite and Paul Winslow who played for Sussex, Rhodesia and Transvaal and was one of the hardest hitters ever seen in Springbok cricket.

At Headingley, South Africa trailed by 20 runs on the first innings but then a big opening stand between McGlew and the left-handed Trevor Goddard set them full steam ahead for a big total. McGlew made 133, Goddard, who was to become the great Springbok all-rounder of the period with his resolute batting and left-arm seam bowling, scored 74, and the pair added 176, a record South African opening partnership in

England. Another left-hander, Natal's Headley Keith, scored 73 and helped McGlew take the score to 265. An unbeaten 116 from Endean saw South Africa to an all-out total of exactly 500. When England tried to make the victory runs, only Peter May, who fell three short of his century, prospered to any great degree, though there was middle-order resistance from Compton, Graveney and Insole. Tayfield and Goddard had five wickets each and England were all out for 256 — 224 runs short of the aggregate and thus giving South Africa an unprecedented second win in the rubber. All now rested on the final Test at The Oval and here it was England who took the honours. For the first time, five Tests in England all reached definite results. South Africa needed nearly 250 to win. Laker (five for 56) and Lock (four for 62) ensured that they failed by 92 runs.

One fine series in England was followed by another in South Africa in 1956-7 when the rubber was again drawn 2-2. Again England won the first two Tests. The First Test was the first to be played at the New Wanderers ground in Johannesburg and a South African record crowd of 100,000 saw England win by 131 runs after Worcestershire's Peter Richardson had scored what was then the slowest Test century. It took him 488 minutes. In contrast, South Africa were shot out for 72 in their second innings, their lowest total in a home Test for nearly sixty years. The Springboks had no answer to the seam bowling of Trevor Bailey. That score of 72 was repeated at Newlands in the Second Test. This time it was Johnny Wardle, with seven for 36, who did the damage. South Africa lost by 312 runs and Russell Endean became the first man given out 'handled the ball' in Test cricket when he diverted a ball from Wardle off his pads and towards his stumps and then knocked it to safety with his hand.

At Kingsmead, the Third Test was drawn, though Hugh Tayfield returned eight for 69 in the second innings, the best figures of any South African Test bowler, and bowled 137 balls without conceding a run, still a record in any first-class match. Tayfield was magnificent and in the Fourth Test at the New Wanderers, it was this player who saw that South Africa gained their first victory over England at home since 1930-1. South Africa had made 340 in their first innings before bowling out England for 251, Tayfield taking four for 79. The Springboks' second innings knock realised only 142 but the target was still too much for England. Tayfield bowled throughout the last day, sending down thirty-five eight-ball overs, and taking nine for 113 as England fell 17 runs short of victory. It was a superb example of off-spin bowling and gave South Africa her first win on turf in the Union. There was now all to play for at Port Elizabeth and on a pitch of quite impossible bounce — the ball hardly ever got above shin height — South Africa's first innings of 164 was the winning score. Once van Ryneveld had won the toss, the result was never in question. Tayfield, who did not take a wicket in England's first innings 110, had six for 78 in the second. They were all out for 130 and South Africa had squared the series with a win by 58 runs. Tayfield's return for the rubber was thirty-seven wickets at just over 17 runs apiece.

Australia were the next visitors, led by Ian Craig, just twenty-two years old. The rubber opened at New Wanderers where McGlew and Goddard put on what is still South Africa's record opening stand against Australia. They scored 176 before they were parted with Goddard falling ten runs short of his century and McGlew going on to 108. Waite made 115 and South Africa closed their innings at 470 for nine. McGlew's declaration was successful in that half the Australia side were out for 62 before Benaud, who made 122, and McDonald rescued them. They were 102 runs short of South Africa's total when their last wicket fell and the fearsome pace of Peter Heine had claimed six for 58. Though Wally Grout held a record six catches when South Africa tumbled to 201 all out — Grout achieved this Test record on his debut — and although Alan Davidson finished with six wickets, the match petered out into a tame draw.

The Second Test was won easily by Australia by an innings and 141 runs as South Africa found themselves totally bemused by the spin of Benaud and Kline, Kline ending the match with a hat trick by dismissing Fuller, Tayfield and Adcock with the scoreboard stuck on 99. At Kingsmead, South Africa could not press home the advantage which Neil Adcock and Peter Heine had given them in bowling out Australia for 163. Adcock, who played with Transvaal and Natal during a first-class career which spanned the decade from 1952, took six wickets with his graceful pace bowling. South Africa made 384, but that was at a cost. McGlew's 105 took nine hours and thirty-five minutes, and though Waite's century came in much quicker time, there was no time left to finish the match. By lunch on the fifth day of the Fourth Test at New Wanderers, Australia needed only a single to give them a ten-wickets win. Heine again had six wickets, but again Benaud and Kline mystified the South Africans. It was much the same in the final Test at Port Elizabeth. Benaud claimed his 100th Test wicket and Australia were home 3-0 with a day to spare. Benaud had thirty wickets in the rubber, Kline fifteen, and with Davidson's twenty-five it was these three who more than made up for the lack of match-winning form which the Australian batsmen had shown.

Nevertheless, this South African side did contain some of the best cricketers ever to represent that country. Players like Tayfield, Adcock, McLean, McGlew, Goddard and Waite were household names in England as well as Australia. It was sad then, that the 1960 tour to England should be one of the most disappointing Springboks' visits on record. They lost three Tests and won none in a damp and miserable summer; and the no-balling for throwing off Geoff Griffin, the blond fast bowler from Natal cast a shadow. Griffin arrived in England with the Springboks shortly before his twenty-first birthday, but there were to be few celebrations for the paceman whose right elbow was bent and could not be straightened naturally. Griffin had first appeared in Currie Cup cricket in 1957-8. In his second full season, 1959-60, he headed the South African national bowling averages with thirty-five wickets at less than 13 runs apiece. He came to England, his 'kinky' elbow, the result of a childhood riding accident, already well-known.

The controversy started when, on the Saturday of the match with MCC at Lord's, Griffin was called for throwing, first by umpire Frank Lee, and then by his colleague, John Langridge; and once he was called simultaneously by both umpires for throwing and overstepping the crease. No further action was taken in the match which was drawn with Griffin taking three for 47 and none for 22 — but the cloud now hung over the young bowler's action. He had, in fact, been called twice in South Africa, once against Transvaal and once against a Combined Border and Eastern Province team. Griffin did not play in the next match, against Northants, but when he was included in the team against Nottinghamshire, the crowd waited anxiously to see what would happen. Griffin was called eight times for throwing — and seven for dragging — and again both umpires were involved. During the match it was announced that Griffin would go to Alf Gover's cricket school for special coaching from the old Surrey and England bowler. Griffin did not play in the next match against Minor Counties at Stoke — when, incidentally, a young Staffordshire wicketkeeper called Bob Taylor made his first-class debut — and when he reappeared at Cardiff he sent down only six overs with his 'new' action. He was not needed as South Africa coasted to an innings and 133 runs victory, the damage being done by 'Pom Pom' Fellows-Smith, the all-rounder from Transvaal who had played county cricket with Northants and who was a double Oxford blue at cricket and rugby football. Known better for his rustic batting techniques, Fellows-Smith had six wickets with his stock medium-pace. Tayfield followed up with five in the second innings and South Africa went into the First Test at Edgbaston with a fine victory under their belts.

For England, Bob Barber, the Lancashire batsman and leg-spinner, and Peter Walker, the fine Glamorgan all-rounder who also played with Transvaal and Western Province, made their debuts. For the Springboks, Fellows-Smith, Sid O'Linn, the Transvaal and former Western Province left-hander, who also played cricket for Kent and soccer for Charlton Athletic, made their first appearances in a Test Match. So did Geoff Griffin. The South African was not called for throwing however. England won the match by 100 runs, a tedious game of cricket highlighted only by some big hitting from McLean and Dexter, two fighting innings from Waite who scored 114 runs for once out, and some fine fast bowling from Trueman, Statham and Adcock. But South Africa came off much the worse and England were home with four hours to spare. Before the Second Test at Lord's, Griffin was again called, this time in the match at Southampton, twice in the first innings and six times in the second. McLean won the match for the Springboks, hooking the first two balls of the last over to the boundary, and South Africa moved to Lord's knowing that they faced problems.

The match proved to be Griffin's last Test. Yet it was one in which he made history by becoming the first South African to do the hat trick, and the first man to do so in a Lord's Test. England made 362 for seven declared. Mike Smith becoming Griffin's first victim of his hat trick when the Warwickshire batsman was just a single short of his century. Griffin was called eleven times for throwing during the innings, all by Frank Lee at square leg. When South Africa batted they collapsed twice, to 157 and 132 all out, and lost by an innings and 73 runs. The match finished just before half past two on the fourth day and an exhibition match was staged. During this 'beer and skittles' encounter, Griffin's first over saw umpire Sid Buller call him four times in five balls. It was now obvious that Buller would continue to call the unfortunate Springbok every time he bowled. After speaking to McGlew, Griffin decided to finish the over by bowling underarm — and was promptly no-balled by Frank Lee for failing to notify of his change of action. It was a sad end to his career, though Griffin stayed with the party as a batsman.

In county games Griffin made 353 runs and was more than useful in the field. More important, he had conducted himself with the greatest possible dignity and it was a great shame that a boyhood accident should eventually rob him of more Test Matches. The Third Test, which saw the debut of Western Province medium-pacer Jim Pothecary, was also lost

South Africa 1961. Back row left to right: E.J. Barlow, K.C. Bland, G.B. Lawrence, H.D. Bromfield, P.M. Pollock, K.A. Walter, W.S. Farrer. Front: M.K. Elgie, R.A. McLean, D.J. McGlew (captain), E.Orchard (manager), J.H.B. Waite, S.O'Linn

when South Africa, in the face of Trueman (five for 27) and Statham (three for 27) were all out for 88 in their first innings, following-on and, despite a gallant 98 from Sid O'Linn, who took over behind the stumps when Waite dislocated a finger, lost by eight wickets. The Old Trafford Test lost two full days to rain and was drawn, as was the Fifth Test at The Oval where Waite became the first South African, and only the third man behind Bert Oldfield and Godfrey Evans, to do the wicketkeeper's double of 1,000 runs and 100 dismissals in Test cricket. After Adcock (six for 65) and Pothecary (four for 58) had earned South Africa a first innings lead of 264, they looked likely to pull back a match. But Geoff Pullar and Colin Cowdrey put on 290 for the first wicket when England batted again and the game was as good as drawn. Only three times had that opening stand been surpassed in Tests and it was then the highest in England. Pullar (175) and Cowdrey (155) ensured that South Africa were never in with a chance.

In 1961-2 South Africa entertained New Zealand for a full five-match rubber. On their previous meeting in 1953-4, South Africa had won four Tests in the Union, though after the First Test, which they lost by an innings, New Zealand were never as bad as the final results would imply. Now New Zealand, led by John Reid, were at a peak, while South Africa's fortunes were in a turmoil. The First Test was played at Kingsmead where seven Springboks made their debuts, including Transvaal's bespectacled batsman, Eddie Barlow, Eastern Province's fine all-rounder Peter Pollock, and the brilliant Rhodesian fielder Colin Bland — one almost forgets he was also a fine Test batsman. Bland's fielding in the covers was unique in its achievement and he must be the only cricketer who could draw crowds to watch him field.

The First Test was won by 30 runs after Pollock took six for 38 in the second innings. Rain on the first day of the Second Test at New Wanderers meant that only an hour or so's play was possible and the game was an inevitable draw, though there was time for the Rhodesian pace bowler Godfrey Lawrence to take eight wickets in his first bowl in Test cricket. Lawrence had figures of eight for 53 in the first innings. The Third Test at Newlands saw New Zealand score their first win over South Africa — and only their second in any Test — when they did not enforce the follow-on but batted again to leave South Africa to score over 400 to win. They failed by 72 runs and the only men who could look back on the match with any real satisfaction from South Africa's point of view were McLean, who made 113, and Syd Burke who, on his debut, took eleven wickets. Burke, of North-Eastern Transvaal and Orange Free State, had a field day with his lively pace. Sadly for South Africa, his efforts were not enough. On the third day of the Fourth Test at New Wanderers, South Africa had bowled out New Zealand twice to win by an innings and 51 runs. This time Godfrey Lawrence had nine wickets in the match, but in the final Test at Port Elizabeth, South Africa lost the initiative in a close-fought match. They trailed by 85 runs on first innings, bowled New Zealand out for 228, but failed by 40 runs to win the match. New Zealand squared a rubber for the first time and there was no doubt that this had been a truly splendid series.

There was now the visit to Australia and New Zealand in 1963-4 and South Africa amazed everyone, including perhaps themselves by sharing the rubber 1-1 with three matches drawn. The main reasons were the bowling of Peter Pollock and Joe Partridge, who made his Test debut after twelve years of Currie Cup cricket with Rhodesia; the batting of Bland, Barlow and Graeme Pollock, left-handed younger brother of Peter, and the captaincy of Trevor Goddard. The First Test in Brisbane, where Australia's Ian Meckiff was called for throwing, was drawn. Australia won the Second Test at Melbourne by eight wickets, Barlow making 109 and 54 for South Africa; and the match found South Africa fielding two pairs of brothers, the Pollocks and the Pellews.

The drawn Third Test at Sydney saw Graeme Pollock, not yet twenty years old, score a magnificent 122. The young left-hander's style seemed so effortless, yet ball after ball was sent crashing to the ropes in ferocious manner. South Africa, set to score 409 to win in 430 minutes, reached 326 for five at the close, Bland and Goddard both scoring 80s. South Africa had enjoyed much the better of the Sydney Test. At Adelaide for the Fourth Test they completed a magnificent ten-wickets victory, thanks almost entirely to an epic stand of 341 for the third wicket between Barlow and Graeme Pollock. Barlow, that busy, bustling cricketer, became the third South African Test cricketer to score a double century. His 201 was a great innings and with Pollock making 175, they raised South Africa from a shaky looking 70 for two, to 411 for three in four hours and forty-three minutes. It remains South Africa's highest stand for any wicket in Test cricket. They ensured that the Springboks' final total was 595 — a lead of 250.

Australia made 331 in their reply, but that left South Africa needing a relatively small handful of runs to complete their victory before lunch on the last day. Fittingly, Barlow was there at the end, 47 not out. South Africa might have won this rubber, but for a frustrating last-wicket stand by Veivers and Hawke who put on 45 when it looked likely that the Springboks would coast home. In the end they needed 171 runs to win in eighty-five minutes, a task that obviously eluded them. In Australia's first innings the patient Joe Partridge took seven for 91 to move forwards towards becoming the Springboks' leading wicket-taker on the tour with sixty-two, including thirteen in three Tests in New Zealand. In Tests against Australia alone, Partridge bagged twenty-five wickets, the same number as Peter Pollock, and on that steamy day in Sydney during the last Test he moved the ball about both ways to become virtually unplayable. In New Zealand, where all the Tests were drawn, South African cricketers had their first taste of things to come. Anti-apartheid demonstrators in Wellington damaged the Basin Reserve pitch but failed to prevent the First Test from starting on time.

The last visit by an official England touring party to South Africa took place in the winter of 1964-5 when Mike Smith's team, although facing a South African side which had some way to go yet before they reached the commanding pinnicle they would enjoy later, won the series by 1-0 with four drawn matches. The series was decided in the very first match when England amassed 408 runs at Kingsmead with centuries from Ken Barrington and Jim Parks. Barrington, the Surrey run-machine, and Parks, the Sussex wicketkeeper, took England from 279 for five before Smith declared, Barrington's 148 giving him the honour of being the only Englishman to score centuries in Tests in all seven countries. South Africa had no answer to the off-spin of David Allen of Gloucestershire and Fred Titmus of Middlesex. It was England's first win in thirteen matches and in the Second Test at New Wanderers they may well have made it two in a row until Colin Bland thwarted them on the last day with a brilliant unbeaten 144 after South Africa had followed-on over 200 runs behind following superb innings from Ted Dexter, who made 172, and Ken Barrington, who hit 121.

Draws in the remaining three Tests were highlighted by Ken Barrington 'walking' after being given not out at Newlands where earlier Barlow and Tony Pithey, a tall right-hander from Rhodesia, added 172 for the second wicket. Pithey shared in another big stand in the Fourth Test at New Wanderers where he and Waite put on 157 for the fifth wicket; in England's innings Parfitt was 122 not out and Mike Smith was given out after Peter van der Merwe threw down his wicket after he had walked out of his crease to prod the pitch. Van der Merwe had received the ball from the wicketkeeper and although umpire H.C. Kidson upheld the appeal, Goddard revoked it and Smith was allowed to continue. Goddard's sportsmanship was repaid when, in South Africa's second innings, he scored his first Test century at the sixty-second attempt. Rain at Port Elizabeth ensured that England would win the rubber when the last Test was drawn, leaving Graeme Pollock with 137, only the second player to score three Test hundreds before his twenty-first birthday.

So the last official England Test team — at least for the foreseeable future — left South Africa. In the final Test, Geoff Boycott, Yorkshire's dour opener, had carved 117 runs. Boycott had made his Test debut in the First Test against the Australians at Trent Bridge in 1964 and here he was making a century in the last recognised Test between England and South Africa in the Republic, as it had been since 1961. It is ironic then that when the next time anything like an England team played in South Africa, Boycott should be the prime mover, though in extreme and controversial circumstances.

Indeed, South Africa now had only three official Test rubbers left before she was cast out of the international arena. In 1965 the Springboks came to England for their last visit, sharing the summer with New Zealand and playing a three-match rubber which they won 1-0. This was a thrilling series with each match going to a close finish. South Africa were always in the ascendancy and in the First Test at Lord's England needed 191 to win in 235 minutes found themselves defending grimly with seven men out and the score still out of reach. To compound England's agony, Edrich could not bat again after being hit on the head by a delivery from Peter Pollock. Fred Titmus and Fred Rumsey guided England safely through a nail-biting last few moments. Earlier, Colin Bland had run out Barrington and Parks with two brilliant pieces of fielding, both of which resulted in direct hits on the stumps from the covers. Transvaal's Dr Ali Bacher made his debut in this game. Small and stocky, Bacher was at his best on the back foot, scoring many of his runs on the leg side. At Trent Bridge South Africa won, thanks almost entirely to the Pollock brothers. A century and a half century from Graeme, and ten wickets from Peter saw them win by 94 runs. Even Colin Cowdrey's first innings century was not enough for England. South Africa now needed a draw at The Oval to win their second rubber in England. They did so, rain foiling England who had been set 399 to win and were within 91 of that target when rain ended play with seventy minutes still remaining. This was Brian Statham's swan song. The Lancashire hero, brought back after an absence of twenty Tests, took seven wickets in his final Test.

That was the last time that England and South Africa met in an official Test. The Springboks now had two series standing between them and the limbo in which they would find themselves, and Australia provided the opposition on both occasions. In 1966-7, Bill Lawry, brought the Australians. South Africa were led by Peter van der Merwe, and in the First Test at New Wanderers he took South Africa to their first home win against Australia in twenty-two matches stretching back sixty-four years. Excitement mounted after Transvaal became the first South African team to beat Australians in the Republic. When the First Test got underway, however, South Africa were bowled out for 199 and when Australia passed that score for the loss of only one wicket, things looked decidedly black for the Springboks. Australia's eventual lead was only 126 and that was when the match turned in South Africa's favour. They batted again and made their highest ever score — 620.

Their biggest hero was the North-Eastern Transvaal wicketkeeper Denis Lindsay who chose this moment to score his first Test century. Lindsay was 182 when his wicket finally fell to Stackpole. This had been quite a match for Lindsay so far — he had already equalled the world Test record of six dismissals in an innings! Everyone seemed to get amongst the runs and now Tom Goddard, freed from the worries of captaincy, took six wickets as Australia were beaten by 233 runs. Australia pulled back in the next Test at Newlands, winning by six wickets with twenty-five minutes to spare. Earlier, Australia had made 542 with centuries from Simpson and Stackpole. Then Graeme Pollock played a phenomenal innings of 209 out of 353 in 350 minutes, yet still South Africa had to follow-on. At Kingsmead, South Africa recovered from Barlow's dismissal to the first ball of the match and won by eight wickets, the debutant Mike Procter taking seven wickets in the match. At New Wanderers, Lindsay scored his third hundred of the series, but when only two wickets stood between Australia and an innings defeat, down came the rains and the match was drawn.

The scales were now tipping in South Africa's favour and at Port Elizabeth they won by seven wickets for their first successful rubber against Australia. It was Tiger Lance who finished the match off, walloping Ian Chappell for a 6 over midwicket on the fourth afternoon. What an incredible series this had been for South Africa. Peter Pollock became the fourth and youngest South African to take 100 Test wickets, and Lindsay, in additional to his swashbuckling batting, held twenty-four catches, the record for a five-match rubber. There was, too, the inevitable century from Graeme Pollock as South Africa ensured a 3-1 win.

So to the historic last rubber played by South Africa prior to their excommunication. Bill Lawry's side were whitewashed 4-0 and it seemed that now, at the very hour of their demise for political reasons, South Africa were at the very peak and poised to become perhaps the world's greatest side, though without competition against all other countries, that is an arguable title. In the First Test at Newlands, South Africa won by an innings and 170 runs; in the Second Test at Kingsmead, the margin of Springbok victory was an innings and 129 runs. Barry Richards, the young Natal batsman who made his debut at Newlands, scored a century. But their real hero was Graeme Pollock. Pollock scored 274, the highest by a South African Test batsman, and the Springboks made their highest score of 622. Richards's 140 had included a century in 116 balls. So the carnage went on. At New Wanderers, South Africa scored a record runs win in any Test — by 307 runs — and then in the next Test, at Port Elizabeth, beat their own record by hammering Australia out of sight by 323 runs. That was South Africa's last Test Match. There were centuries from Richards and from Brian Irvine of Natal and Transvaal; and Mike Proctor, with his unusual 'square-on' action, took six for 73 in the last innings. The side had been led by Ali Bacher and it included Barlow, the Pollocks, Lindsay, Lance, and Athanasios Traicos, Egyptian-born but at university at Natal, and Pat Trimborn, Natal's lively medium-pacer. Those were the players in this historic match. South Africa had just wiped the Australians almost off the face of the cricket map; they were a great side, and they were about to run out of opposition.

One can only imagine to what heights the 1970 South African team might have climbed but for the storm which was to break around their heads and which was to have serious repercussions, not only on Test cricket, but on international sport in general. In 1961 the Union of South Africa withdrew its application for continued membership of the Commonwealth after anti-apartheid demonstrations around the world gathered in force. The South African Cricket Association, formed in Kimberley in April 1890 and one of the three original members of the Imperial Cricket Conference, was also forced to withdraw from the governing body of Test cricket, although Test matches against England, Australia and New Zealand were still played. Because of the apartheid laws, we have never seen the best of the West Indians, Pakistanis and Indians taking on the best of white South Africa.

About the time that the storm over apartheid was gathering force, a young Cape Coloured cricketer, Basil D'Oliveira, was making his way from the sunshine of his homeland to a wet and miserable England. Unable to reach the top in his own country, D'Oliveira was to play for

Middleton in the Lancashire League in the hope that he might eventually make the grade into multi-racial county cricket. At the time, the two events — South Africa's withdrawal and a young coloured cricketer seeking his fame and fortune in more liberal climes — though, of course, related, did not seem to have any special significance, for many young coloured men, cricketers and otherwise, had left South Africa. The difference here was that within seven years, Basil D'Oliveira, after graduating from league cricket to county cricket with Worcestershire, had proved himself good enough to play for his adopted England. With a tour to South Africa drawing close, and the all-rounder set for a place on that tour, the whole cricketing — and political world — waited with baited breath to see just what would happen.

The Tests in England in 1968 were against Australia. From that series would emerge the basis of the touring party to South Africa that winter. The First Test at Old Trafford was won by Australia by 159 runs; D'Oliveira's contribution was 9 and 87 not out, and one for 38 and one for 7. The next three Tests were drawn and each time there was no place for the Worcestershire all-rounder. When the team for the Fifth Test was selected, still D'Oliveira was not included and it seemed that the confrontation would be postponed for the time being. The selectors did not have a pistol at their heads and D'Oliveira was not selected simply because England felt they could do better without him. This was proved beyond all doubt when Northants' Roger Prideaux was taken ill and England skipper Colin Cowdrey immediately asked for D'Oliveira. The MCC now knew that if he was an outstanding success in this last Test Match, then he must certainly be a strong candidate for the tour. It turned out that D'Oliveira was an outstanding success. His 158 was largely responsible for England winning the match and squaring the series. Now the selectors had to select the party for South Africa.

It was announced the very next day — and there was no D'Oliveira. Doug Insole, chairmen of the selectors, felt it necessary to explain why he and his colleagues had not chosen D'Oliveira. It had nothing to do with the political implications, they said. They regarded D'Oliveira as a batsman only on overseas pitches, not as an all-rounder. Put alongside the other batsmen in line for the tour, reluctantly, he and Colin Milburn, the swashbuckling Northants player, had to be excluded. But there then followed a still unexplained event. When Tom Cartwright, the Warwickshire seam bowler, reported unfit, the selectors then called up D'Oliveira to replace him. Now we had a man who the selectors claimed was left out because they regarded him primarily as a batsman, being asked to replace an injured bowler. It did not make sense.

If we could believe there was no underhand business in the original decision not to take D'Oliveira to South Africa because he had failed to make the side on merit, then it strained the imagination to believe that *now* there was not something going on which did not meet the eye. Not unnaturally, the South African Government was also hard put to believe that there was no dirty work afoot. Their premier, Mr John Vorster, announced that D'Oliveira was being used as a 'political cricket ball' and that the MCC party would not be welcome in South Africa because the Republic was not prepared to have a cricket team foisted upon her by people with 'certain political aims'. Vorster's speech at Blomfontein won him few friends outside his own party. Yet people totally opposed to apartheid must have wondered just what had gone on in the minds of that selection committee. All that remained was for MCC to formally cancel the tour, quite rightly so, since, just as South Africa felt that it could not receive a team which it felt was politically influenced neither could England accept a situation where the opposition told them who they could and could not include. Now, of course, the wheel has turned full circle and the England selectors have apparently abandoned that grand principle in banning players who took part in the 'rebel' tour to South Africa in 1982, pre-empting the fact that neither, West Indies, India, nor Pakistan would play against them if Gooch and company were selected.

So the 1968-9 England tour to South Africa was called off. Australia, with no coloured players, had no difficulty in fulfilling the 1969-70 tour to South Africa as we have seen. But as South Africa were hammering them out of sight, a bigger issue was being debated in London, that of the impending visit by South Africa that summer. The first signs of the problems which were to follow came in the summer of 1969 when a private South African team, Wilfred Isaac's XI, had its visit disrupted by demonstrators. The activities of the demonstrators, which included digging up pitches and running on to the field during play, divided Britain as to whether these people, led by Peter Hain, were morally right in what they were doing, or whether, no matter what the validity of their cause, they had no right to disturb people who wanted to play and watch cricket. Hain, then a Young Liberal, now a member of the Labour Party, became chairman of the Stop the Seventy Tour Committee, designed to do exactly that.

Britain had already seen the difficulties involved when violence broke out during the Springboks rugby tour of 1969-70 when it became apparent how difficult it would be to stop a mob which was intent of disrupting a sporting event. The logistics of protecting a Test Match ground for up to six days were infinitely more difficult to organise than the protection of a rugby ground for less than two hours. It was a hideous situation. Right

Barry Richards played only four Tests before his career was cut short at international level

was totally on the side of cricket. If we wanted to play the game against any side in the world, then we should be allowed to do so; yet at what cost? The sight of barbed wire around our peaceful county grounds would be too much to bear; what was the point of trying to play cricket against that kind of backcloth? With a constant and overwhelming police presence, the whole purpose of what is essentially a beautiful game would be destroyed. The Wilson Government was also firmly against the South Africans coming. At last, under heavy pressure, the Cricket Council caved-in. The South Africans' invitation was withdrawn. Many people breathed a sigh of relief, not least the organisers of the Commonwealth Games due to be held in Edinburgh and which African, Asian and Caribbean countries said they would boycott if South Africa played cricket in England.

South African cricket was now isolated. A Springbok rugby tour to Australia in 1970-1 convinced the authorities there — in the same way that a rugby tour had brought about the realisation in England — that they would have to call off the proposed 1971-2 tour by the South Africans. Since then there have been no Test Matches involving South Africa, although great strides have been made in making the sport multi-racial in the Republic. For the next decade, South African cricket had to be content with Currie Cup matches, which took on all the importance of Tests on occasions, and the country was now starved of international sport.

Peter Kirsten has played some brilliant innings for Western Province and Derbyshire and would be an automatic choice for any South African Test team

The feelings of the sportsmen themselves differed from their government. In April 1971, for instance, Mike Procter bowled the first ball of a Transvaal v Rest of South Africa match, Barry Richards hit it for a single, and then the two batsmen, Richards and Brian Bath, and the entire Rest team, led by Procter, walked off the field in protest against the South African Government's refusal to allow non-white South Africans to play for the country. That display at Newlands did much to restore the faith of the ordinary man that perhaps Test cricket with South Africa could be resumed. By the late 1970s and earlier 1980s, a favourite pastime on English county grounds was to while away those hours when the rain came down by selecting a South African team from those who had grown up since apartheid split the game, and a pretty fearsome side it looked too! Peter Kirsten, Garth Le Roux, Clive Rice, all playing in county cricket, would walk into any South African side, and in the first few months of 1982 they had the opportunity to do just that.

For some months there had been whispers that 'something big' was about to happen and talk of large sums of money being offered to tempt an England, or Australian, or 'World' team to South Africa for pirate Tests continually reared its head.

England went to the West Indies in 1980-1 amid controversy over some of the players with South African connections and, although the tour was completed, save for trouble in Guyana, if England had been ostracised there and then, it is conceivable that a South Africa-England series could have been set up. Then came trouble on the build-up to the tour of India. This time it was Geoff Boycott and Geoff Cook who came in for some verbal bullets. But cricket in India transcends politics and it was no surprise when the tour went ahead.

It was on this tour, however, that the final arrangements were made for the bombshell which broke over world cricket on 28 February 1982. That was the day when it was announced that a party of English cricketers, led by Graham Gooch and Geoff Boycott, was in South Africa to play a series of 'Tests' against the Republic. Boycott had apparently been chief recruiting officer before his untimely return to England after scoring the runs which made him Test cricket's greatest run-maker. Hotel rooms in India had been the venues for clandestine meetings to talk about the 'chess matches' — the code-name for the impending tour — and although cash failed to tempt the man who would have been the South Africans' biggest catch — Ian Botham — there were those, particularly players at the end of their Test careers, who excercised their inalienable right to earn their living where they chose. The storm was predictable and intense. The 'Dirty Dozen' as they were dubbed by one politician, consisted of Gooch, the elected captain, Boycott, Amiss, Emburey, Hendrick, Knott, Larkins, Lever, Old, Underwood, Willey and Les Taylor, the Leicestershire opening bowler who has never played for England. Later they were joined by Geoff Humpage, the Warwickshire wicketkeeper, Arnie Sidebottom of Yorkshire, and Bob Woolmer of Kent.

The tour, though ill-advised so far as the English players were concerned, was inevitable. The South Africans had been told that they could not expect another English team until they put their house in order; the all-white South African Cricket Association had been replaced by the multi-racial South African Cricket Union, headed for some time by the late Rachid Varachia, an Indian of great ability; and in 1979 a fact-finding mission, albeit not wholly representative, sent out by the International

Cricket Conference, had found that strides had been made and suggested that a multi-racial touring side should be sent out, and that England should, by direct contact, encourage the South African game. Yet nothing had been done. The South African cricketers felt bitter; they had made a genuine effort and now they had been let down. The problem, of course, was that the emphasis had changed greatly since 1968. Then, it was apartheid in cricket that was the difficulty; fourteen years later it is apartheid in general. There are those who regard multi-racial cricket as a window-dressing to hide the real problems in South African society. The English tourists, later banned by the authorities from playing for England for three years, have apparently been naive in their assumption that the whole thing would be a storm in a teacup. They obviously had no idea of the hornets nest they would stir up.

For the tour itself, ironically it was largely a failure. South African caps were awarded to the players who appeared in the 'Tests', notably Kirsten, Graeme Pollock, Rice, Barry Richards, Vintcent van der Bijl, Jimmy Cooke, Ray Jennings, Stephen Jeffries, Alan Kourie, Garth Le Roux, and of course, Mike Procter who captained the side. Graham Gooch's XI, or the South African Breweries English XI to give them their official title, were whitewashed in the three-match one-day international series, and were largely unsuccessful in their other games, providing some dreary cricket at times and failing to capture the imagination of the South African cricket public who, we were led to believe, would flock in their tens of thousands to watch the return of any form of international cricket.

Just as the 'D'Oliveira' affair had been the watershed of South African Test cricket in 1968, so the 'South African Crisis' of 1982 threatened to polarise Test cricket in black and white. That prospect has largely been avoided by Australia's refusal to back the tour and by England's banishment of its rebels for the immediate future. The legality of that action has, at the time of writing, still to be established, and so, too, has the question of whether this controversial tour might, in the long term, make the return of South Africa to the fold, more, or less, likely. Cricketers everywhere want Test cricket to be open to all the major countries. The price which they are prepared to pay for that remains to be negotiated.

West Indies

Calypso Cricketers

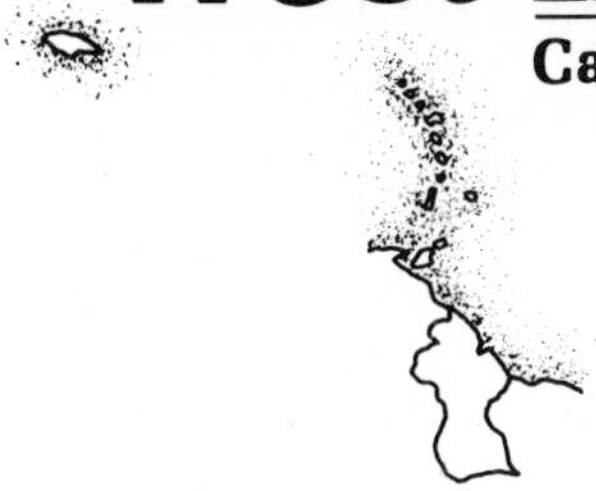

Constantine, Worrell, Walcott and Weekes; Stollmeyer, Headley, Sobers and Lloyd; Richards, Greenidge and Kanhai — the names of great West Indian batsmen ring out down the pages of cricket history. Add to them the spin twins of Ramadhin and Valentine; Lance Gibbs who also weaved a spinner's magic spell; add to them the great pace bowlers, Hall and Griffiths, Roberts, Holding, Marshall, Holder and the rest, and you evoke images of cricket played in the flamboyant style of the calypso stars from the Caribbean. For just as the islands have their golden beaches, crystal-clear waters and cloudless blue skies, just as they have their exotic flowers, fruits and birdlife, so too, do they have their magnificent cricketers. In such glorious surroundings it is little wonder that the West Indians play cricket as, surely, it was meant to be played. Not for them was the game learned in the cobbled streets of a wet Pennine England. Here the game is played in the sun — and it is the sunshine which seems to permeate everywhere in the cricket played Caribbean style.

The climate has played a great part in shaping, not only the attitudes of West Indian cricketers, but also their development. Hard and fast pitches have produced great batsmen. Natural athleticism of the inhabitants has seen to it that the West Indies teams are always brimful of the fastest bowlers in the world. The social climate, too, has ensured that in an area where there is very little work and a high degree of poverty, cricket is the one sure passage to fame and fortune, to a station in life which those lucky enough to possess the greatest ability would otherwise undoubtedly not know. The West Indies have overcome fierce inter-island rivalry to combine into some of the world's greatest teams, and their natural aggressive, attacking play, while it has sometimes worked against them, has, overall, overcome most difficulties set before them in Test Matches against less talented sides who have resorted, occasionally, to tactics not in the best interests of entertaining cricket.

Just when cricket was first played in the West Indies is, like the origins of the game in most other countries, lost in the mists of time though it is mentioned as having been played in Barbados in 1806, and the 59th Foot beat Trinidad Club in 1842. James Lillywhite certainly coached there in the 1860s and the first inter-island match appears to have taken place in February 1865 when Barbados, that island of just 166 square miles which had given the world so many great cricketers, easily beat Demerara, later British Guiana and now Guyana. Cricket, introduced to the islands by the British Army and the trading companies, was more the preserve of the wealthy islanders than the majority of poor people. Trinidad joined the inter-island round of matches in 1869, but Jamaica, far out to the west, was precluded by sheer distance, though club games were being played in Kingston. It was not until the 1880s, however, that cricket took on a more serious and competitive aspect. In 1886 a representative West Indian team visited North America under the managership of G.N. Wyatt of British Guiana, and captained by Jamaica's L.R. Fyffe. The following year the Americans made a return visit to the islands and in 1891, a triangular tournament between Trinidad, Barbados and British Guiana proved so successful that a regular competition was instituted and the trophy, first used in 1893, was competed for until 1939.

So, interest in West Indies cricket was growing and in 1895, the Caribbean game received an enormous boost when an English touring party, captained by R. Slade Lucas of Middlesex, arrived to play sixteen matches, eight of them which can be regarded as first-class. Lucas's team won ten, lost four and drew two (four of the first-class games were won, three lost) and tasted defeat against Barbados, Trinidad, Jamaica and St Vincent. In 1896-7, two separate amateur touring parties from England visited the Caribbean, one captained by Lord Hawke, who had led the Test team to South Africa the previous year, and one led by Arthur Priestley. Hawke's team included 'Plum' Warner of Middlesex, who was born in Port of Spain; Priestley's party included another Middlesex giant, Andrew Stoddart; and both teams were surprised by the standard of cricket played against them.

Lord Hawke's party played fourteen games and won nine and lost two; Priestley's team had sixteen matches, winning ten and losing five. One of the defeats suffered by Priestley's team was a three-wicket loss against a

Sir Pelham 'Plum' Warner played fifteen Test Matches for England. But he was born in Trinidad where his father was Attorney-General. He played one match for the West Indies during their 1900 visit to England.

combined West Indian team. Cricket was now firmly established on the islands and in 1900 the West Indians made their first visit toEngland. The team was captained by 'Plum' Warner's brother, Aucker Warner, and included L.S. Constantine of Trinidad (father of the great Sir Learie), and Charles Augustus Ollivierre, an aggressive batsman from St Vincent whose cutting and driving attracted the attentions of Derbyshire for whom he later qualified and scored some epic innings in the English County Championship.

The first West Indian touring party to England set sail aboard RMS *Trent*, leaving Barbados on 26 May 1900 and arriving in Southampton a record-breaking ten days later. Aucker Warner's selection of the team was hampered by the fact that, instead of picking the strongest party, he was obliged to take a representative selection from all the islands. In addition, his party was seriously weakened in the wicketkeeping department and it was against this background that the tourists played their first match, against London County captained by W.G. Grace, on 11 June at the Crystal Palace. London County was a strong side and it was no surprise when they defeated the West Indians by an innings and 198 runs. L.S. Constantine scored only 2 and 5, but against MCC he hammered a thrilling 113. The early defeats by the English teams largely killed any interest in the West Indian tour and from a financial point, the visit was a sad failure. Yet the Caribbean cricketers had gained valuable experience. Though none of the games were ranked as first-class, the West Indians beat Minor Counties, Leicestershire, Hampshire, Surrey and Norfolk. In the Leicestershire match, 'Plum' Warner played his single game for the West Indians and, opening with Ollivierre, put on 238 for the first wicket before he was out for 113. Ollivierre, meanwhile, marched on to 159. At the end of the tour he had scored 883 runs at an average of 32.70.

In 1902, R.A. Bennett and B.J.T. Bosanquet took out another all-amateur team to the Caribbean. The team won six and lost five of its first-class matches and Bosanquet, inventor of the googly, found the hard, true pitches to his liking. He took eighty-four wickets at less than fifteen runs each, and headed the batting averages with 33 runs per innings to establish himself as the leading player on the tour. Cricket in the West Indies continued to develop and in 1904-5, the first team to include professional English cricketers went out under the captaincy of Lord Brackley. These tours were still private enterprises and it was not until 1910-11 that MCC sent out their first official party. Brackley's side included professionals, Thompson of Northants and Hayes of Surrey, and the West Indians were also delighted at the rare sight of G.H. Simpson-Hayward, one of the last underarm bowlers in first-class cricket.

Brackley's team played twenty games (ten first-class) and were defeated only three times. But those three defeats were in the first-class matches and the West Indian cricketers were now acquitting themselves well. R. Ollivierre, brother of the man who was now making his name with Derbyshire, scored 99 against the English tourists during the game with St Vincent, and then took ten wickets in the match for only 57 runs. But the best performance by a West Indian bowler was that of C.P. Cumberbatch who took eight for 27and five for 30 when the England team was rattled out for 92 and 100 against Trinidad. His right-arm medium-pacers were too much for the tourists and underlined, once more, just what rapid strides cricket in the West Indies was making. The results of this visit by the English team left West Indian cricketers full of optimism for their visit to England in 1906 when an ambitious programme of thirteen first-class matches was arranged.

The team was led by Major H.B.G. (later Sir Harold) Austin and included the brilliant left-handed batsman and slow left-arm bowler S.G. Smith, who later played for Northamptonshire. The tour began at Crystal Palace, scene of the West Indian's huge defeat at the hands of London County in the opening game of their previous English tour. This game was to follow the same pattern for Grace's team won by an innings and 247 runs. In the same week, the tourists led Essex by 153 on first innings, but still contrived to lose the match. In a second-class fixture, the West Indians beat the Minor Counties, and then triumphed in a game against South Wales whom they beat by 278 runs. They suffered defeat at the hands of Lord Brackley's team, and other reversals came in games against MCC, Derbyshire, Kent, Surrey and Hampshire. Their biggest success of the tour came, however, in the match against Yorkshire at Headingley. It has to be admitted that the Tykes were not at full strength, yet even so, the West Indians' performance caused a sensation. Batting first, they made 270 and then bowled out Yorkshire for just 50 runs, Ollivierre taking seven for 23 and Smith three for 27. When the West Indians batted again Percy Goodman made 102 not out and they were able to declare at 305 for six, leaving Yorkshire an improbable 526 for victory. Though Denton made a century for the county, the task was never on and the tourists won by 262 runs.

In the very last match of the tour, West Indies claimed their third first-class victory against Northamptonshire. Goodman scored another century and Smith took twelve wickets in the match as the tourists won by 155 runs. The performance by Smith was no doubt instrumental in Northants offering him a place and he helped them to second place in the County Championship table in 1912 before he eventually emigrated once more, to New Zealand. But before Smith could take the county almost to the Championship in 1912, he had an important engagement in the West Indies during the English winter of 1910-11 when MCC sent out its first official party under the captaincy of A.F. Somerset of Sussex, who had played with Lord Brackley's team in the Caribbean seven years earlier.

This was an historic tour, for on 5 April 1911, in the tourists' third match with Jamaica at Kingston, there occurred a tie. MCC batted first and made 269, bowled out Jamaica for 173, made 131 in their second innings, and then bowled out the home side once more, this time for 227 with the total scores standing exactly equal. The MCC party played eleven first-class matches and won only three of them to underline just what improvements had come about in the West Indians' game. From the start of the tour it had been apparent that the MCC team was not strong enough and they lost to Barbados twice, each time by an innings and twice being bowled out for less than 100. Trinidad joined in the fun, beating MCC twice at St Clair, once by an innings and once by seven wickets, and the full truth about the state of West Indian cricket was dawning.

In 1912-13, MCC returned to the islands, still led by Somerset, and were again soundly thrashed by Barbados. MCC might have felt that their opening score of 306 was good enough. Barbados felt otherwise and with Walter Gibbs scoring 129 not out and George Challenor 188, made 520 for six to go on to win by an innings. In the return match there was further humiliation for the English players, though the match itself turned out to be a thrilling one. Albert Relf scored 41 in MCC's first innings, which was as well since the rest of the tourists could muster only 24 runs between them including extras. Then Challenor scored another century, and with Percy Tarilton making 157, Barbados amassed a big lead with 447. In their second innings MCC were 246 for nine before W.C. Smith and Somerset raised a fine last-wicket stand to take the tourists to 372 before Smith was out for 126 and Barbados had yet another innings win, this one with 10 runs to spare. The brilliant left-hander, Harry Ince, then made 167 for a West Indian XI, but here was one of MCC's rare successes and they won the representative match.

Here, however, West Indian cricket had to pause a while. World War I was but a few months away and cricket in the islands had to take a back seat. It was not until 1923 that a team from the West Indies made another tour to England. Major H.G.B. Austin brought over his second side. Austin's task in selecting the side was made even more difficult than usual because the inter-island matches, which he could have used as a guide to form, mostly fell victim to heavy rain. His team was picked mostly by recommendation and Austin stepped off the boat full of trepidation for his largely unknown team. One of the players to make the trip was George Francis, born in Barbados in 1897 and a fast, uncomplicated bowler who fired in at the stumps with no thought of swing or swerve. He played in every game on the 1923 tour, took ninety-six wickets, and with George John formed the first of what was to be a long and distinguished line of West Indian opening attacks. A measure of their ferocious skills can be drawn from the fact that at Scarborough, H.D.G. Leveson-Gower's team was set only 31 to win the match and reached that paltry target, only after losing six wickets to the combined efforts of Francis and John.

In all, the West Indians played twenty first-class matches and won six and lost seven. One of their greatest wins was at The Oval where Surrey, who included such great names as Sandham, Fender, Jardine, Ducat and Shepherd, were shot out for only 87 to set up the West Indians for a ten-wickets win. George Challenor made 155 undefeated runs in a West Indian first innings total of 305. In the second innings, Challenor (66 not out) and Percy Tarilton scored 121 for victory without losing a wicket. Challenor finished the tour with an average of nearly 52, putting him third in the English averages of 1923, behind Hendren of Middlesex and Mead of Hampshire. Challenor's contribution to the tour was immense. He scored six centuries in first-class matches with his all-round class — an aggressive style backed up by copy-book defensive technique.

Another great success on the 1923 tour was Learie Constantine, son of the man who had scored a century at Lord's twenty-three years earlier. Constantine had English crowds gasping at his astonishing fielding at cover point. He had played in the same Trinidad team as his father in 1922 and when he boarded the *Intaba*, he was full of youthful high spirits for the adventure which lay ahead. Poor Constantine's hopes were to be set back by the English weather, however. He recalled later:

> I shall never forget that so-called summer! The rigours of it robbed us of our captain, froze up poor George John's bowling, upset Victor Pascall, and chilled the rest of us into pessimism. Being naturally exuberant, we fought against it; but it lay in wait for us and trickled down our necks, damped the clammy sweaters we tried to hide in, and made our

> wrinkling flesh creep. I recall miserable journeys in freezing trains from one damp hotel to another; dressing rooms with their own private chills laid on, and afternoons in the field when it was impossible to pay attention because one kept thinking about overcoats.

This, then, was Learie (later Sir Learie) Constantine's first impression of England. Yet he looked forward keenly to the game against Lancashire (in which county he would become a great and legendary figure in the league). Lancashire had, at that time, two great bowlers in Cecil Parkin and Dick Tyldesley, and Parkin in particular, intrigued Constantine, for he knew that the bowler was trying to get the last few wickets which would take him to 100 for the season. Lancashire batted first and made their usual large total before reducing the West Indians to 26 for four. That was the scene of desolation which met the loose-limbed all-rounder from Trinidad, Joe Small, who, despite his name, was a tall, distinguished-looking player.

It was a scenario which would have seen most batsmen get their heads down and make a concerted effort to lose no more wickets. But this was not the way in which Joe Small approached his cricket. He went out to meet every ball, cracked Parkin and Tyldesley all around Old Trafford, and reached 94 in less than 100 minutes, half his runs coming in boundaries. Even in the 'nervous nineties', Small did not alter his cavalier approach, and this proved his downfall. Just short of what would have been a grand century, he fell, perishing as he had prospered — by the sword. Old Trafford rose to him and even Lancashire's hard-pressed bowlers slapped him on the back. In the second innings, Small made 68 and although his efforts were not enough to save the West Indians from defeat, they set him on the road to personal glory during the tour, scoring one glorious innings of 131, and reaching around the 50 mark on ten occasions.

In the last game of the tour, at the Scarborough Festival, came that amazing collapse by Leveson-Gower's XI. Jack Hobbs was among the English batsmen who found the sheer pace of Francis too much to handle. Hobbs had already been dropped, but to Francis it was no matter.A simple, straight ball was just too fast for the Surrey master and he departed lbw. The game was lost but the tour was hailed as a great success. The West Indians returned home in elated mood. It had been many years since a Caribbean team had visited English shores. They had accounted for themselves with great skill and proved to the world that they could produce cricketers who were as good as any in the game. The scene was now set for one more MCC tour to the islands — and then surely the West Indians would be able to push home their claim for full Test Match status alongside the great international teams.

In the 1925-6 English winter, the first English team to visit the West Indies since before World War I arrived in the Caribbean under the leadership of the Warwickshire amateur, the Hon F.S. Calthorpe. The party comprised fourteen players, eight of them professionals, and included some of the great names of English cricket at that time. Wally Hammond, Fred Root, Percy Holmes, 'Tiger' Smith, Lionel Tennyson, Roy Kilner and Ewart Astill were among the touring party. The team lost only one first-class match, but the West Indians found seven players who were good enough to make centuries against the tourists, though the top score of the tour belonged to Percy Holmes who scored a magnificent 244 in

Jamaica, while Wally Hammond was not far behind him with 238 not out in Barbados.

The final representative game of the tour was played in British Guiana where West Indies batted first and made 462 on a perfect pitch after six had been hit in the first over of the match to set the pace. When MCC batted they could muster only 264 after Holmes had fallen to Constantine's wiles. The English team followed on and again Holmes and Constantine came face to face. This time the Englishman stonewalled until the last over of the day. Constantine sent down three good-length straight balls, each one of which was pushed safely back to the bowler. Off the fourth ball, the West Indian found the outside edge of Holmes's bat and the wicketkeeper accepted a simple chance. Alas for the West Indians, the weather robbed them of what would have been an historic victory, MCC were only 45 ahead with just two wickets remaining when the rains came down and ended the match. Lionel Tennyson was to bring private sides to Jamaica in the future, sides which included a good sprinkling of Test players, but this last match of the 1925-6 tour was the last unofficial 'Test' between West Indies and an English XI. In the summer of 1928, West Indies were at last to join the ranks of the world's best as equal members.

The decision to admit West Indies to full Test Match status was made and in the early summer of 1928 the party, captained by Karl Nunes of Jamaica, arrived in England. Nunes, a fine left-handed opener had been in the eleven at Dulwich College and was vice-captain of the West Indian team which toured England in 1923. Five years later he returned to lead a full Test side of which he was also wicketkeeper. Learie Constantine was also back and again he found the English weather in particularly spiteful mood. The opening game of the tour was against Derbyshire. It was a real thriller and gave the West Indians great confidence for what lay ahead. In the fourth innings, the tourists needed 189 to win but found the Derbyshire bowlers in fine form. With two wickets standing, the West Indians still needed a further 40 runs for victory. Constantine appeared at the wicket and took complete charge of the match, hitting five 4s and a 3, then 8 runs in one over. The first match of the tour was duly won and the West Indians received their much-needed injection of confidence.

Alas, the success was not to last out. Disappointment followed disappointment and at the summer's end, only five out of thirty first-class games were won. Three Tests were played — and in each one of them England won by an innings. The first match was played at Lord's on 23-26 June 1928 when eleven West Indians made their Test debuts. They lined up against one of the greatest of all England Test elevens. Names like Sutcliffe, Tyldesley, Hammond, Jardine, Chapman, Tate, Larwood and Freeman — the team read like a Who's Who of English cricket. Ernest Tyldesley made 122 — scored in 160 minutes — and England totalled 401. West Indies had no answer to that and they were bowled out for 177 and 166 to lose their first-ever Test Match by an innings and 58 runs. Throughout the Tests the West Indian batting was no match for England's bowlers. George Challenor, who had been the great hope, was now forty years old and well past his best. His scores in six Test innings were 29, 0, 24, 0, 46, 2. In the Second Test at Old Trafford England won by an innings and 30 runs; at The Oval they won by an innings and 71.

After that early win over Derbyshire, the West Indians had enjoyed little success prior to the First Test and had even been beaten by Ireland. Against Essex, Constantine scored 94 in his first hour at the crease at

Leyton and went on to make the tour's first century — 130 — following that up with 60 not out against Surrey to save the game. Constantine tore a muscle in the game at The Oval, but was determined to play in the next match against Middlesex. He said later 'I knew the tour had so far failed to cover costs and that Mr O'Dowd of British Guiana, who had financed it, looked like losing a lot of money. I was the draw card and was determined to play.' Play Constantine did, coming to wicket at 79 for five after Middlesex had knocked up a big score, and making 86 in under an hour. When Middlesex batted again, Constantine grabbed the ball for a second spell and took six for 11. West Indian hopes were dashed when they batted a second time and lost half the side for little more than 100. Then up stepped Learie Constantine once more. He made a century in just about one hour and the West Indians were home by three wickets. What an epic performance had come from Constantine. His first innings spell of six for 11 had given him innings figures of seven for 57, and pulling and driving with incredible power, his second innings 103 had included two 6s and twelve 4s.

But 1928 was a summer of stark contrast for the West Indians. Nowhere were their fortunes lower, or their moral deeper in the pit of despair, than in the game with the Minor Counties at Exeter. The Minor Counties had been forced to follow-on in the face of Francis and Herman Griffith and their second innings looked likely to fold as quickly as the first, when their skipper, Lockett, came in at number five and hit 154. Not only did the Minor Counties avoid an innings defeat, they set themselves up for an extraordinary win. The West Indians were rattled out for 103 and lost the match only days before the First Test. It was a stunning blow to the tourists hopes and they never recovered. Constantine became the first West Indian to achieve the double of 1,000 runs and 100 wickets in a season and he alone had more than made up for the public's disappointment.

Apart from the feats already mentioned, Constantine also weighed in with a hat trick at Northampton against the county. It was another match in which this irrepressible West Indian was never out of the action. In the first innings he took seven for 45 as Northants slumped to 100 all out, then scored 107 before taking the ball again and with six for 67, ensuring that the tourists won by an innings. His hat trick came on the last day when Woolley, Walden and Matthews were dismissed in successive deliveries. For the latter pair it was the second time in the match that Constantine had claimed their wickets for nought. Older Northamptonshire fans still remember that match over half a century ago, which underlines what a legendary figure Learie Constantine had become, even in his own playing days. He alone stood head and shoulders above the rest of this first West Indian Test team.

For the rest it had been a largely disappointing tour, though it must be remembered that it was also a very strenuous one. The West Indian fast bowlers in particular were not used to plugging away, day after day, week after week in this manner. They were tired and they were aching by the time the tour ended and they left England's shores for their home islands. For Constantine there was the knowledge that he would soon return to play for Nelson as a Lancashire League professional. His feat of beating Middlesex almost single-handed had seen to it that the offers came in. One can only imagine what kind of figures a man of Learie Constantine's calibre would command if he were playing today. There would not be an English county, Yorkshire excepted, nor an Australian state, which

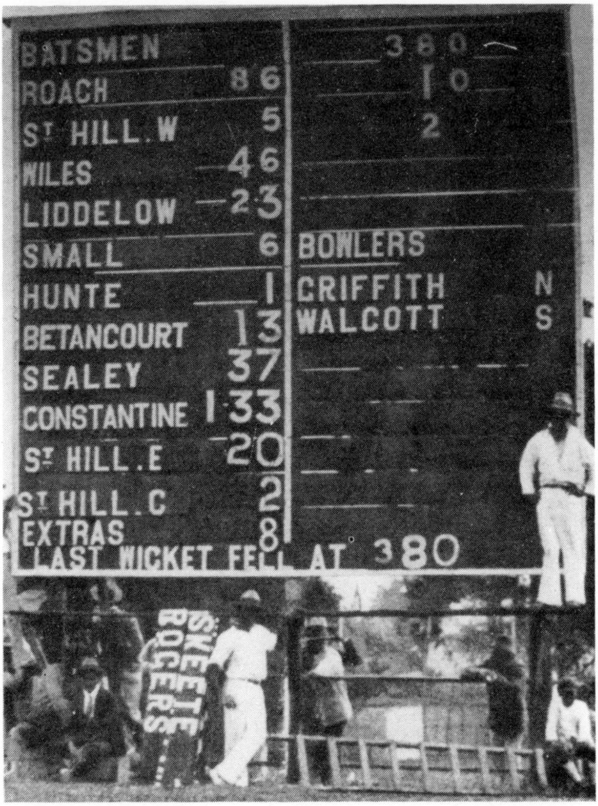

Scoreboard shows Learie Constantine's record-breaking last match as an amateur in 1929 when he scored 133 against Barbados to break his father's Trinidad Inter-Colonial record score made in 1912

would not almost bankrupt itself to parade the talents of a Constantine. Not that they would bankrupt themselves, of course; any outlay for such a player today, if he existed, would surely be repaid by increased gates receipts and membership fees. Constantine was a unique cricketer, and in the West Indian season of 1929-30 he would be lining up against England again, this time on the grounds of his beloved Caribbean.

Yet the first England side to play official Tests in the West Indies was certainly not the strongest that MCC could muster. To begin with, New Zealand had also been awarded her full Test spurs and an English team set sail for Australasia to play four Tests in New Zealand as well as some first-class games in Australia itself. That touring party was captained by Harold Gilligan and included famous names like Frank Woolley and Duleepsinhji. In addition, regular Test players like Hobbs, Sutcliffe, Larwood, Hammond and Tate had all opted for a winter's rest after the rigours of the English County Championship season. Nevertheless, the England party to the West Indies did include players like Hendren, Sandham, Rhodes, Ames, George Gunn, Stevens and Voce, under the captaincy of the Hon F.S.G. Calthorpe.

In the opening games in Barbados, MCC gave the West Indians a taste of their quality when Patsy Hendren scored two consecutive double centuries. In fact Hendren, who was now forty years old, had an incredible tour and in all matches he averaged 126; in the Tests alone he made 693 runs at an average of 115. The West Indians were still suffering from inter-island rivalry over who should captain their Test side and the matter was only resolved when it was decided that each island should stage a Test and nominate its own captain for that particular game. The First Test began on 11 January 1930 at Kensington Oval, Bridgetown, Barbados with the local player Teddy Hoad, a defensive right-handed batsman and leg break bowler, in charge. Another player to make his debut in the match was Jamaica's George Headley. Headley was born in Panama but arrived in his mother's home island at the age of ten. Soon he was showing great prowess as a schoolboy cricketer and his Test debut in January 1930 was the start of a run which would see this 'Black Bradman' as the outstanding West Indian batsman for the next twenty years.

Hoad won the toss and West Indians naturally took first use of a perfect Bridgetown pitch. The home side made a splendid start and reached 303 for three with Clifford Roach of Trinidad scoring the first official Test century against England with 122 runs scored with a powerful array of cuts, hooks and drives. The middle and late order West Indian batsmen could not capitalise on this fine start and the Middlesex leg break and googly bowler, Greville Stevens, picked up five of the last seven wickets as West Indies slumped to 369 all out. England replied with 467 to give themselves a comfortable lead after Andrew Sandham contributed a fine 152. Now the scene was set for George Headley, just twenty years and 230 days old, to stride to the rescue of his side. Headley scored 176 before Wilfred Rhodes, over thirty years his senior, claimed the wicket of this brilliant young West Indian. Headley had added 156 with Clifford Roach, and 142 with Frank de Caires of British Guiana, to ensure that England had no chance of pressing home their advantage. Derek Sealy of Barbados and later Trinidad, who had made 58 in the first innings, was the youngest player to appear in a Test Match at the age of seventeen years and 122 days. Clearly, with Sealy and Headley to lead the way, the West Indies had much to anticipate. Sealy had already given MCC something to think about with a century in the game between Barbados and the tourists.

The tourists moved to Trinidad and in the colony game, Patsy Hendren reached 96 and was looking for the first century against Trinidad's bowling on that island. Ellis Achong, the slow left-arm bowler of Chinese descent, put down a good length ball and Hendren's bat flashed it hard and wide of first slip and although the Middlesex man was thinking of the boundary which would give him the record, the ball flew to Learie Constantine who snapped up one of his five catches in that match. The West Indian had to choose between catching Hendren's fierce shot, or having a hole drilled through him. He chose the former and Hendren marched off muttering, as Constantine recalled later, 'one or two of the more red-hot words of the parade ground!'

The West Indians went into the Second Test at Queen's Park Oval, Port of Spain, the next day, their hopes sky-high. They led on the first innings, having reduced England to 12 for three at one stage, but Hendren, who had scored 77 in the first innings, made 205 not out in the second and when Bill Voce added seven for 70 to his first innings four for 79, England were home by 167 runs. The highest West Indian scorer was Errol Hunte, captain of Trinidad, and poor Clifford Roach, who had scored 122 and 77 in the First Test, bagged a 'pair' in this game, falling each time a victim of Bill Voce. As for Learie Constantine, he could only contemplate on the fact that he had dropped Hendren when he had scored less than 40. His remaining runs on the way to that double century were just about the margin of England's victory.

 All this gave no hint of the drama which was to unfold at Georgetown,

British Guiana, where the local hero, Marius Fernandes, took charge of the side. Fernandes, a steady right-hand batsman, had the ill luck to contract malaria in, of all places, Ireland, during the West Indians visit in 1923. Charles Jones, British Guiana's left-hand bat and left-arm slow bowler, was the one new face in the West Indies side, while England brought in Derbyshire all-rounder, Leslie Townsend, for his first Test Match. This match proved just how fickle the fortunes of cricket can prove. Clifford Roach, after failing to score a run in the previous Test, became the first West Indian to hit a double century. He made 209 before Townsend had him caught by Haig. George Headley made 114 and West Indies were all out for 471. When England batted, they had no answer to the bowling of Francis and Constantine who each took four wickets. England were 33 for three at one stage and all out for 145 to give the West Indians a massive lead. When they batted again, West Indies made 290 and Headley's 112 made him the first West Indian to score two separate centuries in a Test Match. He had now scored three Test centuries before his twenty-first birthday and there was now no doubt of the outcome of this match. Despite Hendren's brave 123, England were bowled out to lose by 289 runs, though it was not until fifteen minutes from the close that Voce became the last victim. Constantine returned five for 87 and West Indian cricket moved into a new era.

The final Test at Kingston, though drawn, was a remarkable match for several reasons. It broke records, all subsequently beaten, for the longest Test Match, highest total, highest individual score, highest individual match aggregate, and provided the youngest player to score a double century in a Test. England began by making 849, with Andrew Sandham's 325 then the highest Test score. They led after the first innings by 563 runs but did not enforce the follow on, instead setting the West Indies an incredible 836 to win. Now George Headley scored 223 and the West Indians reached 408 for five before the match was left drawn after nine days, the last two of which saw no play due to rain. West Indian cricket had come of age; and George Headley, still almost a schoolboy, had collected a double century and three centuries against the victors. His aggregate for the series was 703 runs and his average 87.

Perhaps the most significant part of the tour was, however, the dropping of Learie Constantine for the last Test. Without his bowling — he had nine wickets in the previous Test — England massacred the West Indian attack to the combined total of well over 1,000 runs. The bowling figures of the Jamaican all-rounder, O.C. 'Tommy' Scott, make fascinating reading. In the first innings at Kingston, Scott's leg-spinners took five wickets for 266 runs in eighty overs and two balls, just thirteen of them being maidens! The other interesting point of the match is to ponder why Calthorpe, having got the West Indians on the rack, did not put them in to bat again. The only possible explanation must be that people like Gunn and Rhodes, both in their fifties, did not relish the prospect of fielding again after the West Indians had made 286 in their first innings. If Calthorpe had enforced the follow-on, then perhaps England might have won. Instead, the West Indians were level at one game each in the four-match rubber. It was the springboard for cricketers from the Caribbean to launch themselves fully on to the world circuit. In November 1930, they set sail for Australia and a new adventure.

In truth, the West Indians could hardly have picked a worse time to visit Australia for cricket there was at its high noon with players like Bradman,

West Indies party in Australia 1931. Back, left to right: R.H. Mallett (manager), E. St Hill, F. de Caires, T. Scott, H. Griffith, G. Francis, L. Constantine, J. Selheult (Asst Secretary). Middle: G. Headley, O. Wright, L. Birkett, G. Grant (captain), F. Martin, C. Roach, I. Barrow. On ground: L. Bartlett, E. Hunte, J.E.D. Sealy

Ponsford, Jackson, Kippax, McCabe, Woodfull, Fairfax, Oldfield and Grimmett holding the stage. The West Indians set sail through the Panama Canal and into the Pacific under the captaincy of the Cambridge University batsman, G.C. 'Jackie' Grant who, not only was he inexperienced as a captain, had never seen the team now under his command in action. The party docked at Wellington for a two-day game against what was virtually a full New Zealand Test side. Constantine, who had spent the summer with Nelson in the Lancashire League, found his form at once and took six for 24 as the New Zealanders were dismissed for under 200. The West Indians were 128 for four when rain stopped play and they left the match unfinished and set sail once again.

Grant soon welded his side into a fighting unit and two days after landing in Australia the West Indians faced New South Wales, one of the strongest sides in the southern hemisphere who, of course, included Donald Bradman. The Australians were soon to be treated to some vintage Caribbean cricket as their visitors rattled up 339 in 250 minutes, and then shot out New South Wales for 206, of which Bradman scored only 10. Constantine took six for 45. Batting a second time, the West Indians increased their lead with Constantine making 59 in thirty-five minutes before winding himself up for the biggest hit of his life, only to see the New South Wales bowler stick out a hand and catch a ball which must have been travelling like a rifle bullet. Catches were dropped and the New South Welshmen got home by four wickets. Monty Noble, writing in the *Sydney Sun* commented: 'Constantine hit four 6s and four 4s. Australians have to travel back to times before 1914 to recall such a sensational innings as this one.'

Grant hoped that his side would prosper on the fast pitches of Australia with the bowling of Constantine, Herman Griffith of Barbados and George Francis, also of that famous cricketing island. Yet the First Test, at Adelaide Oval, was lost by ten wickets. Grant had a successful match, becoming the first West Indian to score an undefeated 50 in each innings of a Test Match, and catching Bradman off Griffith after the great Australian had made only 4 runs. Bradman's previous Test innings, incidentally, had been 232 off the England attack at The Oval four months earlier. But the leg-spin of Clarrie Grimmett proved to be the deciding factor in the First Test. Grimmett took eleven wickets in the match and Ponsford and Jackson scored the 172 Australia needed for victory without being parted. In the Second Test, played at Sydney, the West Indians enjoyed no luck at all. Australia won the toss and batted first on a perfect pitch which took them to 323 for four at the end of the first day — New Year's Day 1931. The following day was lost to rain and when the game resumed on the 3 January, the pitch had completely altered in character. Australia lost their last six wickets for 46 runs and when Eddie Bartlett caught Kippax at mid on, he crushed a finger and was unable to bat. The West Indians, a man short and caught on a wet pitch, were bowled out twice to lose by an innings and 172 runs.

The tourists moved to Brisbane where they beat Queensland by over 200 runs in a match in which Constantine scored 75 and 97. The Third Test was played on the same Exhibition Ground and the West Indians had an immediate success when Francis trapped Archie Jackson leg before for a duck. It might have been an even greater breakthrough when Bradman, who had scored just 4, steered Constantine straight to first slip. The fielder spilled the ball and Bradman went on to make 223, adding 229 for the second wicket with Bill Ponsford. It was then the highest score made by an Australian in a home Test and though Headley scored the first century by a West Indian against Australia, Grimmett was largely responsible for the tourists falling by an innings and 217 runs.

Against the lower class of opposition the tourists prospered. In a minor game against Combined Country Districts at Newcastle, Constantine scored 147 in ninety-three minutes from just sixty-seven balls and the West Indians won by an innings. But back in the Test Match arena, at Melbourne, the Caribbean cricketers reached rock bottom. Bowled out for 99 and 107, they lost by an innings for the third time in succession (the First Test had, remember, been lost by ten wickets). It was a sad and disillusioned party which made its way to Sydney once more for the Fifth Test. Just before the final Test, West Indies played New South Wales again and this time decided to get the bit between their teeth and go for all out attack. They batted first and made just under 350, not a big score when batsmen like Bradman, Kippax, McCabe and Fingleton were playing for their opponents. Constantine, however, was in rampant mood. He took six wickets, including that of Bradman who had made 10, and New South Wales were all out for 190. When the West Indians batted again they lost three wickets for 37 before Sealy and Constantine collared the bowling and enabled them to declare, leaving New South Wales to score nearly 600 for victory. Bradman refused to be tempted again and scored 73 carefully amassed runs; Kippax and McCabe both scored centuries; but New South Wales could muster no more than 466 and the West Indians went into the final Test with renewed optimism.

Their high spirits were justified. Batting first, they made 350 for six declared, 'Freddie' Martin, the Jamaican left-hander scoring 123 and Headley weighing in with 105. Grant now had the best use of a sticky pitch, and after Australia had been bowled out for 224 he was able to declare a second time at 124 for five, leaving his bowlers time to rattle out Australia to win by 30 runs. The last wicket to fall was that of Herbert Ironmonger. Fairfax called him for a run, but Martin's throw to Grant was straight and true. The bails flew off and West Indies had beaten Australia for the first time.

Thus, the West Indians began to establish themselves. After four huge defeats they had settled down to prove that, on their day, they were as good a side as any on the Test Match circuit. What they did lack was assurance and strategy. Too often they had played solely by instinct and had learned that this was not enough to see them through. The batting order was not always correct and some of the batsmen who might have seen them to victory were not always selected to play. The reason for that was simple enough. The team was a fragmented collection from several islands who were unused to playing together. Moreover, Grant did not know his team at the start of the tour. For Constantine, of course, there was the usual fine record. During the Australian tour, on which he had missed only one match, Constantine scored 948 runs with an average of over 40, and took fifty wickets at around 20 runs apiece, also holding twenty-three catches. Young George Headley had scored 1,000 runs on the tour, the first West Indian player to achieve that feat, and from the series, West Indian cricket had emerged with some fine individual players who might now be welded into a team which, with the right strategy, and the confidence which is born out of success, could take on the world.

In 1933, the West Indians returned to England for their second visit as a Test side. Their performance against England in the Caribbean in 1929-30 led English cricket followers to hope that the side would have improved greatly on that which previously visited English shores. But the improvement was only marginal and not helped by the fact that Nelson declined to release Constantine regularly to play for the tourists. In fact, he played in only one Test and was unable to form the fast bowling partnership with 'Manny' Martindale which might have seen the West Indians to greater feats. Martindale, from Barbados, was a small man for a fast bowler, but his speed and ability to swing the ball into the batsman made him a lethal weapon who took fourteen Test wickets and 103 victims in all first-class matches on the tour.

In the First Test, played at Lord's, Martindale and Cyril Merry, the brilliant right-hander from Trinidad, made their debuts and the West Indians brought in George Francis to replace Constantine. Francis was playing as a professional with Radcliffe in the Bolton League, but his knowledge of English conditions proved of little value and he failed to take a wicket in the match. England needed to bat only once, making 296, and then bowled out West Indies for 97 and 172 to win by an innings and 27 runs, Walter Robins taking six wickets with his leg-spin in the first innings. In the Second Test at Old Trafford, Constantine came into the side and the West Indians batted first. At one stage they were 226 for one with Headley and Jamaica's wicketkeeper and opening batsman, Ivan Barrow, both scoring centuries. The rest of the innings folded, however, and totalled only 375. When England batted, Martindale and Constantine gave them a display of 'bodyline'. Wally Hammond retired with a cut chin, but Douglas Jardine's 127 ensured that England were only one run behind when their last wicket fell. Constantine had not wanted to bowl bodyline, but Grant insisted. The game, however, ground to an inconclusive finale with West Indies 225 all out in their second innings and England having no time to begin their reply.

At The Oval, the Third Test, which was the final game in the rubber, again saw the West Indians without Constantine. England won the toss and spent the first day making 312, of which Fred Bakewell of Northamptonshire scored 107. On the second day, a Monday, the West Indians found themselves with the worst of the conditions and were skittled for 100. When they batted a second time they failed to score the runs needed to avoid an innings defeat and were 17 short when Griffith was caught and bowled by Kent's leg-spin and googly bowler, Charles Marriott. For Marriott it was his one and only Test appearance, yet he marked it with eleven wickets. Few players can have been so successful on their only appearance for their country.

Without Learie Constantine, the West Indians had needed to depend too much on Martindale and Headley on the 1933 tour. Both had delivered the goods, George Headley making 2,000 first-class runs that summer and averaging over 66; Martindale, as we have seen, took 100 wickets. But the rest were really nowhere. Only five games out of thirty were won and Freddie Martin had the misfortune to injure a leg while fielding in the county match against Middlesex at Lord's. The Jamaican all-rounder had been taking wickets and scoring runs up until then, but the injury forced him out of the Tests and the balance of the West Indian team was upset. The loss of both Martin and Constantine, both fine all-rounders, meant that they were seriously weakened in most matches.

In 1934-5, an MCC party captained by R.E.S. Wyatt set sail for the Caribbean and four Tests, the first of which, played at Bridgetown, produced some remarkable cricket on a sticky pitch. This England party was by no means the best that MCC could have mustered and it was now apparent that any side visiting the Caribbean would have to be very much on its mettle to succeed. Constantine had been in India that year, invited by the Maharaj Kumar Vizianagram to take part in the Gold Cup Tournament. At the last moment the Maharaj Kumar's team was withdrawn and Constantine instead found himself playing with a team entered by the Maharaj Kumar Ali Rajpur, and alongside such great Indian players as Merchant. A brilliant century by Amarnath wrested the cup from the grasp of Constantine's team, but it had been a welcome jaunt for the West Indian who now went off to join his colleagues for the Tests against England. Strangely, Constantine had not been originally selected and had arrived back in England from India two days before Christmas 1934 with the England party having already sailed. He received a telegram inviting him to follow them and arrived in the West Indies too late for the First Test at Bridgetown.

What an incredible game that First Test turned out to be, with only 309 runs scored in the match and only one innings fully completed. The West Indians made 102 in their first innings with Ken Farnes taking four for 40. Half the home side had fallen for 31 and it was only the skill and courage of George Headley, who scored 44, which saw them to anything like a respectable score. Leslie Hylton of Jamaica was the only other player to get into double figures. The pitch had been badly affected by rain and with Farnes in particular almost unplayable early on, every run was a bonus. England fared no better and at the close of the day had limped to 81 for five, Wally Hammond emulating Headley by scoring 43 to become England's lone saviour.

Play could not begin until after tea on the second day, due to more rain, and after Hylton took two more wickets without a run being added, Wyatt declared the innings closed, anxious to get after the West Indies again. His ploy worked beautifully. The first three wickets fell with the score at 4, and six were down for 51 after Headley had fallen for a duck. Middlesex bowler Jim Smith, had five for 16 at this stage when Grant took the biggest gamble of his life. He declared, leaving England to score just 73 to win. It was a stunning decision, but at 48 for six — Martindale doing almost all the damage with five of the wickets — Grant was set to become the West Indies national hero. But it was not as simple as that. Wyatt had opened the England second innings with Smith and Farnes in the hope that the lower order men would belt precious runs. So Wyatt and Wally Hammond were still at the wicket and it was they who guided England to a four-wicket win in this most astonishing of Test Matches. The game had, however, been a lottery and was no guide to what might still be a close fought series. Indeed, with Learie Constantine to come into the side, there was every chance that the West Indians would score the greater successes in the rubber which had just got underway.

Wally Hammond had won the First Test for England by hitting Martindale for 6. But it was the last real success that the English team was to taste on this tour. Before the Second Test at Port of Spain, England suffered a blow when Ken Farnes injured his neck and was unable to play at Queen's Park Oval. West Indies, on the other hand, were strengthened by the inclusion of Constantine, who had arrived from England, and he, together with Martindale and Leslie Hylton, proved to be the scourge of England. Constantine was back on his home ground, the picturesque cricket ground where thousands paid good money to sit on baked grass and under a blazing blue sky, confident that 6s galore would soon speed from their local hero's bat. Wyatt won the toss for England on the morning of 24 January 1935, and to the astonishment of almost everyone, put the West Indians into bat. They padded up gleefully, looking forward to batting on a perfect pitch and against an England attack shorn of one of its best bowlers.

Yet early on, it seemed that Wyatt's gamble was justified when two wickets fell for 38, and then four men were out for 115. Sealy had other ideas, however, and when he was joined by Constantine the runs began to flow. Sealy reached 92, scoring runs all around the wicket before getting out to one of Wyatt's innocent-looking breaks. It was an innings which would be remembered by those who saw it for the rest of their lives. Constantine went on to 90 before his old foe Patsy Hendren caught him out. The West Indies tail had offered scant support and the all-out score of 302 was not a particularly good one on this wicket. There was sensation to follow, however. David Townsend of Oxford University and Durham made his Test debut in this match — the last man to play for England without ever representing a first-class county — and he opened the innings with Wyatt. With 15 on the board, Constantine trapped Townsend leg before and the procession began. Eight runs later, half the England side were out — 23 for five — and the crowd was ecstatic. Wyatt, Hammond, Ames and Leyland were the men to join Townsend in the pavilion as Constantine, Hylton and Martindale wreaked havoc. It took brave and defiant batting from Hendren (41), Iddon (73) and Errol Holmes (85 not out) to pick up the pieces and see England to the calmer waters of 258 all out.

When the West Indies batted again, Jim Smith and George Paine captured an early wicket apiece before Sealy and Headley got together and proceeded to blast the ball all around Queen's Park Oval. Headley went on to a magnificent 93 — there were no centuries in this match — before he was lbw to Smith. The others gave steady, if not spectacular, support and Grant was able to declare at 280 for six, leaving England to score 325 to win in about three and a half hours. It was at this point that Wyatt made his second extraordinary decision of the match and all but turned his batting order upside down. The Lancashire wicketkeeper, Bill Farrimond, who had batted number ten in the first innings and scored 16, opened with Townsend. With 14 runs on the board he was caught by Headley off Hylton. The rest of the tail followed and only Townsend, the one recognised early-order batsman, prospered, scoring a steady 36 before Achong tempted him and Da Costa took the catch. When England were 75 for six they had no chance of saving the game. Errol Holmes and Maurice Leyland were the last pair, brought together at 103 for nine.

Earlier there had been more sensational events when Constantine, after bowling some short-pitched stuff at Ames, was spoken to by umpire Arthur Richardson, the former South Australian Test player who had played with Constantine in the Lancashire League. Richardson claimed that Constantine was bowling 'bodyline'. Constantine counter-claimed that if he had been on the receiving end of this kind of bowling, then the ball would have been swatted over the pavilion for 6. Richardson had his way and, after complaining to Grant, had Constantine removed from the attack. It was of no consequence so far as the result was concerned, though the final few moments were gripping. There were only five minutes to play when Holmes, who had scored 85 unbeaten runs in the first innings, came out to join the experienced Leyland. Four byes were taken off Hylton and with one minute remaining. Constantine was allowed back to bowl the last over of the Test. The first four balls were each left well alone by Leyland. The fifth moved just a fraction, Leyland was too late to get down on it, and the ball rapped his pads. Constantine recalled later that the appeal could have been heard in New York. Leyland was out and West Indies had won by 217 runs.

With one ball left, West Indies had gone one ahead in the rubber. It was a good result, for a draw would have flattered England who had been outplayed throughout, particularly, one has to say, in the art of captaincy. The Third Test at Georgetown was an anti-climax. Rain delayed the start of the match and in a low-scoring game, West Indies were set to score 203 to win in less than two hours. They reached 104 for five by the close and the game was drawn. Only three players scored 50 or more in the match and it was the Warwickshire leg-spinner, Eric Hollies, who had most to recall with seven for 50 in the first innings.

In the Fourth Test at Sabina Park, Kingston, there was a very different tale. West Indies batted first and found George Headley in magnificent form. The legendary young batsman scored 270 runs in just over eight hours, a score which remained the West Indians' highest individual effort against England until Lawrence Rowe's 302 in 1973-4. Headley's effort — he put on 202 for the third wicket with Sealy, and 147 for the seventh with Rolph Grant — came under a blazing sun which poured down like molten gold across the billiard table which is Sabina Park. Against the backcloth of the hazy Blue Mountains, it was an innings of unique brilliance. The scoreboard rattled on under the sun as white figures flitted across the scorched grass, chasing a red leather which had been despatched with equal fire by Headley and his partners. Eventually, after almost two days of remorseless torture, the England fielders were spared further agony as Grant declared at 535 for seven. Headley was still there at the close, and the West Indians, now certain of not losing, had to work out a plan to win the game and take the rubber.

In the face of Martindale and Constantine, England folded completely. In the very first over, Martindale sent down a ball of incredible speed. Wyatt failed to pick it up and there was a sickening thud. The England captain had fractured his jaw and was led away to take no further part in the Test. It was a fair delivery, but just too fast for any human being to avoid. England collapsed to 26 for four, then 95 for five, with Wyatt unable to bat. Only the later order batsmen proved equal to the task that had defeated their specialist colleagues, and what a splendid job they made of it. Leslie Ames, the Kent wicketkeeper, led the way with 126, Iddon made 54, Hendren 40, and the last four wickets raised a further 176 runs. Even so, a follow-on was inevitable and this time there were no heroics from anyone. England collapsed to 103 all out to lose by an innings and 161 runs. Constantine had the honour of leading his country in the final moments when they won their first rubber, for George Grant had twisted his ankle in the field and was forced to hand over the reins. The difference between the two sides had been the batting of George Headley, which was undoubtedly world-class, and the bowling of Constantine, Martindale and Hylton. This fearsome trio had snapped up forty-seven English wickets between them in the rubber. Martindale had nineteen English wickets, Hylton thirteen, and Constantine fifteen, and the West Indians had established their credentials as a top-class Test side.

Yet the West Indies had to wait four years before they were able to put their new-found status to the test. Not until the fateful summer of 1939 did they play another Test Match when they came to England, a country hurtling headlong towards war with Germany. The tour started in the most miserable weather. It ended prematurely as the last few moments of peace choked agonisingly away in the clammy, humid atmosphere of a late English summer. The three-match series went to England who won the First Test at Lord's by eight wickets with the other two drawn, the Test at The Oval, which ended on 22 August 1939, being the last such match for six and a half years.

The Lord's Test was notable for several reasons, not least because West Indies lost, despite George Headley scoring a century in each innings, the first time the feat had been performed in a Test at cricket's HQ, and Headley thus became the first West Indian to perform it twice in a Test. But Headley's efforts were overshadowed by 196 from Len Hutton and 120 from a young Denis Compton. England's skipper, Wally Hammond, was able to declare at 404 for five in reply to West Indies' 277, and Derbyshire's red-haired pace bowler, Bill Copson, followed up his Test debut performance of five for 85 in the first innings with four for 67 in the second. Copson's first ball in first-class cricket had accounted for the great Andrew Sandham and, but for Hitler, he might well have played many more times for England. So, though they were a convincing force in their own islands, the West Indies were still comparative novices abroad. Even the selection of their side, always a difficult task when taking into account players from islands scattered over a wide area of the Caribbean, did not please all their cricket followers. It did, however, contain some names which would become great favourites when cricket was resumed after the war.

Headley was there, of course, and making his Test debut in the first match at Lord's was Jeff Stollmeyer. Stollmeyer, from Trinidad, a tall and distinguished opening batsman, made 59 in his first Test innings and would go on to captain his side in the post-war years. Stollmeyer's international career, though interrupted by the war, was kept alive by some splendid performances in the Inter-Colonial games. In 1946-7 he added 434 for the third wicket against British Guiana in the company of Gerry Gomez, Stollmeyer's own score being 324, the highest individual effort in these games. Gomez, too, made his Test debut in England in 1939, playing in the Second Test at Old Trafford, though with little personal success. He was to go on, however, to become one of the West Indies' leading Test all-rounders, as well as a radio commentator and administrator with the West Indies Cricket Board of Control.

For the rest of the 1939 debutants — Cameron, Clarke, Weekes, Williams, Johnson and V.H. Stollmeyer — there were to be no illustrious Test careers, though Tyrell Johnson, a fast left-armer from Trinidad, had the distinction of taking a wicket with his first ball of the tour, and then a wicket with his first ball in Test cricket when he bowled the Nottinghamshire batsman, Walter Keeton, at The Oval. Jeff Stollmeyer's elder brother, Vic, also made his debut in the last Test, scoring a brilliant 96 in his only Test innings. Troubled by illness on the tour, Stollmeyer senior did not play for his country again. It is one of the ironies of cricket that players like Vic Stollmeyer and Tyrell Johnson should enjoy great personal success on their Test debuts and then, for one reason or another, never have the chance to play again.

By the time West Indian Test cricket resumed in 1948, a whole new generation of cricketers had come of age in the sunshine islands. When England began their tour in January 1948, they were faced by Everton Weekes and Clyde Walcott, both of Barbados, and both making their Test debuts. Walcott and Weekes played in the First Test at Bridgetown; for the second, at Port of Spain, they were joined by Frank Worrell, also of Barbados, and the legend of the 'Three Ws' was born. Other West Indians were starting out on their Test careers in this series, players like John Goddard, a left-handed bat and medium-pace bowler from, yes, Barbados. There, too, was Robert Christiani of British Guiana, stroke-playing batsman and brilliant fielder who had been unlucky not to be selected for the 1939 tour. These were the players who would carry West Indian cricket to the pinnacles of success. Up until 1939 the West Indies had played twenty-two Tests and lost twelve. In the first three series after the war they played thirteen Tests and lost only one, beating England five times in eight meetings.

Constantine's first-class career had ended in 1945 after he had scored 4,451 runs, took 424 wickets and held 133 catches. It seems incredible to look back and realise that this great West Indian cricketer played in only eighteen Tests, though that was enough for him to score 635 runs, take 58 wickets and hold 28 catches. His last Test Match appearance had been at The Oval in 1939 when he scored 79 at a run-a-minute and took five for 75. After doing social work among coloured people in England during the war, in 1945 Constantine captained the Dominions team which beat England at Lord's. For Learie Constantine, a new career, just as distinguished as his cricketing one had been, then opened. He was called to the Bar by the Middle Temple, returned to his native Trinidad where he became MP and Minister of Works, and later returned to England as High Commissioner for Trinidad and Tobago. Still the honours were poured upon him. He was awarded the MBE, was knighted, and then created a Life Peer — Lord Constantine, Baron of Maravel and Nelson. When he died in 1971, aged sixty-nine, Trinidad posthumously awarded him that country's highest honour, the Trinity Cross. Lord Learie Constantine was not just a great West Indian cricketer, he was a great statesman.

Back,however, to Bridgetown in the new year of 1948. England, too, had a young debutant playing for them, the Surrey off-spinner Jim Laker. Northants' Dennis Brookes also made his debut in the game, but it was Laker who would go on to become a legend and it was somehow fitting that his own Test career should start alongside those of Clyde Walcott and Everton Weekes. West Indian cricket was now taking positive shape and although tropical rains ended the First Test on the last morning, there was still time for 'Foffie' Williams to score one of the fastest Test fifties, hitting 6, 6, 4, 4, off his first four balls from Laker who, incidentally, had taken Williams's wicket in the first innings when the off-spinner enjoyed seven for 103 in his first Test bowl.

This MCC touring party had left out players of the calibre of Edrich, Compton, Hutton, Yardley and Bedser, despite the incredible performances which the West Indian players had been chalking up in the Inter-Colonial games of the previous few years. The absence of Doug Wright, the Kent leg-spinner who was a major part of England's attack on tour, was especially surprising. In January 1946, just two years before the MCC party arrived in the West Indies, the islands' batsmen began signalling the sort of thing that visitors could expect. Barbados were 45 for three in their second innings against Trinidad when Walcott joined Worrell. Walcott scored 314 not out, Worrell 255 not out, and Barbados were able to declare at 619 for three! The fourth-wicket partnership had realised 574 runs scored in under six hours. In 1943-4, Frank Worrell, then aged just nineteen, had produced a fourth-wicket stand of 502 with John Goddard. This was the sort of run scoring which was going on in the West Indies. Even after the plunder by Worrell and Walcott against Trinidad, their opponents were not outdone altogether and Gerry Gomez, with 213, and the eighteen-year-old Ken Trestrail, who scored 151, and who shared in a Trinidad record second-wicket stand of 207 with Andy Ganteaume, saw to it that their side was not humiliated.

Ganteaume and Worrell made their Test debuts in the second match of the rubber at Port of Spain where there was another drawn game. After Billy Griffith had scored his maiden first-class century in his first Test innings for England — the first man to do so — Ganteaume (112) and George Carew (107) put on 173 runs for the first wicket when West Indies replied. It was an opening stand which gave the home team the chance to build a lead of 135. George Carew played only four Tests for West Indies and they were as far apart as his debut in 1934-5 and his last game in India in 1948-9. The First Test had seen George Headley captain West Indies. He had to miss the Port of Spain match and Gomez took over. Rain had robbed West Indies of victory in the First Test. Set to score 141 in less than an hour, they settled for a draw in the second after losing three wickets.

Len Hutton flew out to join the injury-hit MCC party in time for the Third Test at Georgetown, though the fact that the game against British Guiana had been abandoned without a ball being bowled, suggested that the pitch would be unhelpful and that the tourists would need more than even the efforts of Yorkshire's great batsman to keep them in the hunt. West Indies batted first and Frank Worrell found no devils in the pitch, hitting 131 to enable Goddard, who failed with the bat, to declare at 297 for eight. But with the ball Goddard was a demon. He took five wickets as England tumbled to 111 all out, Hutton making the top score of 31. With a lead of 186, and with England caught on a drying pitch, Goddard asked them to bat again. Although the pitch was now much easier, allowing England to score 263 in their second innings, this still left West Indies to score only 78 for victory and, although they lost Carew, Goddard and Christiani with only 26 scored, Walcott and Gomez knocked off the remaining runs with ease to give their side a victory by seven wickets.

At Sabina Park, West Indies exposed the frailty of the England party, winning by ten wickets. The splendidly-named Hophie Horace Hines Johnson marked his first Test appearance — at the age of thirty-seven — by taking five wickets in each innings. The only England success was Lancashire's Winston Place, who scored 107, but when Everton Weekes made 141, seeing West Indies to 490 and a lead of 263, even Place's second innings century was not enough to prevent the West Indians from taking the rubber without the loss of a second innings wicket. Even though England had sent none of the great players on who they largely relied upon in Tests, the winning of the rubber so emphatically, underlined the strides which West Indian cricket had made since before the war. Even *Wisden* was moved to comment: 'On current form the West Indies must be the strongest cricketing body apart from Australia . . . .'

This was certainly the last time that England would dare send a below-strength team to the Caribbean. But before the West Indians were to visit England again in 1950, they had new ground to explore on a visit to India, where the first Test Match between the two countries was played at Feroz Shah Kotla, Delhi, on 10-14 November 1948. The brilliant left-hander from Jamaica, Allan Rae, made his debut here, but scored only 8 of the West Indians' 631 in the first innings. It was left to Walcott (152), Weekes (128), Christiani (107) and Gomez (101) to lead the way to this mammoth score. The Indians fared not too badly either, scoring 454 with the little Hemu Adhikari scoring a century. The Indians followed on and had made 220 for six when the inevitable draw was declared.

Indeed, four of the five Tests were drawn; Goddard's side, which lacked Frank Worrell, who did not tour for personal reasons, triumphed in the Fourth Test at Madras by an innings and 193 runs. This was the last tour by George Headley, now thirty-nine years old. It was Everton Weekes, averaging 111 with four Test hundreds, who dominated the batting however. In West Indies' win in Madras, Weekes made 90, and with an opening stand of 239 between Rae (109) and Stollmeyer (160), West Indies scored 582 before bowling out the Indians twice. It had been a hard tour against an Indian side which included players of the calibre of Amarnath, Mushtaq Ali, 'Vinoo' Mankad, and Vijay Hazare, and had been made even harder by the often uncomfortable and difficult travel in post-war India, as well as pitches which gave bowlers like John Trim of British Guiana, Prior Jones of Trinidad, and Gerry Gomez little help. Jones, however, did persevere to take fifty-one wickets in all first-class games and seventeen in the Tests, a testimony to his incredible stamina. But a wearing wicket in the Madras Test, when India were caught in their second innings, was the reason behind West Indies' victory in their first rubber on the sub-continent. If India had been a little more fortunate in the last Test in Bombay — where they fell just 6 runs short of scoring 361 in 395 minutes for victory — then the series might have ended all-square. It was certainly a thrilling Test Match and worthy of two fine sides.

The West Indians' next overseas tour was to England in 1950 when they were to gain the tag 'Calypso Cricketers'. It was an unforgettable summer when cricket was played to the sound of oil-drum music and the joyous songs of West Indian supporters who transformed hitherto staid cricket grounds all over England into citadels of noise and sheer enjoyment. The previous West Indian season had seen the emergence of a young spin bowler from Trinidad, Sonny Ramadhin, standing just 5ft 4in tall and beguiling batsmen with a curious mixture of leg and off-spin bowling, all of it coming from the fingers. In his first match for Trinidad, in 1949-50, Ramadhin had taken eight wickets against Jamaica. Poor Jamaica were on the receiving end in that match. Trinidad amassed the amazing score of 581 for two (Stollmeyer 261, Trestrail 161 not out, and Ganteaume 147). Indeed, with Weekes, Walcott and Roy Marshall of Barbados all scoring heavily, and Christiani of British Guiana also in rampant mood with the bat, the West Indian selectors' only headache appeared to be who to leave out of the touring party for England. The hitherto unheard of Ramadhin made the trip; and so did another spinner, Alf Valentine, the Jamaican left-armer. Unheard of at the start of the tour, the names of Ramadhin and Valentine were soon to be on everyone's lips and would even be committed to song.

Ramadhin and Valentine made their debuts in the First Test at Old Trafford where England won by 202 runs. It was a relatively low-scoring game for a Test — but one in which the bespectacled Alf Valentine wrote himself into the record books. Goddard's side had the misfortune to bat last on a bad pitch. But in the first innings, Valentine — on his Test debut — took the first eight wickets to fall and at one time had reduced England to 88 for five, and this was the man who had been selected for the tour on the strength of first-class figures of two for 190! A century by Godfrey Evans rescued England and gave them the whip-hand in the match. But Valentine — who had taken eight for 26 and five for 41 on the same ground immediately before the Test, against Lancashire — had eleven wickets in this Test and a place in cricket's gallery of fame. It was an incredible start by a man whose selection had surprised everyone not directly involved in naming the tour party.

Before the Second Test at Lord's, the West Indian batsmen tore the county attacks apart. Everton Weekes made 279 at Trent Bridge; Stollmeyer (198) and Rae (179) opened with 355 at Hove. So, with his batsmen in grand form — and spinners likely to dominate the Lord's game — John Goddard was not too worried about the loss of Hines Johnson, who had been injured in the First Test, bowling only ten overs in the match. Goddard won the toss and Allan Rae, with 106, was the mainstay of a West Indies first innings score of 326. Though Worrell and Weekes made half centuries, the West Indians felt that they had missed the boat on this plumb Lord's pitch.

Then, up stepped Ramadhin and Valentine. The spin pair who had been selected for the tour after only two first-class games each, then set to and charmed out England's batsmen for 151 — and that was only after Yorkshire's Johnny Wardle had clubbed 33 runs batting at number nine.
 Alf Valentine just trundled down straight and true for four for 48; Sonny

Ramadhin's 'magic' bowling claimed five for 66 as England's best batsmen failed to read his hand. Though the leg-spin of Worcestershire's 'Roley' Jenkins claimed the first three West Indian batsmen when they batted again, Clyde Walcott dispelled any fears about the pitch with a brilliant and undefeated 168. With Gomez (70) he put on 211 — a record stand by the West Indians in a Test in England — and with 63 from Everton Weekes, Goddard could declare at 425 for six, setting England an impossible 601 to win. Only Cyril Washbrook stood firm against Ramadhin and Valentine. He made 114 before Ramadhin bowled him. England were all out for 274 to lose by 326 runs. Ramadhin had six for 86, Valentine three for 79, and the scenes of joy which burst over Lord's gave birth to the Calypso Cricketers. The massive win set the Caribbean alight, put the West Indies into the status of world champions, gave the West Indian community in Britain fresh heart, and, perhaps most of all, elevated Sonny Ramadhin into the realms of the mystical. From Taunton to Middlesbrough they debated the apparently unique skills of this young Trinidadian.

There were no defeats between the Lord's Test and the game on that bowler's graveyard of Trent Bridge. This time, however, it was Johnson and Worrell who did most of the damage, taking three wickets each as the West Indians did well to bowl out England for 223. Rae and Stollmeyer knocked off 77 before they were parted and then the scene was set for an extraordinary innings by Frank Worrell. Worrell scored an astonishing 261 in five hours and thirty-five minutes. It was then the highest score for the West Indies in England. Worrell shared a record fourth-wicket partnership of 283 in 210 minutes with Everton Weekes (129) and the tourists totalled 558 — their highest total in any Test against England and the highest total by either side in England. In all, Worrell shared in seven records during his innings and although England replied with an opening stand of 212 — Hutton and Simpson's being England's highest opening partnership against West Indies — England's final total of 436 still left West Indies to score only 102 to win — a total which Rae and Stollmeyer knocked off with ease to give West Indies a ten-wickets win and the lead in the series.

England had to win the last Test at The Oval to level the series and Warwickshire raised their hopes at Edgbaston by becoming the only county to beat West Indies that summer, winning by three wickets on what was best described as an 'interesting' pitch. But as soon as the West Indians batted at The Oval, it was obvious that they had won the series. Rae (109) and Worrell (138) steered them to 503 all out; and although Len Hutton became the first England batsman to score a double century (212) in a home Test against the West Indians (and also to carry his bat through a completed innings against them), the rest of England's batting collapsed to 344 all out and the follow-on. Valentine had four wickets in the first innings; now he took another six and England toppled to 103 and defeat by an innings and 56 runs.

Even if you were not a West Indian supporter, the 1950 series had been a great one. There had been epic batting, great bowling, and, most important, cricket played at the highest level, but played with the infectious enthusiasm that the West Indians had brought with them. The gamble to play Ramadhin and Valentine had paid off handsomely. Between them they captured fifty-nine England Test wickets; the nearest to them were Worrell and Goddard with six each. Thus, though the West

Indian's one weakness was in the pace department — and that seems incredible in these days of five West Indian pacemen operating for hours at a time — they did not need speed in 1950. The legend of Ramadhin and Valentine — and that of the 'Three Ws' had been born and carried them to greatness. John Goddard's captaincy had been truly magnificent and only in the First Test, where the West Indians were unlucky to lose the toss, were they outplayed. A new era had been forged.

Yet that lack of first-class fast bowlers in the early 1950s was to prevent West Indian cricket from making the strides which it had promised. When they visited Australia in 1951-2 — their first Tests against the Australians since the inaugural series of twenty-one years earlier — they found Ray Lindwall and Keith Miller in their path. Only Don Bradman was missing from the great Australian side of the immediate post-war years and against them the West Indians lost four Tests, winning only the third game at Adelaide. Ramadhin, hero of 1950, had a poor tour — fourteen wickets costing nearly 50 runs apiece in the Tests and although Valentine did better (twenty-four wickets at 28 each to become the leading West Indian wicket-taker) — the overall performance was far behind that of their hosts. The sole West Indian victory was achieved on a wet pitch at Adelaide where Worrell (six for 38) and Goddard (three for 36) bowled out Australia for 82. West Indies made 105 in reply, then Valentine took six for 102, leaving his side to score 233 to win, which they did with six wickets to spare. Their winning runs came on Christmas Day — the first time that Test cricket had been played on 25 December. The 'Three Ws' had failed in the Tests and Gomez headed the batting averages. The West Indians were clearly still not 'world champions'.

Two Tests were played against New Zealand on the way home, the first game between the two countries on an official Test level taking place at Christchurch on 8-12 February 1952. The second day brought a record

'Those two little pals of mine . . . .' Sonny Ramadhin (left) and Alf Valentine, two spinners who weaved a magic spell over England in 1950 when they had a calypso composed in their honour

Christchurch crowd of some 18,000 people who saw the West Indians on their way to a five wickets win. The game was interesting because the Trinidad wicketkeeper, Simpson 'Sammy' Guillan, played against New Zealand and scored 54 — his highest first-class score to that date. Guillan became a permanent resident in New Zealand, played with Canterbury, and appeared in three official Tests for New Zealand against his former side in 1955-6. The Second Test, played at Eden Park, Auckland, saw the West Indians declare at 546 for 6 with Stollmeyer, Worrell and Walcott each scoring centuries. Again there was an interesting incident when Allan Rae, who was 9 not out, fell while backing up. The ball was returned to Moir, who could have run out the opener but instead sportingly allowed him to regain his crease. Rae went on to make 99 and one can hardly imagine that sort of thing happening today! New Zealand were bowled out for 160, and were 17 for one when rain prevented any play on the last day and saved them from an innings defeat.

In 1952-3, India made their first visit to the Caribbean and lost the series one game to nil with four drawn. Both sides decided to indulge themselves in an orgy of runs and the only match to achieve a positive result was in Barbados where rain before the start helped the West Indians to a 142-run victory in a low-scoring match. Everton Weekes averaged 102 in the Tests and in many ways the series was similar to the West Indians' first visit to India in 1948-9, though the Fifth Test at Sabina Park promised to be a thrilling affair when the West Indians needed 181 to win in 145 minutes. But after losing both openers for 15, and already being one up in the series, they decided not to bother. In their first innings, Frank Worrell had scored 237, one of six three-figure innings in the Test.

The visit of MCC to the Caribbean in 1953-4 provided a series which saw the last game of George Headley and the first by Gary Sobers. It also provided some fascinating cricket — and some incidents which cricket could well have done without. The decision to bring back Headley at the age of forty-four was strange to say the least. He played in the First Test, made 16 and 1, and was never seen in a West Indian cap again. This was a bizarre match. Surrey's Tony Lock became the first player since South Australia's Ernest Jones (in 1897-8) to be no-balled for throwing in a Test. The wife and son of umpire Burke were the subjects of physical attack when the official gave out the local hero, John Holt, leg before to Statham when Holt was but six runs short of his century; and the West Indians won by 140 runs after Jeff Stollmeyer had been the victim of much criticism for not enforcing the follow-on. In the Second Test at Bridgetown West Indies, who were without Weekes, made 383 when Clyde Walcott made 220 — his only double century in a Test. They had England at 25 for three before Hutton brought them round to 181 all out, the England skipper contributing 72. West Indies batted again, this time Holt reached his century, going on to 166, and Stollmeyer could declare at 292 for two. This time England batted with much more early composure and Hutton (77), May (62), Compton (93) and Graveney (64 not out) served them well. But this was a bleak time for English cricket and 258 for three became 313 all out to give West Indies victory by 181 runs.

At Georgetown, England fought back to win by nine wickets. Alf Valentine — at the age of twenty-three — took his hundreth Test wicket, but Hutton's 169 gave England a firm base from which they reached 435. When West Indies batted they could manage only 251 and that only after a record eighth-wicket stand of 99 between Holt and Clifford McWatt of

British Guiana. When McWatt was run out for 54, bottles were thrown, and only the sight of Hutton standing his ground averted an even uglier situation. West Indies followed-on, but could set England only 72 to win, a score they achieved for the loss of Peter May.

Now England were a match down in the rubber with two to play. They were not to draw level at Port of Spain where there was a Test which produced 1,528 runs. No Test had been completed on this ground since the jute matting was put down in 1934. West Indies scored 681 for eight declared (Weekes 206, Worrell 167, Walcott 124) and England replied with 537 with centuries from May and Compton. Weekes and Worrell shared a record third-wicket stand of 338 and the game dragged on to an inevitable draw. So West Indies were sure of not losing the series, though at Sabina Park, caught on a lively pitch on the first day of the Fifth Test, they started the slide which saw them lose their first Test in Jamaica and allow England to square the rubber. Trevor Bailey took seven for 34 as West Indies tumbled to 139 all out. Garfield Sobers, an eighteen-year-old Barbadian, played in his first Test and batting number nine scored 14 not out. When England replied, it was Len Hutton who took on the West Indian bowling almost single-handed. His 205 was almost half of England's total of 414 — the next-highest scorer was Wardle with 66 — and though the West Indians made 346 in their second innings, with a century from Walcott, England needed only 72 to win. They lost Graveney, bowled by Frank King of Barbados, without a run scored, before May and Watson saw them to a remarkable victory.

In 1954-5, Australia made their first visit to the Caribbean and won three Tests, drawing the other two. The tour was unusually late in the West Indian season — from March to June — but the Australians proved

Gary Sobers on his way to a world record Test score at Sabina Park in 1957-8

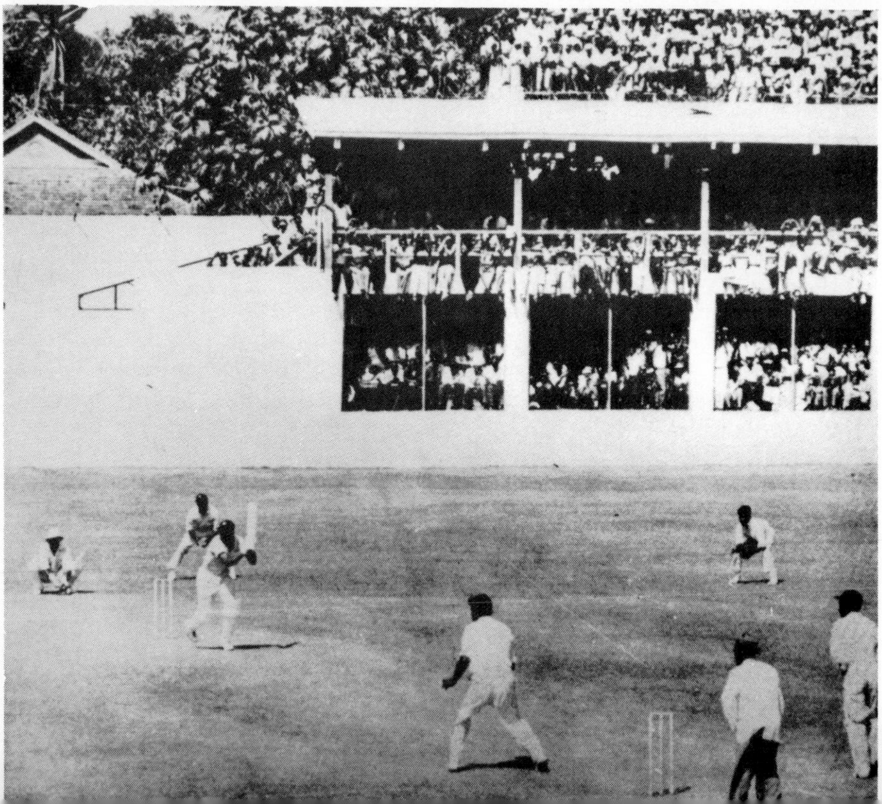

popular visitors. Though the West Indians matched their visitors for runs — Walcott making five Test centuries — it was the bowling of Lindwall, Miller, Benaud and Johnson which proved to be the undoing of the home team. Australia won the First, Third and Fifth Tests easily, but at Bridgetown in the Fourth Test, West Indian hopes were raised when Denis Atkinson (who made 219) and Clairmont Depeiza (122) scored a world record 348 for the seventh wicket. They batted for more than a day and took West Indies from 147 for six to 494 for seven in the face of an Australian first innings total of 668.

In 1957 the West Indians returned to England, having made their first full-scale tour to New Zealand in 1955-6. West Indies won that series three games to one, their first defeat against New Zealand coming in the last Test at Auckland which was the Kiwis' first victory in an official Test. This was the tour in which Guillen played against his old comrades, though he was officially unable to do so. But a jaunt against the Test novices of New Zealand did not hide the fact that the West Indies' post-war heyday was over, and when John Goddard brought his side to England the following year, they lost by three clear games. There were new faces to England — Roy Gilchrist, Gary Sobers, Wes Hall, Rohan Kanhai, 'Collie' Smith to name but some of them. But they were part of a West Indian side which was in a transitional stage.

The turning point came as early as the First Test at Edgbaston where England started their second innings 288 runs behind the West Indies. Ramadhin had taken seven for 49 and it looked as though he would rattle out England again to give the tourists a wonderful start to the rubber. But in that second innings Ramadhin bowled an incredible ninety-eight overs and took two for 179. England were 113 for three when Peter May and Colin Cowdrey came together. Between them they wore down Ramadhin, adding a record 411. May's unbeaten 285 was the highest by an England captain. Cowdrey made 154 and the match was saved. From that moment on the tide had turned against West Indies. England won three Tests by an innings, only the third game at Trent Bridge was drawn when Worrell (191) became the first West Indian to carry his bat through a Test innings, adding a last-wicket West Indies v England record of 55 with Ramadhin. In the last Test at The Oval, West Indies' ignominy was complete. They were bowled out twice, for 89 and 86, to lose within three days. For most of the West Indian players, the tour had been a disaster.

In the First Test between West Indies and Pakistan, at Sabina Park, Kingston, in 1958, Garfield Sobers, then aged twenty-one, recorded the highest score in Test cricket with an unbeaten 365. Sobers hit thirty-eight 4s and batted for ten hours and fourteen minutes. His stand of 446 with Hunte (260) was the second-highest for any Test wicket and West Indies totalled 790 for three declared. This was Sobers's first three-figure Test innings, but by the end of the series he had scored 824 runs, including centuries in each innings of the Fourth Test.

West Indies would not have the opportunity to exact revenge over England until 1959-60. Before then they played three series against the cricketers of the Indian sub-continent. In 1957-8 Pakistan made their first trip to the Caribbean and lost the first series between the two countries by three Tests to one; in 1958-9, West Indies visited India where the fast bowling of Hall and Gilchrist, who took fifty-six wickets between them, earned the tourists an easy series victory by three games to nil; at the end of that tour the West Indies made their first visit to Pakistan. After their relatively easy three-month visit to India, the West Indians found things in Karachi much different. On the matting wicket they found Fazal too much for them and lost by ten wickets; in Dacca, West Indies bowled out Pakistan for 145 and 144, but still lost by 41 runs, Fazal taking six for 34 and six for 66 as West Indies tumbled to 76 and 172. Only in the final Test, at Lahore, did West Indies get the upper hand when Rohan Kanhai scored 217 before both Pakistani innings were interrupted by rain, West Indies winning by an innings and 156 runs.

So England came to the Caribbean in 1959-60. This time the West Indians had Wes Hall, now more mature, heading a formidable battery of fast bowlers. Coupled with that, England's skipper, Peter May, was unwell and had to return home before the final Test. Yet it was England who won their first series in the West Indies. The First Test saw Sobers (226) and Worrell (197 not out) add a record 399 for the fourth wicket in the drawn match; the last three Tests were drawn, and it was the dramatic Second Test at Port of Spain which decided the rubber. On the very first day, Hall was warned by the umpire for short-pitched bowling. England, with centuries from Ken Barrington and Mike Smith, made 382; Trueman and Statham bowled West Indies out for 112; then May declared at 230 for nine and bowled out West Indies once more for England to win the match by 256 runs.

The match was played in an ugly atmosphere and on the third day, bottles rained on to the ground and brought play to a premature end after Charran Singh, the local boy, was given run out for a duck. Riot police were used to quell the disturbances and the game was all the poorer for the disgraceful scenes. The series thus went to England, but Gary Sobers had much about which to be pleased; his Test average was 101.28 with scores of 226, 0, 31, 147, 19, 145, 92 and 49 not out.

So the beginning of the 1960s saw West Indian cricket defeated. Yet the decade was definitely 'swinging' so far as Caribbean cricket was concerned. Between 1960-1 and 1967-8, the West Indians played thirty-three Test Matches and were on the losing side in only six of them, and though the 1960-1 series in Australia was lost by two Tests to one, it will always be remembered for the Brisbane game which resulted in the first tied Test Match in history. The game is fully detailed in the Australian section of this book, since they were winners of that series, and it is sufficient to record here that Australia, needing 233 for victory, saw their last man run out with the scores level and one ball remaining. India came to the West Indies in 1961-2 and were beaten in all five Tests, losing their skipper, Nari Contractor, after he was struck on the head by a bouncer from Charlie Griffith of Barbados. Contractor's skull was fractured and for a while his very life hung in the balance. Griffith was perhaps the world's most feared fast bowler at that time. In the same match he was no-balled for throwing, but still went on to take ninety-four wickets in twenty-eight Tests. West Indies won the Test at Bridgetown by an innings and 30 runs after Lance Gibbs, the off-spinner from Guyana, had the remarkable second innings spell of 15.3-14-6-8. Gibbs had made his debut against Pakistan at Port of Spain in February 1958 when Waqar Hassan became the first of his record 309 Test victims.

In 1963, West Indies went to England and won the rubber by three games to one. Although it was generally acknowledged that West Indian cricket had risen once again, no one really expected their victory over England to be so emphatic. They won the First Test by ten wickets to have six consecutive Test wins for the first time. After declaring at 501 for six — Conrad Hunte scored 182 — they bowled out England twice, Gibbs taking eleven for 157 — and then needed just one run, scored by Hunte, to claim a comprehensive victory. The Second Test at Lord's was drawn, yet it was one of cricket's most dramatic games. With the last ball to be bowled, any one of four results was still possible. England needed six runs to win with their last pair at the wicket. Allen played Hall's last ball defensively to draw the match, while at the other end, his partner, Colin Cowdrey, had his broken left arm in plaster and had intended to resume his innings by batting left-handed, using only his right arm, if required.

England levelled the series by winning the Third Test at Edgbaston where the seam bowling of Trueman, Shackleton and Dexter saw them to victory by 217 runs. But with the last two Tests, West Indies got back into their stride with wins by 221 runs and by eight wickets. The final scenes at Lord's were amazing with the gates closed on nearly 26,000 people. When the winning runs were struck, thousands swarmed on to the field to acclaim Frank Worrell's team. His reign as skipper of the West Indies had ended after fifty-one Tests in which he had scored 3,860 runs, taken sixty-nine wickets, and held forty-three catches. The following year he was knighted, became a senator in the Jamaican Parliament, and when he died in 1967, his life was honoured with a memorial service at Westminster Abbey. He was the last of the 'Three Ws' to play for West Indies. Everton Weekes had played his last game in 1958, retiring after scoring 4,455 Test runs, and Clyde Walcott bowed out in 1960 with 3,798 Test runs. West Indies cricket would not see their likes again. Walcott, with twelve centuries in twelve consecutive Tests, was awarded the OBE for his services to cricket, managing several West Indies touring sides in the 1970s. Weekes, too, became an OBE.

When the Australians visited the Caribbean in 1964-5, the series was billed as an unofficial 'world championship' and clearly, the West Indians, then at the height of their powers were favourites to take the crown. They soon proved to be the better side, winning two of the first three Tests to take a clear lead in the series. In the First Test, at Sabina Park, Sobers captained West Indies for the first time and took his hundreth Test wicket in the match, though it was Wes Hall's nine wickets that ensured victory for the home side by 179 runs. After Bobby Simpson became only the second captain to put West Indies in to bat in the Caribbean, the Second Test at Port of Spain was drawn.

West Indies second victory came in the Georgetown Test where Lance Gibbs took his hundreth Test wicket, the last Australian batsman falling to him with the second ball of the fifth day, West Indies winning by 212 runs. The Fourth Test, at Bridgetown, was a run glut. Lawry and Simpson, who both scored double centuries put on an Australian record opening stand of 382, and with centuries from Cowper, Kanhai and Nurse (who hit 201) the draw was inevitable. What a difference there was in the last Test. On a wicket where the ball kept low, only Kanhai prospered, with 121, as West Indies were bowled out for 224; Australia made 294 (Griffith six for 46) and then McKenzie took five wickets to leave Australia to score only 61 for victory, a feat they managed without losing a wicket. It had been a fine series, though not, of course, living up to the incredible 'Tied Test' series of 1960-1; and it was marred by continued Australian criticism over the bowling of Charlie Griffith, who, they felt, threw the ball. It was to Hall and Gibbs that West Indies had to pay thanks, however; these two, together with the batsmen, Sobers, Nurse, Kanhai, Hunte and Butcher, had seen them hailed as 'World champions'.

In the 1965-6 season West Indian domestic cricket saw the introduction of the Shell Shield, an inter-island competition which replaced the old knockout tournaments which were played largely in one centre. Barbados, Combined Islands (Leeward and Windward), Guyana, Jamaica and Trinidad met each other in four-day matches to bring domestic cricket in the Caribbean into line with that of other Test-playing countries. Barbados were the first winners; then the West Indians set out for their 1966 visit to England. In a wet summer they repeated their 1963 success of a three games to one victory in the rubber. Yet this was an ailing West Indian team, held together largely by captain Sobers, who scored 722 runs and took twenty wickets in the Tests. He scored 161 as West Indies won by an innings and 40 runs at Old Trafford — Gibbs had ten wickets in the match — and in the Second Test at Lord's, West Indies were staring at defeat on the fourth day when Sobers (163 not out) and his cousin, David Holford (105 not out) added a record sixth wicket 274, taking West Indies from 95 for five to 369 for five declared to draw the match. It was Basil Butcher, with an unbeaten 209, and Sobers, with 94, who set up a 139-runs win in the Third Test at Trent Bridge; and Sobers again, with 174, and Nurse (137) in the innings and 55 runs win at Headingley where Gibbs took six for 39 in troubled England's second innings. Only in the last Test, after West Indies had won the rubber handsomely, did England triumph.

A short, three-match tour of India followed and the West Indies won by two matches to nil, thanks largely to Sobers, who averaged 114 and took fourteen wickets, and Gibbs, who took eighteen. The First Test, at Brabourne Stadium, Bombay, saw the debut of Guyana's Clive Lloyd. The tall left-hander scored 82 and 78 not out in his first Test to signal the start of his brilliant career. Triumphs against India were, however, not going to disguise the fact that this great run by the West Indians was all but over. When England visited them in 1967-8, it became obvious that the cracks which had shown through the 1966 West Indian tour to England were now becoming gaping holes.

England, under the superb captaincy of Colin Cowdrey, who also batted brilliantly, won the series with a single victory in Trinidad when a remarkable declaration by Sobers set them to make 215 in 165 minutes. Boycott was the anchor man with 80 not out, Cowdrey scored 71, and England raced home with three minutes to spare. Sobers came in for sharp criticism, especially since Griffith was injured and Hall dropped. Nevertheless, it was a declaration which was right for cricket, for Sobers reasoned that to break the deadlock after three drawn games, he must give England a chance to go for the runs so that his side had an opportunity to bowl them out. Indeed, until the bottle-throwing incident midway through the fourth day, England had the upper hand in the Second Test at Sabina Park. West Indies still needed 29 to avoid an innings defeat when Butcher became the fifth man out, caught by Parks diving down the leg side. On came the bottles, followed by tear gas, and off went the players. Though seventy-five minutes was added on a sixth day, England had clearly lost the initiative; Sobers rescued West Indies with 113 not out and it was England who struggled at the end, being 68 for eight when stumps were drawn.

Beaten by England, West Indies went to Australia and New Zealand in 1968-9 and although they started in grand style, winning the First Test at Brisbane, Griffiths and Hall were over the hill and Australia is clearly not the place for ageing fast bowlers. West Indies lost the next two Tests — by an innings and by ten wickets — and though the fourth match, at Adelaide, was drawn, it produced the most exciting finish of the rubber when Australia made a bold effort to score 360 in less than six hours. They looked like doing so until four batsmen were run out; with their last pair at the crease they were just 21 runs short when the final over was completed. Sheahan and Connolly were happy to survive the last twenty-six balls. In the end just 20 runs separated the sides in a match in which 1,764 had been scored. In the Fifth Test at Sydney, West Indies were crushed by 382 runs. Starting with this series, West Indies were to win only two Tests out of eleven to confirm their fall from power.

They came to England in 1969, sharing the summer with New Zealand, and with a team shorn of names like Hall, Griffith, Hunte, Kanhai and Nurse, lost a truncated rubber two games to nil with one drawn. Sobers led an inexperienced side which lost by ten wickets at Old Trafford and by 30 runs at Headingley, though they were 219 for three, chasing 303 to win with Sobers to bat. Though Butcher made 91, Sobers was out for a duck, playing on to Barry Knight, and the surge died with him. Indeed, Sobers had, by his own Olympian standards, failed on this tour, averaging only 30 and his eleven wickets costing nearly 30 runs each. For some time Sobers had been the difference between the West Indians being an ordinary side and a match-winning team. When he failed, so did they.

Their previous overseas tour had ended in defeat in Australia, with a 1-1 draw in the three-match series in New Zealand which followed. After England in 1969, they entertained India in 1970-1 and although Sobers found form with the bat, scoring 594 runs at an average of 87, they could not bowl out the Indians. Four of the Tests were drawn, but in the second, played at Port of Spain, India won by seven wickets when the Indian spinners won the day. It was the first time India had beaten West Indies in a Test and so the first time they had returned victorious from a series with them. Thirty-five-year-old Trinidad off-spinner, Jack Noreiga, who had not played first-class cricket for eight years, was called up for his Test debut to replace the out-of-form Lance Gibbs in the First Test. Noreiga stayed in the side for four matches, taking nine for 95 in the first innings of the Second Test, the first West Indian to take nine in an innings. It is of such delightful episodes that cricket's story is made more magical.

The thought of losing to India in the Caribbean was bad enough; but when New Zealand came for their five-match rubber the following season, West Indian cricket hit rock-bottom when they could not beat the New Zealanders once on their home soil. All the first-class matches of the tour were drawn and the New Zealanders had more to smile about than their hosts. Dropped catches in the Third Test probably cost them an historic victory; for West Indies, the brightest spot was Lawrence Rowe of Jamaica making 214 and 100 not out on his debut in the First Test at Sabina Park. Rowe was the first player to achieve this feat, though sadly he has been one of the great enigmas of West Indian Test cricket since then.

Early in 1973, Australia flew into the Caribbean for a five-match rubber, fortified by the presence of Lillee, who, with Massie, had done so well in England the previous year. But Lillee injured his back and was unable to play after the First Test; Massie was unable to move the ball about in the thinner West Indian air, took only eighteen wickets in six games, and did not play in a Test. Australia did not miss them unduly. Playing against a West Indian side which lacked Sobers — he had a knee injury and Kanhai led the side — they played positive cricket, batted better than their hosts, and won the Third and Fourth Tests to take the series. The other Tests were drawn and only Lance Gibbs, with twenty-six wickets, could look back on it with any satisfaction from a West Indian point of view. Lawrence Rowe fell and injured his ankle in the Third Test and took no further part in the rubber.

By the time West Indies landed in England in the summer of 1973 for their three-match rubber — again, they shared the summer with New Zealand — they had not won a Test in eighteen attempts, and only twice had they been successful in their previous twenty-six Tests. In addition, Sobers was playing county cricket with Nottinghamshire, though he did say that he would play in the Tests if required. Sobers was required, Rowe discovering that his ankle was still not healed, and Steve Camacho returning home after a ball from Hampshire's West Indian paceman, Andy Roberts, fractured his cheek. The party, led by Kanhai, thus had Sobers back in the fold, and Ron Headley, son of the great George, left his county, Worcestershire, to join the party.

It was Clive Lloyd who hammered the runs in the First Test at The Oval, scoring 132, and Alvin Kallicharran made 80 as West Indies totalled 415. Barbados and Essex seamer, Keith Boyce, took five wickets as England were bowled out for 257; and when Kallicharran hit his second 80 of the match, aided by a half century from Sobers, West Indies were well on the way to their first victory for twenty matches. Though Lancashire's Frank Hayes made a brave century, the West Indies won at half-past two on the fifth afternoon, Boyce adding six wickets to his match tally. The Second Test at Edgbaston was drawn when England reached 182 for two, being set 325 to win in 227 minutes. Unfortunately the Test was marred when umpire Arthur Fagg went on 'token strike' after Kanhai's dissent when Fagg turned down an appeal for a catch by Murray which would have dismissed Boycott. The last Test at Lord's saw the West Indians beat England by an innings and 226 runs — their largest margin of victory against England. West Indies scored 652 for eight declared (Sobers 150 not out, Bernard Julien 121) and then bowled out England twice. The sad days of West Indian cricket were at an end. A new combination had been forged to work new victories in the 1970s.

On 7 February 1974, West Indies won the First Test against England in Port of Spain to end a run of twenty-two home Tests without victory. Set to score 132 for victory after Gibbs had taken six second innings wickets, they did so with seven wickets in hand. The match contained centuries from Amiss (174) and Kallicharran (158), but it will be remembered best for the incident in which Tony Greig ran out Kallicharran off the last ball of the day with the little Guyanan having set off for the pavilion thinking 'time' had been called. The umpire had no option but to give the batsman out, but wise counsel prevailed and the appeal was subsequently withdrawn, Kallicharran adding a further 16 runs to his score before Pocock had him caught by Underwood. There was no suggestion of any gamesmanship by Greig; but the future of the tour was more important.

The next three Tests were drawn, for both sides had powerful batting line ups. At Sabina Park, Amiss hit 262 not out, and Rowe 120; at Bridgetown, where Andy Roberts became the first Antiguan to play for a West Indies Test side. Greig made 148, Fletcher 129 not out, but both were totally overshadowed by Lawrence Rowe who scored 302 in 612 minutes for the first triple century by a West Indian against England. His stand of 249 with Kallicharran was the highest for the second wicket by West Indies in the series. Naturally, there was no result, though the match did produce a Test record of ninety-nine no-balls. At Georgetown, Amiss became the first Englishman to score three centuries in a rubber against West Indies, but rain claimed most of the game and the first innings was not completed. So to the last Test, at Port of Spain once more, and here England squared the series. Sobers played in the last of his ninety-three Tests for West Indies — and became the first West Indian to take 100 wickets against England — but it was Greig who won the match, taking five for 70 as West Indies were bowled out 27 runs short of victory with an hour to spare. In the first innings, Greig had taken eight for 86, though Rowe (123), Fredericks (67) and Lloyd (52) had the measure of him.

So a series which had been dominated by batsmen was, inevitably, won by bowlers — Gibbs, who finished the series with eighteen wickets, and Greig, who had twenty-four, making the breakthrough in the two games which saw a result. Before they flew to England for the first-ever 'World Cup', the 1975 Prudential trophy, West Indies went to India and Pakistan. In India, they took the first two Tests with Clive Lloyd in charge of his first tour. At Bangalore, two batsmen made their debuts. Gordon Greenidge, a Barbadian who came to England at the age of twelve and who played with Hampshire, and Vivian Richards, from the Leeward Islands, who was to become one of the greatest batsman that cricket has ever seen. Greenidge had a fine start — scores of 93 (when he was run out) and 107; Richards fared less well with only 4 and 3. Kallicharran's 124 in the first innings, and 163 from Lloyd in the second, steered West Indies to a win by 267 runs. At Delhi, Richards found his form, hitting 192, and with Gibbs, who took six wickets in the second innings, sending his side to an innings victory.

But then there was a remarkable turnaround in the series. Two games down and 32 for three in the Third Test, India recovered to level the series. They won their first home Test against West Indies by 85 runs, then drew level with a 100-runs win at Madras, despite Andy Roberts's feat of twelve wickets in the match. The series was now alight with everything to play for in the last Test at Bombay. West Indies now took the lead again, making 604 for six declared, thanks to a brilliant unbeaten 242 from skipper Lloyd, 104 from Fredericks, and 90s from Kallicharran and Richards. Gibbs took seven wickets to give West Indies a lead of almost 200; and when Lloyd declared at 205 for three, it was Vanburn Holder, the paceman from Barbados, who wrapped up a great rubber with six for 39 and the West Indians were home by 201 runs. Lloyd had averaged over 79 with the bat, Roberts, Holder and Gibbs took seventy wickets between them, and after two drawn Tests in Lahore and Karachi, West Indians went to England for further triumphs.

The concept of a one-day 'World Cup' was an exciting one and in a rare scorcher of an English summer, the West Indians took the crown. They topped the qualifying competition with three wins out of three, against Australia, the runners-up, Pakistan, and Sri Lanka, while England, who also had a one hundred per cent record, and New Zealand, overcame the weaker challenges of India and East Africa. In the semi-final West Indies, who had removed Australia from top spot in the previous match, met New Zealand at The Oval. Though New Zealand were at one stage 92 for one, they folded to 158 all out and West Indies marched into the final for the loss of five wickets, most of them being lost in a cavalier chase for runs. They faced Australia, who had put out England, in the first world final at Lord's. The West Indians started with a cruel piece of luck when Roy Fredericks hooked Lillee for a mighty 6 but, in doing so, trod down his wicket. Soon they were 50 for three and in big trouble. But then came Clive Lloyd. The giant hit 102, his second 50 coming off only thirty-two balls, before Marsh caught him off Gilmour — a dismissal which involved the adjudication of both umpires, Harold Bird and Tom Spencer, to rule that the wicketkeeper had taken the ball cleanly. Lloyd's great innings — which had started with 6 and 4 off Lillee — ensured that West Indies' bowlers had a target to bowl at; Australia needed 292 to win and what a great effort they made, falling just 17 runs short. Clive Lloyd, Man of the Match, took the cup from HRH the Duke of Edinburgh, President of MCC, and the new world champions had their crown to prove it.

That winter West Indies went to Australia for a six-match rubber, which they lost by five games to one. Only in the Second Test, at Perth, did they triumph when 169 from Fredericks and 149 from Lloyd gave them enough runs to bowl out Australia twice to win by an innings. Andy Roberts ripped out the heart of Australia's second attempt with seven for 54, the best analysis by a West Indian against Australia. The First Test had been lost by eight wickets, despite second innings centuries from Rowe and Kallicharran, and so the disasters continued after Perth. The tour was highlighted for West Indies, however, by some personal feats including that of wicketkeeper Deryck Murray, of Trinidad, who became the first West Indian to score 1,000 runs and make 100 dismissals. But the greatest cheer was reserved for Lance Gibbs. In the Fifth Test at Adelaide, Gibbs dismissed Mallett to equal Fred Trueman's record of 307 wickets in Tests; in the final Test at Melbourne, first innings figures of two for 68 gave Gibbs a new world record. With that he bowed out of international cricket.

West Indies returned home from Australia and one month later found themselves doing battle with India. They won the series 2-1 with one match drawn. The First Test went to West Indies by an innings and 97 runs after centuries from Richards and Lloyd at Bridgetown; Richards was again a century maker in the drawn Second Test at Port of Spain; but neither his 177 on the same ground in the Third Test, nor Kallicharran's 103, could prevent India from winning by six wickets with the highest fourth innings score to take a Test. West Indies took the rubber on an unpredictable pitch at Kingston when short-pitched bowling from Michael Holding of Jamaica found Bedi twice declaring India's innings closed to save his batsmen from further injury — Viswanath, Gaekwad and Patel were all taken to hospital. In fact, it was later recorded that the Indian second innings had closed because four batsmen were absent hurt. Whatever the reason, West Indies needed only 13 to win which they scored with ease.

When the West Indians visited England in 1976 they found the weather as good as the Caribbean. For the second year running, the sun scorched down mercilessly from clear blue skies and the British Government found

Viv Richards, the brilliant batsman from the Leeward Islands who scored a record 1,710 Test runs in just eight months of 1976

it necessary to appoint a 'Minister for Drought'. There was no run drought for West Indies, though, and they won the five-match rubber, 3-0 with two drawn. At Trent Bridge, Viv Richards scored 232 to take his Test aggregate for the calender year past 1,000 runs. The game was drawn, as too was the Second Test at Lord's where West Indies needed 323 to win in a minimum of 294 minutes. At 210 for two, with eleven overs left, Lloyd claimed the last half-hour. When he was out he wanted to end the match at 233 for four, but Greig insisted on continuing and the final score was 241 for six. Then the tide turned totally West Indies way. At Old Trafford they shot out England for 71 and 126 to win by a massive 425 runs. Greenidge hit two centuries, Richards one, and then the fearsome pace battery of Roberts, Holding, and Wayne Daniel of Barbados did the rest. At Headingley, West Indies won the series, taking the Fourth Test by 55 runs. Again the pacemen were among the wickets and Roberts took his hundreth Test wicket in record time — two years and 142 days and only nineteen Tests. There were centuries from Fredericks and Roberts at Leeds; and at The Oval, that incredible man Viv Richards struck 291 to bring his total of Test runs for the year to 1,710. Though Amiss made a double century for England he was on the losing side. Holding had eight for 92 and six for 57, and West Indies were home by 231 runs to ram home their utter supremacy.

In 1976-7 West Indies won the series against Pakistan by two Tests to one. In the First Test, at Bridgetown they needed 306 for victory and lost nine men for 237 before Roberts and Croft survived fifteen minutes plus the last twenty overs. Colin Croft of Guyana and Joel Garner of Barbados made their debuts to add to the long line of West Indian pacemen, taking seven and six wickets in the match respectively. In the Second Test, Croft took eight for 29 in Pakistan's first innings and they never recovered, West Indies winning by six wickets. The Third Test was drawn, Irving Shillingford of the Windward Islands making 120; and then Pakistan drew level at Port of Spain.

They made 341, shot out West Indies for 154, declared at 301 for nine, and then had the West Indies tumbled out once more to score only their second victory in the West Indies by 266 runs. At Kingston in the Fifth Test, West Indies came back to win the rubber. Gordon Greenidge scored exactly 100 out of 280 in their first innings; then Croft took four wickets as Pakistan fell for 198. A second innings total of 359 by West Indies left Pakistan with too much to do. Though Asif Iqbal scored a century, they were still 141 runs short of victory when Wasim Bari became the last man out. Colin Croft, with thirty-three wickets, had emulated Alf Valentine in his first rubber. By the time their next series was underway, West Indies were caught up in the storm over Kerry Packer's World Series Cricket. Unlike England and Australia, however, they could not afford to axe their stars and so the WSC men lined up for the official West Indies visit by Australia in 1978. They struck gold immediately, bowling out Australia for 90 at Port of Spain where Croft (four), Garner (three) and Roberts (two) did the damage. Kallicharran hit a century, West Indies made 405, and poor Australia lost by an innings and 106 runs when Roberts took five for 56 in their second innings.

Inside three days West Indies had won the Second Test at Bridgetown by nine wickets, but before the Third Test at Georgetown, a dispute between Lloyd and the West Indies Board of Control led to the entire band of WSC cricketers withdrawing from the team. With six debutants in their side, West Indies lost by three wickets, though there were centuries from Larry Gomes, of Trinidad and Middlesex, and from Basil Williams of Jamaica, who was playing in his first Test. The West Indian 'second string' was more than equal to its task at Port of Spain, however, winning the Fourth Test by 198 runs with a day to spare, thanks mainly to the bowling of Holder in the first innings and Derek Parry of the Leeward Islands and Ralph Jumadeen of Trinidad in the second. The last Test at Sabina Park was drawn, though Australia might have felt robbed of victory when, with West Indians at 258 for nine and needing 368 to win, the match was virtually abandoned after the crowd rioted following the dismissal of Holder. There were still thirty-eight balls to be bowled but umpire Gosein would have no more.

World Series Cricket, which had wrecked the West Indies team during the Australian rubber, also took its toll on the team which toured India and Sri Lanka in 1978-9. The team was young and inexperienced, only five of them having appeared in West Indian teams before the Packer players, and one of them, Vanburn Holder, would have already ended his Test career under normal circumstances. Their feat in losing only one of the six Tests against India was, therefore, a creditable one. In the Tests, Sylvester Clarke topped the bowling averages with twenty-one wickets at 33.85 apiece, two more victims than Norbert Phillip. Alvin Kallicharran headed the batsmen with an average of almost 60, followed by Jumadeen, Bacchus and Gomes. Kallicharran might have given more opportunities to the off-spinner, Derek Parry, who showed that he could extract a considerable amount of turn from the Indian pitches. The West Indian skipper instead relied too heavily on the pace of Clarke, Phillip and Holder who responded magnificently, despite suffering from dropped catches. There were two innings of particular note from the West Indians. Kallicharran scored a highly polished 187 in the First Test at Bombay; and in the final Test at Kanpur, after India had made 644, Faroud Bacchus responded with 250 on the benign pitch, just saving West Indies from the follow-on in what had become a match of purely academic interest.

Twelve months later, with their Packer men now reinstated, West Indies went to Australia and boosted by the experience of the WSC men — who had played there for the previous two seasons — they won their first rubber in Australia and the Benson and Hedges World Series Cup. The three-match Test series found Australia wanting badly. Lloyd's side, meanwhile, went from strength to strength, their pace battery of Roberts, Holding, Garner and Croft holding the balance of power. Viv Richards apart — and he was the outstanding player in both the full Tests and the Benson and Hedges World Series Cup one-day competition which West Indies won — their batting was not as sharp. But with superb bowling, athletic fielding — and the incomparable Richards — it mattered little. The First Test at Brisbane was drawn, thanks to some safety-first batting by Australia in their second innings which followed 140 by Richards to give West Indies a lead of 173.

West Indies went to Melbourne knowing that they had lost all of their previous seven Tests on the MCG. Now they took control from the start, bowled Australia out for 156, took a first innings lead of 241 with Richards top-scoring with 96, and then bowled out Australia again for 259 before scoring 22 for victory with ten wickets and a day to spare, to lay the jinx of Melbourne. West Indies went to Adelaide needing only a draw to take their first series in Australia. Instead they won by 408 runs. Richards made 76 and Lloyd recovered his form to score 121 in their 328; Australia toppled to 203 all out and then found themselves on the receiving end of a Kallicharran hundred as West Indies set them an impossible 574 to win. Not one Australian batsman seemed interested in saving the game and the West Indies cruised to an emphatic victory in both this match and the rubber. The bowling averages tell their own tale about the series. Garner: fourteen wickets at 21.50; Holding: fourteen at 22.78; Croft: sixteen at 23.62; Roberts: eleven at 26.90. In three Tests, Richards scored 386 runs and averaged 96.50, with Lloyd, who played in two, averaging 67, and Kallicharran 50.50 from three matches.

West Indies went to New Zealand without the injured Richards, were guilty of some boorish behaviour, and lost the First Test by one wicket, drew the last two and so lost the rubber. It was a strange series, perhaps summed up by the fact that Roberts topped the batting averages, and Kallicharran the bowling! Both, of course, enjoyed freak statistics, but it served to underline the fact that the West Indians came to New Zealand with less interest in their tour than might reasonably be expected.

Clyde Walcott, the great West Indian batsman, and manager of the 1976 team, took charge of the party to tour England later in 1980 after Willie Rodriguez's handling of the New Zealand tour came into question. Walcott's team once more relied heavily on the use of pace, and for England's batsmen that summer there seemed no respite from over after over of seam bowling, a facet of the West Indians game which drew condemnation for its attendant slow over rate. Sometimes as few as a dozen or so overs were bowled in an hour and the rate rarely topped fourteen. Cricket fans deserve better and everyone knew it, though no one seemed prepared to do anything to rectify the matter. The rubber was won in the First Test at Trent Bridge where West Indies started the last day needing only 99 to win with eight wickets in hand. That they won by only two was due to Bob Willis who set the match alight with five for 65.

Dropped catches actually cost England a probable victory, for rash batting by the West Indians gave the few hundred spectators who turned up for the last morning some thrilling cricket. A century by Gooch at Lord's was countered by a brilliant stand of 223 between Richards (who reached his hundred in 125 minutes and went on to make 145), and Haynes, whose 184 was overshadowed for the most part by the brilliance of Richards. Gooch's maiden Test hundred was a splendid innings, but after the genius of Richards and the magnificence of Haynes, it was only rain which saved England from probable defeat.

Bad light and rain took a large slice out of the drawn Old Trafford Test, and at The Oval another complete day was lost to rain. Here, though, West Indies almost pulled off a great victory. After Gooch's splendid 83 gave England the base for a first innings of 370, West Indies trailed by 105. But in their second innings England were 92 for nine and heading for defeat when Peter Willey and Bob Willis rescued them to the point where Botham was able to make a token declaration of 209. Willey was 100 not out and his last-wicket stand of 117 with Willis saved the day. Rain ruled out play

Controversial Geoff Boycott was one of the leading lights in the 1982 'rebel' England tour to South Africa. Ironically, Boycott was a great favourite in the West Indies and here he extends his hand to two young black fans

Cricket is the West Indians' greatest love. An impromptu game on a Barbados field

on the first and fourth days of the Headingley Test and England had no chance of levelling the series. Throughout, the funereal over rate maintained by the West Indians was a blot on the rubber. Garner topped the bowling with twenty-six wickets at 14.26 each, and he and Roberts, Marshall and Holding claimed seventy-two batsmen between them. Richards was at the head of the batting as usual with an average of over 63. The 1980-1 visit to Pakistan saw the West Indians again win a rubber 1-0 with the other Tests drawn. It was their first win in a Pakistan rubber, achieved once more with the fierce battery of pace bowlers which they were now content to rely on. It was effective, but oh, for the sight of a Ramadhin, Valentine or Gibbs!

Politics always seems to be with cricket these days and the 1980-1 England tour to the Caribbean sparked off yet another row which resulted in Robin Jackman, the Surrey all-rounder, being made unwelcome in Guyana, due to his South African links, and what should have been the Second Test in Georgetown being called off. It was yet another sad moment for cricket and served only to make one wonder, at the very height of the crisis, just where international sport was going to in the context of world politics. How refreshing it would be if all sporting organisations were totally free from the political pressures now exerted upon them.

Jackman's problems apart, this would have been a sad and depressing tour anyway, for during it, Ken Barrington, the former Surrey and England run machine and as likeable a man as anyone could wish to meet, died suddenly. The death of England's popular assistant manager cast a shadow over the whole tour which, for the record, West Indies won 2-0 with two Tests drawn. Their victories came in the first two games, in Port of Spain and Bridgetown, and by wide margins, and once more it was the pace bowling of Roberts, Holding, Croft and Garner which did the damage. West Indies won the First Test by an innings and 79 runs; the Second Test by 298 runs. At St John's, Antigua, a new Test venue, the loss of the fourth day's play to rain, and a second innings opening stand of 144 between Gooch and Boycott, ensured a draw; and in the last match at Kingston, a brilliant innings of 154 by Gower, in which the young lion allied massive concentration to his natural ability, saved England. Earlier, Gooch scored 153 to auger well for England's future. Alas, subsequent events were to prove that he would have little immediate future in the England team. For West Indies, Viv Richards was again his brilliant self with an average of 85; and though Holding topped the bowling averages with seventeen wickets at 18.53, it was Croft, with twenty-four, who claimed a new record for West Indies-England Tests in the Caribbean.

West Indies were the undisputed world champions and Boxing Day 1981 saw them start the First Test against Australia in Melbourne, favourites to extend their winning run. In the final analysis it was the luck of the toss which decided the result on an unpredictable MCG pitch. Having called successfully, Greg Chappell elected to bat with a side largely unchanged from that which had crashed by an innings to Pakistan. Australia began disastrously in the face of Holding's pace and three wickets were down for eight runs. Half the side was out for 59 but Kim Hughes held firm for a magnificent unbeaten 100, helped by Alderman who stayed bravely while Hughes scored the last 29 runs he needed. Holding had five for 45 and West Indies set about reducing Australia's 198. But by stumps West Indies themselves had crashed. They stood at 10 for four, Lillee taking three for 1 in eleven balls including the prize of Viv Richards. Though Gomes rescued West Indies with a brave half-century the following day, he became Lillee's 310th Test victim, thus giving the Australian his world record. West Indies were all out for 201 with Lillee moving on to seven for 83. Holding added seven for 62 to his first innings figures, giving himself the best match analysis for West Indies against Australia, and the tourists were set 220 to win. They failed and Australia won by 58 runs — a fine victory in a fine Test Match.

The Second Test at Sydney was drawn, though it threw up several individual achievements, notably Gomes's 126, Dyson's unbeaten 127, and a brilliant catch by that player to dismiss Clarke. West Indians now needed to win to level the series and at Adelaide they played more like their old selves than at any other time on the tour. Holding and Roberts destroyed Australia for 238, and then Gomes, with another excellent innings of 124, helped West Indies to 389. This time it was Garner, with five wickets, who broke through the Australians, leaving the West Indies to score 236 to win. They lost Haynes quickly, but then 100 partnership between Richards and Greenidge pulled them to within range. Lillee, who left the field after 4.5 overs of the first innings with an injury, came back but his gentle medium-pace troubled neither Lloyd nor Bacchus. West Indies got home by five wickets and retained their world crown. It sits easily on the heads of the cricketers of the Caribbean.

New Zealand

Kiwis Calling

Cricket in New Zealand has always suffered from one big problem — geography. In relation to almost all the other Test-playing nations, New Zealand is out on a very long limb. Only Australia can be counted as a neighbour — some 1,400 miles of ocean separate the two countries — and yet, amazingly, up to December 1973, only one full Test had been played between them. For encouragement at Test level, particularly in her formative years, New Zealand has had to rely solely on England who fostered international matches at a time when the Kiwis would otherwise have stood alone in the world. Even then, they have had to rely on MCC stopping over after a long and arduous tour of Australia. With a low crowd potential, until quite recently the lack of any real star names, and the large costs involved in visiting other countries, New Zealand has been the Cinderella of Test-playing countries. Happily, towards the end of the 1970s and into the 1980s, much progress was made by New Zealand, particularly when more and more of her players began to gain experience in English county cricket, and the Kiwis are now no longer the whipping boys that perhaps they once were.

The seeds of cricket were planted here by the British, about the same time that cricket in Australia was gaining a foothold. In the 1830s cricket was played and there is record of a match between the Reds and the Blues at Wellington towards the end of 1842. The first recorded match in Auckland took place in 1845, and in March 1860 the first inter-provincial match between Wellington and Auckland was played at Mount Cook Barracks with a return game two years later. Cricket was now flourishing and it inevitably followed that George Parr's side became the first English team to visit New Zealand when they went there from Australia in 1864. Parr's team played four matches, all against odds, won three and drew one. James Lillywhite's team came in 1876-7 and again played against odds and went undefeated; and the following year, the first Australian visitors to England also visited New Zealand, winning five and losing one of their seven matches against odds.

Though largely isolated, the cricketers of New Zealand were intent on furthering their game and as more England parties visited the islands, the Kiwis saw the need for professional coaches. They engaged players from both England and Australia in an attempt to polish up their game. By 1894, cricket in New Zealand had progressed to the stage where it was felt that a national body should be organised to co-ordinate the game into a properly established national sport. In December of that year the New Zealand Cricket Council was formed and within four years, New Zealand had sent her first side abroad when a team visited Australia. The first New Zealand representative team had already taken the field by then, selected by Mr A.M. Ollivier on behalf of the Canterbury Association to meet New South Wales at Christchurch in February 1894. They lost by 60 runs, being bowled out for 79 in their second innings, but won a second game at Christchurch in January 1896, when they defeated New South Wales by 142 runs to gain the first success by a representative New Zealand XI.

In 1896, Harry Trott's Australians, on their way home from England, fielded a team against fifteen of New Zealand at Christchurch and won by five wickets with such famous names as Trott himself, Iredale, Gregory, Darling, Giffen and Trumble in their side. In 1896-7, Queensland played eight matches in New Zealand and when the 'international' was played at the Basin Reserve, Wellington, New Zealand triumphed by 182 runs. New Zealand's second innings began in rip-roaring fashion with Cuff and Holdship setting the pace with 74 runs in 37 minutes. The 200 came up in 137 minutes and although Queensland might have settled for a draw — they had lost six wickets when the appointed finishing time was reached — they sportingly agreed to play on so as not to deny the local side a well-deserved victory.

Thus, when the first New Zealand side went to Australia in 1899, they had already gained some experience of playing as a national representative team. The Kiwi tourists were captained by L.T. Cobcroft who had captained New South Wales against New Zealand in 1895-6. The Kiwis played four matches, two first-class games against Victoria and against

The first New Zealand team to play abroad. These players played in Australia in 1898-9. Back, left to right: F.C. Raphael (manager), H.B. Lusk, F.S. Frankish, J.Baker, G. Mills, A. Sims, F.L. Ashbolt, I. Mills, E.F. Upham. Seated: A.D. Downes, L.T. Cobcroft (captain), C. Boxshall. On ground: D. Reese. Absent: A.H. Fisher

New South Wales, and two non-first-class against North Tasmania and South Tasmania. The game at Melbourne was lost by an innings and 132 runs, despite the fact that Victoria did not field Trumble and McLeod. The New Zealand bowlers were slaughtered by the Victorian batsmen. McAlister hammered 224 before being last out at 602, and the gulf between the two sides was immense, though before McAlister began his assault, the Kiwis had five Victorian batsman out for 129. New South Wales fielded almost their strongest side for the match at Sydney and only Gregory, Kelly and McKenzie were missing. Again the Kiwis were in for a battering. They were bowled out for 140, saw New South Wales amass 588 with the great Victor Trumper making 253, and then fell to the slow-medium pace of Tom McKibbin who took seven for 30 as New Zealand were beaten by an innings and 384 runs.

The pattern of New Zealand cricket throughout the years before World War I was now not only that of visits by teams who called in on the islands after tours elsewhere but also by teams which made New Zeanland their main destination. In 1902-3, a strong team organised by Lord Hawke (who was himself unable to tour), captained by 'Plum' Warner, and containing the famous player B.J.T. Bosanquet, played eighteen matches, seven of which were first-class, and won all three of the representative games against South Island at Dunedin, and against New Zealand at Christchurch and Wellington. There were now other developments taking place in the New Zealand game. In January 1904, South Island won the first inter-island match by two wickets in a rousing finish at Wellington; and in 1907-8, the Plunkett Shield came into being as an inter-province competition. Presented by the then Governor-General of New Zealand, it had been first presented to Canterbury in 1906-7 for performances during that season. Thereafter it was played for under a challenge basis until 1921-2 when it was competed for on a league system until superseded by the Shell Shield in 1975, becoming instead the trophy played for between North and South Islands.

Things were now moving along at a faster pace and in 1906-7 MCC sent its first team to play in New Zealand when Captain E.G. Wynyard captained a party of fourteen amateurs which included J.W.H.T. Douglas. Two 'Tests' were played and in the first, at Christchurch, MCC won by nine wickets after New Zealand-born opener, P.R. Johnson, scored 99 for the tourists. At the Basin Reserve it was New Zealand's turn to taste success. MCC needed 255 to win and lost both openers with 4 scored. Thereafter wickets fell regularly, though Douglas and Page raised 50 for the fifth wicket, and Curwen and May 41 for the last, and New Zealand were home by 56 runs, the Otago bowler A.H. Fisher taking five for 61. Warwick Armstrong brought the Australians in 1909-10 and played nine matches including two 'Tests' which were both won by the tourists.

The period before World War I was especially important to New Zealand cricket. In 1913-14 the Kiwis sent their first team to Australia since 1898-9. Four state games were played — against Queensland, New South Wales, Victoria and South Australia — and New Zealand were triumphant at Brisbane in the first of these. The New South Wales match was lost by an innings and 247 runs, and the Victoria match by an innings and 110 runs, all of which was in sharp contrast to the thrilling 12-run victory over Queensland. The last first-class match, against South Australia at Adelaide, was drawn. It was after this visit to Australia that New Zealand set up a visit by an Australian XI in the early part of 1914.

Arthur Sims, the former Canterbury and New Zealand player, told Monty Noble and Frank Laver that if they would take an Australian team to the islands, he would finance the venture and any money left over from gate receipts would be shared among the players. Though the Australian board objected, a determined bid by the players saw the tour get underway. The Australians had a fine team — Trumper, Armstrong, Collins, Noble and Mailey among them — and amassed some phenomenal scores both in the first-class and the minor games.

They scored 658 against Auckland, 653 against Canterbury — when Trumper (293 in 190 minutes) and Sims (184 not out) added a world record 433 for the eighth wicket — and 922 against a South Canterbury XV when the former England Test star Jack Crawford, who played with Surrey and South Australia, totalled 354. The first 'Test' was played at Dunedin in March 1914 and New Zealand were in trouble immediately when Snedden and Hemus were unable to travel from Auckland. Arthur Mailey's second innings seven for 65 ensured that Australia needed only 84 to win, which they scored for the loss of three wickets. For the second match, at Eden Park, New Zealand made seven changes and after a strong case had been put for the inclusion of players from other cricketing centres, Wanganui's Chester Holland, and Leslie McMahon, who had scored 87 not out for Poverty Bay against the tourists, were included. The new players made little difference to New Zealand's fortunes however. In perfect conditions they lost three wickets for 13 runs and although E.V. Sale scored an unbeaten 109, Australian batsmen took complete control. With centuries from Waddy and Dolling, Armstrong and Crawford, they reached 610 for six before Sims declared. Even then New Zealand might have saved the match. They were 201 for five with only ninety minutes remaining when the tail collapsed and they were beaten by an innings and 113 runs.

After the war, more visits by touring sides were arranged. In 1920-1, the Australian board sent its first official team which was skippered by Vernon Ransford and which included V.Y. Richardson, Kippax, Hornibrook and Ironmonger, and which played nine first-class matches, two of which were against a New Zealand XI. In the first of these, New Zealand were set an impossible 217 to win in 100 minutes and the game was drawn; in the second, the Australians hit a 600-plus score to win by an innings and 227 runs. In 1922-3, MCC, led by A.C. MacLaren, visited New Zealand. They included a future England skipper, A.P.F. Chapman, and the great leg-spinner from Kent 'Tich' Freeman. MCC won six of their eight first-class matches and were twice successful by an innings in the 'Tests' at Wellington. In the first match, MacLaren, now aged fifty-one, hammered the Kiwis for 200 not out.

After further visits by New South Wales and Victoria, New Zealand struck out for foreign shores themselves. In 1925-6 they played nine matches in Australia, four of them first-class, and in these state games lost by an innings to Queensland and then drew with Victoria, South Australia and New South Wales. In the minor games they twice enjoyed innings victories, against Goulburn and Wagga Wagga, and returned home much the wiser for their trip, especially since the side captained by W.R. Patrick had contained so many young players. One of the most encouraging features of the trip had been the batting of Cyril Alcott, the left-handed all-rounder from Auckland who scored centuries against both Victoria and New South Wales.

Two years before New Zealand first played Tests and the first time the Kiwis visited England. The left-arm medium-pace of E.H.L. Bernau beats Derbyshire's Harry Storer during the tour match at Derby in 1927

From the platform of this successful trip to Australia, New Zealand now took their biggest plunge yet, and in 1927 went to England with a side selected from players who had at least ten years of cricket ahead of them. Captained by Tom Lowry, the party included C.S. 'Stewie' Dempster, the opening batsman from Wanganui who was to become one of New Zealand's greatest players, Milford Page, the Canterbury right-hander, John Mills, left-handed opener from Auckland, all-rounder Bert McGirr (Wellington), and Roger Blunt (Otago), left-arm paceman Matthew Henderson of Wellington, and wicketkeeper Ken James, also of Wellington. All these players would go on to win full Test caps when the time came for the Kiwis to be accepted into the fold on equal footing. The itinerary for the New Zealanders' first visit to England did not include any Tests, official or unofficial, but twenty-six first-class matches were played, including one against MCC at Lord's in only the second fixture of the tour.

The first match was against H.M. Martineau's XI in a non-first-class encounter at Holyport where the Kiwis scored 586 for nine declared in the drawn game. So to Lord's and the opening first-class match of the tour. MCC, including Gubby Allen, A.P.F. Chapman, J.W.H.T. Douglas, Hon F.S.G. Calthorpe, and Nigel Haig, batted first and made 392. When New Zealand replied, two middle order centuries from Dacre and Lowry saw them to 460, though Allen had seven for 120, and then MCC declared their second innings closed at 426 for four after centuries from Lyon and Allen.

When New Zealand closed at 224 for four in this drawn match, they had contributed to a record Lord's aggregate of 1,502 runs and established themselves as sturdy opponents. Seven of the first-class matches were won and only five ended in defeat, one of their best displays being a win at Derby over the county by an innings and 240 runs. Dempster headed the first-class batting averages for the tour with 1,430 runs at 44.68 each, Blunt had 1,540 at 441 and another four batsmen topped 1,000 runs. Merritt, who sent down 768 overs, took 107 wickets at 23.64 each, Ken James had sixty-four wicketkeeping dismissals during the summer, and New Zealand set sail for home, well pleased with their overall performance so far from home.

Indeed, they had not long to wait for their ticket into full Test Match cricket. On their way home from England, the Kiwis stopped off at Sydney, where they lost by ten wickets to New South Wales, and that Australasian summer, a strong Australian team captained by V.Y. Richardson and including Woodfull, Kippax, Oldfield, Ponsford, Jackson and Grimmett, the latter a New Zealander by birth who had played for Wellington fourteen years earlier, toured. The Australians won the 'Test' series by 1-0 with one drawn and Bill Woodfull ended the tour with an average of over 130. New Zealand now wanted full Test status and in 1929-30 they were granted that wish when MCC sent a team to play in a four-match rubber which had been accorded full international status.

Even the fact that this was far short of England's strongest side — another team was representing England in the West Indies — did not detract from the fact that the Kiwis were now full partners. The MCC party did include Duleepsinhji, Frank Woolley, Ted Bowley, Fred Barratt, and Geoffrey Legge, all of whom had played Test cricket before this tour. Arthur Gilligan was forced to drop out and his brother Harold took over the captaincy of the MCC party. New Zealand's first full Test began at Lancaster Park, Christchurch on 10 January 1930.

They were led by Tom Lowry who won the toss and elected to bat on a fast pitch. The Kiwis were in trouble from the start and lost their first three wickets to the Essex fast bowler, 'Stan' Nichols, who sent back Foley, Roberts and Page with only 15 scored. But there was even worse to follow for New Zealand. Maurice Allom, Surrey's medium-pacer, made Test Match history by doing the hat trick on his debut. He had four wickets in five balls to reduce the Kiwis to 21 for seven and only a brave 45 not out by Blunt enabled them to crawl towards a modest 112. At the close England were 147 for four in reply and although rain prevented any play on the Saturday, the game resumed on Monday morning on a soft pitch on which Blunt, with a spell of three for eight, wrapped up the England innings at 181. On New Zealand's reply, only Dempster, Page and Lowry looked capable of coping with the drying conditions. They helped New Zealand to 131 but that still left England needing only 63 to win in 105 minutes. Dawson and Gilligan soon went, but Duleepsinhji and Woolley opened their shoulders and got the runs with 55 minutes to spare to record New Zealand's first defeat in Test cricket.

The last three Tests were drawn, the fourth match being added after rain robbed the Third Test at Eden Park of any play on the first two days. In the Second Test at the Basin Reserve, Dempster and John Mills of Auckland gave the Kiwis a brilliant start of 276, a record which would stand until 1971-2. Dempster became the first Kiwi to score a Test century and Mills the first New Zealander to score a century on his Test debut.

Though the match was drawn, Dempster and Mills had done much to wipe out the memory of the first match.

In holding England in three of the four Tests in their inaugural rubber, New Zealand had proved that they were not going to be cannon-fodder at the highest level. In 1931 they made their second visit to England, their first at full Test level, and although only one Test was scheduled — at Lord's in late June — the Kiwis' form in that match, and in the county games, led to two extra Tests being arranged. Against Douglas Jardine's side at Lord's, New Zealand trailed by 230 runs on first innings. But when they batted again, even after Mills was bowled by the second ball of the innings, they did more than enough to earn a comfortable draw. Dempster took charge to score 120, Page also scored a century, Blunt was four runs short of his hundred, and Lowry was able to declare at 469 for nine, setting England to score 240 in 140 minutes. They did not attempt that target and the match ended in a draw at 146 for five.

England won the next Test by an innings, giving debuts to Freddie Brown and Hedley Verity, and this time the Kiwi batsmen had no answer to a total of 416, of which Sutcliffe, Duleepsinhji and Hammond had all contributed centuries, before Jardine declared with only four wickets down. The Oval Test was followed by a match at Old Trafford where rain allowed for only half a day's play on the last afternoon. In all first-class matches New Zealand had won six and lost only three out of thirty-two. Dempster was again top of the averages with 1,778 runs at nearly 60. Blunt scored almost 1,600 and again four other Kiwis reached the 1,000 mark. Merritt was again the leading wicket-taker, this time with ninety-nine, though he was way down the averages which were topped by the Kiwi captain and manager, Tom Lowry, whose fifteen wickets at 18.26 edged out 'Giff' Vivian (sixty-four at 23.75). Apart from a visit by the South Africans in 1931-2, who played two Tests at the end of their Australian tour and won them both, all the other Tests involving New Zealand up to the outbreak of World War II were against England.

MCC made one more journey to New Zealand before the war and again it was at the end of an Australian tour when they played two Tests in March and April 1933. England had just emerged from the infamous 'bodyline' tour and although both Tests in New Zealand were drawn, they produced some interesting cricket. At Christchurch, Horace Smith bowled Eddie Paynter with his first ball in Test cricket. Poor Smith then finished with figures of one for 113, was bowled by Tate for 4, and never played in another Test Match. Wally Hammond (227) and Les Ames (103) added 242 runs for the fifth wicket in 145 minutes before Jardine declared at 560 for eight. The Kiwis made only 223 and followed-on, but England had no time to bowl them out and they were 35 for no wicket when a combination of a dust storm, rain and bad light prevented further play.

At Auckland, Mills was out to the first ball of the match and when Gordon Weir fell to the second, a sensational opening hat trick from Bill Bowes looked in prospect. Dempster averted further disaster and stayed to score 83 not out in the Kiwis' total of 158. The second day saw England resume at 127 for one with Wally Hammond on 41. From that moment, the Gloucestershire giant was in magnificent form. He flayed New Zealand's bowlers to all parts of the ground in scoring what was then the world Test record of 336 not out. Hammond's 300 came in only 287 minutes, the fastest-ever triple Test century, and his last hundred was posted in just forty-seven minutes. As soon as Hammond had passed Bradman's record, set at Leeds two and a half years earlier. Jardine declared, but rain ended the match almost a day early with New Zealand's second innings barely underway. Though there were to be no further Tests in New Zealand before the war, MCC did pay a visit in 1936-7 under the captaincy of G.O. Allen. They came, yet again, after a visit to Australia and played three matches. In the first, at Dunedin, New Zealand were bowled out for 81 and MCC then made 653 for five declared with centuries from Parks, Barber and Langridge, before the Kiwis hung on at 205 for seven to survive with bad light again saving them; it was a fine defensive innings by Langridge that denied New Zealand victory at Wellington; and at Auckland, big scoring by both sides meant that a draw was inevitable.

New Zealand's last Tests before the war were against England in the three-match series of 1937 which introduced Len Hutton and Denis Compton to the international scene for England, and blooded Martin Donnelly and Walter Hadlee for New Zealand. Donnelly, then playing for Taranaki, was blossoming into one of the greatest left-handed batsman that the world had ever seen. His driving, hooking and pulling were a pleasure to behold, according to contemporary writers, and the previous year he had made his debut in the Plunket Shield, playing for Wellington at the age of nineteen. Hadlee, from Canterbury, was a tall, bespectacled opening batsman and father of Dayle and Richard, who won full Test caps, and of Barry who played for New Zealand in the Prudential World Cup.

The First Test of 1937, played at Lord's, saw Hadlee and Donnelly pitched into the action along with four other debutants, Denis Maloney, the all-rounder from Manawatu, Eric Tindill, Wellington's wicketkeeper, and the Auckland pair, fast bowler John Cowie and batsman Walter Wallace. Walter Robins won the toss and elected to bat. For nearly a quarter of an hour, Len Hutton stayed on nought. Then Cowie beat him for sheer pace and the man who was to enjoy such a magnificent Test career was gone for a duck. Cowie accounted for Parks at 31, but then Hammond and Joe Hardstaff took control. They added 245 for the third wicket, both reaching splendid centuries, and with Eddie Paynter adding 74, England were all out for 424. Just as Hutton had failed, so Donnelly, too, was out for a duck on his Test debut. It was left to the middle order to rescue New Zealand who trailed by 129. England set them 356 to win, and at 15 for three they looked a beaten side. But then John Kerr of Canterbury, Wallace, Donnelly and Albert Roberts, the Canterbury medium-pacer who had scored 66 in the first innings, took the Kiwis to a draw at 175 for eight. In the Second Test at Old Trafford, Norman Gallichan, the hard-hitting batsman and slow left armer from Manawatu, made his debut when Tom Goddard bowled England to victory by 130 runs. Cowie had taken six wickets in England's second innings, but Hutton's first innings century had tipped the balance. The final Test at The Oval was affected by rain and a draw was inevitable. Debutant Denis Compton made 65 before he was run out and Donnelly made a half century for the Kiwis who, thanks to Moloney, Vivian and Tindill, left England insufficient time to score their victory runs.

In all, New Zealand had played thirty-two first-class games on this tour and won nine, lost nine, and drawn fourteen. Six batsmen reached 1,000 runs, led by Wallace who had 1,641 and averaged over 41. Donnelly had 1,414 and Moloney, Kerr, Hadlee and Vivian, the vice-captain to Page, all joined them on a four-figure aggregate. The bowlers were led by Cowie with 114 wickets at less than 20 runs each, and Tindill, keeping wicket for New Zealand with great skill, had forty-six dismissals. On their way home from England, New Zealand played a one-day match against All Ceylon in Colombo, and then took on South Australia, Victoria, and New South Wales, all of whom beat the Kiwis handsomely. There was very little time left to organise any more international cricket. Sir Julien Cahn brought out a private team which played nine minor matches and one first-class game — against New Zealand in which rain limited play to one day — and his side included 'Stewie' Dempster who was now playing English county cricket with Leicestershire, and Nottinghamshire hero Joe Hardstaff.

International cricket everywhere now took a back seat while Hitler, Mussolini and company were defeated, and New Zealand domestic cricket was punctuated by matches such as South Island Army versus North Island Army, New Zealand Army versus Royal New Zealand Air Force, and a New Zealand XI versus a New Zealand Services XI. The latter match was played at the Basin Reserve in March 1944. In March 1945, North Island beat South Island at Eden Park, and normal service was about to be resumed. It was ironic, then, that when peacetime cricket was restored, it was Australia who should provide the opposition in what was the first official Test between the two Pacific neighbours. It took place at the Basin Reserve and after Walter Hadlee had taken first use of a rain-affected pitch, the Kiwis were never in with a shout. Toshack and O'Reilly shot them out for 42, their lowest-ever Test score, and then Australia scored 199 for nine before declaring and rattling out New Zealand again to win by an innings and 103 runs. Martin Donnelly was absent in England and Australia lacked only Don Bradman from an otherwise full-strength line-up. Bill O'Reilly was almost unplayable and in his farewell Test took eight wickets. It was a pity, though, that the first official Test since the end of the war should be played on such a poor pitch.

After the disastrous defeat in their first Test for nine years, New Zealand waited almost exactly one year before their next match. Wally Hammond brought the England party which had lost the rubber in Australia. It was Hammond's last Test Match and rain spoiled his farewell. For the Test, which was played at Christchurch, New Zealand brought in six debutants, three from Auckland and three from Canterbury. The Auckland trio were Bert Sutcliffe, on the threshold of becoming one of the most brilliant left-handed openers in the world, Don Taylor, a right-hander, and Colin Snedden who bowled medium-pace off breaks. From Canterbury came batsman 'Runty' Smith, all-rounder Roy Scott, and slow left arm bowler Tom Burtt who was to have such a fine summer in England in 1949. Smith replaced 'Stewie' Dempster who was originally selected but who withdrew from the side.

Hammond won the toss and put New Zealand in to bat on what might have appeared a difficult track. But Walter Hadlee and young Bert Sutcliffe found it all too easy. They put on 133 for the first wicket, Sutcliffe going for 58, and Hadlee marching on to 116. The Kiwi skipper reached his 50 in eighty-seven minutes, his century in 130 minutes, and when on 97 hit the fence in an attempt to reach three figures with a 6. Though Alec Bedser got among the middle order, New Zealand's close of play score of 306 for eight was more than satisfactory. They closed the following morning at 345, Cowie scoring 45 in his ninety-minute stay which had started the previous evening. When Cowie had Washbrook caught by Smith off the last ball of the first over, New Zealand had their tails up, but at close of play, England had reached 265 for seven when Hammond, who marked his last Test with 79, declared and put in prospect a fascinating last day's play. Alas, that was to be the end of the match. It rained on the Monday and although an extra day's play was arranged — the first time that had been done in a Test — rain again prevented any play and what was up until then a magnificent cricket match, ended in a draw.

New Zealand would never know if they could have beaten England in 1946-7, and in 1949, when they played four Tests, the mistake in limiting Tests between the two countries to only three days meant that there was again no positive result in any of the matches. For the First Test, at Headingley, the Kiwis brought in Harry Cave, Wanganui's medium-pacer; Frank Mooney, Wellington's wicketkeeper; and Geoff Rathbone, the all-rounder from Wellington who had already proved himself a versatile bowler in the Plunkett Shield. At one stage New Zealand looked in real trouble at 80 for four in reply to England's 372, which included centuries from Hutton and Compton. Trevor Bailey had taken a wicket — that of Verdun 'Scotty' Scott — with his eighth ball in Test cricket, and the Kiwis were on the rack when Smith joined Donnelly. Together, these two added 120 in only eighty-six minutes before Donnelly was out for 64. 'Runty' Smith went on to 94 before Bill Edrich had him caught by Compton, and with late-order resistance from Mooney and Cowie, the Kiwis were only 31 runs behind. Their joy was even greater when Hutton fell to Cave — the second ball of the innings — but Washbrook, with a century, and Edrich stepped into the breach and Freddie Mann was eventually able to declare at 267 for four, leaving New Zealand 299 in 150 minutes for victory. Sutcliffe and Scott started off in a determined bid to get the runs. Eighty-two runs came in an hour, but after Scott went at 112, the innings slowed and though Smith counted two 6s in his 54 not out, the match was drawn with New Zealand still 104 runs short at the close. Sutcliffe had scored a brilliant 82 and the Kiwis had entertained the discerning Yorkshire crowd every inch of the way.

At Lord's, New Zealand were again in great form. They had England at 112 for five before Bailey joined Compton and the two added 189 for the sixth wicket. Compton was 116 when Burtt claimed his wicket, and Bailey seven runs short of his maiden Test century when he fell to Rabone. Mann declared with seven men out for 313, and Bert Sutcliffe reached his 50 in an hour as the Kiwis went to 137 for three. Now Martin Donnelly arrived at the wicket to play the greatest innings of his career. Donnelly ensured that New Zealand would remember this match for ever. He gracefully stroked his way to a double century, being the last man out when he had scored 206 and taken the Kiwis to a lead of 171.

Donnelly had pulled and cut anything short, driven the rest, and taken complete charge of the innings from the moment he had arrived at the crease 355 minutes earlier. He now had the distinction of having scored a century at Lord's in a Test, in a Varsity Match, in a Gentlemen versus Players match, and for the Dominions against England when his 133 at HQ in 1945 had won the game. He was the star in a fine batting side and though this meant entertainment for the crowd when he was at the crease, it also meant that the Tests could not achieve a result in three days. Robertson scored a century when England replied and at 306 for five, the result was another inevitable draw. It was the same at Old Trafford where John Reid of Hutt Valley, the man who was to become perhaps the greatest all-rounder that New Zealand has ever seen, made his debut and scored 50. Donnelly made 75, and after Reg Simpson's century for England gave the home side a lead of 147, the Kiwis had no difficulty in batting out time when Sutcliffe hit a fine century. Donnelly was again in great form with 80, and this pair added 78 in only an hour for the fourth wicket to send New Zealand en route to 348 for seven at the close. But perhaps the player who remembers that game most is the former Yorkshire and Somerset skipper, Brian Close, who, at the age of eighteen, became England's youngest-ever cricketer. Runs were still being scored in plenty at The Oval. The final Test found Sutcliffe and Scott opening with a century partnership in only eighty-eight minutes and the Kiwis eventually reached 345. Then it was England's turn to pile on the agony. Len Hutton scored a double century and with Bill Edrich took England from 147 for one to 365 for two. Their stand helped England to a lead of 137, and although the Kiwis had lost four wickets before knocking off the deficit, Reid, Wallace and Rabone carried New Zealand to the point where Reid, captaining New Zealand in only his second Test, could declare at 308 for nine, though there was no time for England to reply.

This hot, dry summer had been ideal for cricketers, though perhaps not always for the spectators who were often denied a result. Tom Burtt had found the English conditions in 1949 especially pleasing and in all first-class matches he claimed 128 wickets. Donnelly and Sutcliffe led the batting, each with over 2,000 runs. Martin Donnelly topped the averages with nearly 62 per innings out of 2,287 runs; Sutcliffe was the leading runmaker with 2,627; and Wallace, Reid, Scott, Hadlee, Rabone and Smith all totalled over 1,000. The side had played thirty-two first-class matches and lost only one — by 83 runs to Oxford University — and they had been victorious on thirteen occasions. After the customary festival games at Hastings and Scarborough, the Kiwis enjoyed a seven-wickets win over Combined Services in the unusual cricket setting of Bad Oeyhausen in Germany, and then set sail for home, well satisfied with their tour.

Australia played a match at Dunedin in March 1950 and almost beat New Zealand in a 'non-Test'. The Kiwis were nine men down at 67 and still needed a single to avoid an innings defeat when George 'Fen' Cresswell came in and helped stave off disaster. Creswell, who did not play first-class cricket until his mid-thirties, had been a big success on the 1949 tour with his medium-pace bowling which claimed sixty-two wickets. Against this Australian XI he had eight for 100 in their only innings and when England played two Tests in 1950-1, at the end of another unsuccessful Australian visit, he again found himself facing a strong batting side, but this time on a lifeless pitch. A total of 1,013 runs were scored for the loss of only twenty-one wickets. Bert Sutcliffe scored 116 in New Zealand's 417 for eight declared, and when England batted their hero was Trevor Bailey who scored what was his only Test hundred with 134 unbeaten runs coming in the face of some fine bowling by debutant leg-spinner Alex Moir. Moir, who played with Otago, took six wickets, though in doing so, he was hit for 155 runs off fifty-six overs as England ploughed on to take full advantage of the dead pitch. The match had given Brian Statham the first of his 252 Test wickets. At Wellington, rain — and even a slight earthquake — could not save New Zealand. Roy Tattersall bowled England on the way to a six-wickets win, though the winning runs

New Zealand take the field at Wellington for the First Test of 1953 against South Africa. Players from left are: A.M. Moir, F.E. Fisher, L.S.M. Miller, W.M. Wallace, R.W. Blair, F.L.H. Mooney, B. Sutcliffe, J.G. Leggett. J.R. Reid, E.M. Meuli, and T.B. Burtt are hidden

were struck with less than a quarter of an hour to play.

With the 1950s came new opposition for New Zealand. In 1951-2, West Indies, again following the routine of visiting the islands after an Australian tour, played two Tests. The inaugural meeting between the two sides drew 18,000 spectators to Christchurch to see names like Stollmeyer, Worrell, Weekes, Walcott, Ramadhin and Valentine take the tourists to a five-wicket win. At Auckland, the match was drawn after West Indies scored 546 and rain left the final day blank. After West Indies, South Africa made their first visit since 1931-2, winning the First Test at the Basin Reserve by an innings and 180 runs after Jackie McGlew's great double century put the game beyond the reach of New Zealand. A draw at Auckland gave the Springboks the rubber, and in December 1953, just nine months after the series in New Zealand, the Kiwis paid their first visit to South Africa. They lost the rubber by 4-1, Geoff Rabone captaining New Zealand for the first time. Only Rabone, Reid, Sutcliffe and Mooney had experience of overseas conditions and the Kiwis fell far short of the standards required to do well in the Union.

The tour ended with the Kiwis playing three state games in Australia, beating Western Australia and South Australia, and drawing with Victoria. Gordon Leggett, the Canterbury batsman who had the unique experience of playing against four different countries in his first four Tests, topped the tour averages after joining the side in Australia to replace the injured Rabone. In reality, though, it was Sutcliffe, with 1,653 runs at over 52, who stood at the head of the batsmen, with Reid nudging him close. When England arrived in New Zealand in 1954-5 after regaining the Ashes, the Kiwis knew that they faced a tough time against Hutton's supremely confident side. It was reflected in the results when England won both Tests, by eight wickets and by an innings and 20 runs. The first game was Dunedin's first Test and even rain, which wiped out two full days, could not stop England. There was even worse to follow at Auckland where New Zealand were utterly humiliated when they were shot out for a record low Test score of 26 in their second innings. Only Sutcliffe reached double figures, the innings was all over in 104 minutes, and England won with over two days to spare.

Undaunted by this setback, New Zealand broke still more new ground in 1955-6 when they went to the Indian sub-continent under the captaincy of Henry Cave. Their first taste of cricket there came with a drawn game against the Pakistan Chief Commissioner's XI in Karachi, whereupon they were pitched into the First Test in the same stadium. Otago's John Alabaster was one of three debutants as Zulfiqar Ahmed's off-spin bedazzled the Kiwis on the matting pitch and the last four wickets went down for only 6 runs to send them tumbling to an innings defeat. Noel Harford, the neat Central Districts batsman, and Auckland's wicketkeeper Eric Petrie, both made their debuts in the next Test at Lahore where Pakistan won again, scoring 116 at over a run a minute for their six wickets win.

A draw at Dacca in the rain-affected Third Test, saw New Zealand move on to the Indian part of their tour and an immediate defeat against West Zone at Poona. It was a sorry prelude to the first Test that New Zealand had ever played against India, but the pitch beat both sides at Hyderabad. Central Districts' John Guy, playing in only his second Test, stonewalled for over seven hours in making 102 and the game was drawn. Polly Umrigar scored India's first double century, Kripal Singh scored a hundred in his first Test, and Manjrekar also joined the centurions. Bert Sutcliffe was not to be left out and coasted to 137 not out as the game drifted to a draw. The Second Test at Bombay again found an Indian batsman in double century form and this time Mankad was the man, making 223 to equal Umrigar's record set in the previous Test. This time, however, New Zealand could not shore up their defences and defeat by an innings and 27 runs was the result. In Delhi, it was Bert Sutcliffe's turn. His 230 not out, in a New Zealand total of 450 for two declared, ensured no further disasters. With Reid (119) he added 222 runs in an unfinished third wicket partnership. With India's reply in excess of 500, and here there was another fine century by Manjrekar (177), there was stalemate again; at Calcutta, New Zealand, set to get 235 in ninety minutes, settled for 75 for six and the draw after a collapse had threatened them with defeat.

But there was to be no escape in Madras. The match belonged to India from the start as they piled on a world Test record of 413 for the first wicket with Mankad, who went on to make 231, and Roy (173) establishing an unbeatable position. Umrigar was able to declare at 537 for three and New Zealand were bowled out twice to lose by an innings and 109 runs. Though both rubbers had been lost, this tour had opened up new horizons for New Zealand cricketers who now knew what it was like to bat and bowl on the flat, docile pitches of the Indian sub-continent. They arrived home to find the West Indians ready for a full fifteen-match tour of New Zealand which included four Tests. The Kiwis lost the first three heavily, succeeding only at Auckland where Cave, Alabaster and Don Beard bowled the West Indians out for only 77. This was more than just a consolation victory at the end of a rubber — it was New Zealand's first victory in an official Test since they had been upgraded in 1929-30. Twenty-six years and forty-five Tests after their first match at full status, it tasted very sweet. At one stage, after John Beck ran out Sobers, West Indies were 18 for five, and New Zealand forgot for a moment that they had lost the rubber. This victory was now so much more important.

John Reid's touring party to England in 1958, despite including such experienced players as Reid himself, Bert Sutcliffe, Harry Cave, Tony

MacGibbon, the fast bowler from Canterbury, Alex Moir, Auckland paceman John Haynes, Hutt Valley's seamer, Bob Blair, and the left-handed opener from Wellington, Laurie Miller, did not do at all well. Several young players were blooded on the tour, including John D'Arcy from Canterbury who had made a big impression as a batsman in the Plunkett Shield, Trevor Meale, a left-hander from Hutt Valley. John Sparling, the all-rounder from Auckland, and Canterbury wicketkeeper John Ward. It was a damp and miserable English summer and the Kiwis lost four of the five Tests, being bowled out for scores of 94, 47, 74, 67 and 85. Only rain saved them from a complete whitewash and New Zealand cricket found itself at a low ebb.

New Zealand touring party to England 1958. Back row, left to right: J.T. Ward, J.C. Alabaster, N.S. Harford, W.R. Playle, A.R. MacGibbon, T. Meale, R.W. Blair, J.T. Sparling, A.M. Moir. Front: E.C. Petrie, L.S.M. Miller, J.A. Hayes, H.B. Cave, J.R. Reid (captain), J.H. Phillipps (manager), B. Sutcliffe, J.W. D'Arcy

Seven months later, England, under the captaincy of Peter May, won the First Test at Christchurch by an innings and 99 runs after a splendid century by Ted Dexter and some equally fine bowling by Tony Lock who took eleven wickets in a match which attracted a record 20,000 to watch the second day's play at Lancaster Park. That gave England the rubber, for the Second Test at Auckland was almost completely ruined by high winds and rain. Though Australia continued to supply occasional opposition at non-Test level — Ian Craig's team played six first-class games, including four against New Zealand, in the islands in 1959-60, the next Test series was against South Africa in 1961-2.

The previous season, MCC had played a full-scale tour of twenty-two matches in New Zealand under the captaincy of Dennis Silk. Three of MCC's ten first-class matches were against New Zealand, the Kiwis winning an unofficial rubber by 1-0 after their 133-runs win at Wellington. Dick Motz, the fast bowler from Canterbury who took a wicket in the second over of his first-class debut in the Plunkett Shield of 1957-8 (and two more in his third over) impressed and was ready to take his place in the party to tour South Africa. It was a successful tour for both Motz and the rest of the team. New Zealand won their second and third

Tests to draw the rubber — the first time they had squared a series — and Motz topped the bowling averages of this tour, which also included a few matches in Australia, with eighty-five wickets at less than 19 runs each. John Reid was head and shoulders above the rest of the batsmen with over 2,000 runs at an average of 61.26. His nearest rival was Graham Dowling, the Canterbury batsman who had just entered the Test arena where he would stay for the next decade. Dowling's return was 929 runs at almost half Reid's average. There had been Test centuries from Reid, Parke Harris of Canterbury, and Paul Barton of Wellington.

When Ted Dexter brought MCC to New Zealand in 1962-3, his side included some of the great names in English cricket — Cowdrey, Barrington, Illingworth, Trueman, Sheppard and Titmus. England won all three Tests, the first two by an innings, and engulfed New Zealand in every department of the game. In the face of an England total of 562 in the First Test at Auckland, New Zealand had to follow-on 304 runs behind and could then muster only a further 89 as Larter and Illingworth ripped through them; at Wellington it was the same depressing story — defeat by an innings and 47 runs — and at Christchurch, even a brave 100 by John Reid failed to save New Zealand. Fred Trueman took seven for 75 and two for 16 to end the Test with 250 victims and go way in front of Brian Statham's previous record of 242. South Africa were the next visitors, in 1963-4, drawing all three Tests, though in the last match at Auckland, New Zealand were eight wickets down and needed another 118 runs to win when rain saved them. Bob Cunis of Auckland, playing in his first Test, and wicketkeeper Arthur Dick were together when salvation came from the heavens.

That was the last time that New Zealand met South Africa in a Test Match to date. The New Zealanders' next opponents were Pakistan who also drew their three-match series in 1964-5. New Zealand, however,

Bert Sutcliffe, of New Zealand, Auckland, Otago and Northern Districts, was one of the greatest left-handers in the world. From 1941-66 he scored 17,283 runs in all first-class cricket and in forty-two Tests made 2,727

looked likely to win the Second Test at Auckland when they were set 220 in 240 minutes and raced to 68 in seventy-three minutes. But when Pervez took four wickets for no runs in ten balls, the Kiwis were thankful to settle for another draw. Two players who were to become great names in the New Zealand side, made their debuts in the series. Bev Congdon, the little all-rounder from Nelson, and Richard Collinge, from Wairarapa, who stood 6ft 5in tall and bowled left-arm fast medium, were included for the First Test. Collinge was soon among the wickets and kept up a good striking rate throughout his career until he was the Kiwis' most prolific wicket-taker.

The Pakistanis played the last Test at Christchurch in February 1965. By the end of that month, New Zealand were in India at the start of a long and arduous tour which took them through Pakistan and on to England in time for the 1965 English season. Four Tests were played in India, India winning the series 1-0 after the first three were drawn, before the Kiwis moved on to Pakistan where they lost 2-0 in the three-match series. Vic Pollard of Manawatu made his debut in the First Test, batting well down the order and being used more for his off-spin bowling. In the Second Test at Calcutta, Graham Vivian, a left-handed batsman and leg-spinner from Auckland played in what was his first-class debut, making 43 and adding 81 with Vic Pollard for the eighth wicket in nearly even time. Big Bruce Taylor, the Canterbury all-rounder, also made his debut in Calcutta, becoming only the second Kiwi to score a century in his first Test, and followed that up with five for 86 to establish a new record. Taylor had five wickets in the Third Test when India were dismissed for 88, though when they followed-on, the Indians made 463 for five before the Nawab of Pataudi declared, setting New Zealand 255 in 150 minutes. They were happy to achieve a draw after the Indians had them on the canvas at 80 for eight. At Delhi, India scored 73 in double quick time to win the rubber with a seven-wickets victory.

When they moved to Rawalpindi, the New Zealanders lost to Pakistan by an innings and 64 runs after slipping to 79 all out in what was John Reid's fifty-third consecutive Test — a new record. A drawn Test at Lahore gave the Kiwis a chance of squaring the rubber at Karachi. Instead, they lost by eight wickets and now looked towards the cooler climes of England and a three-match rubber. But things were just as difficult in a more hospitable climate. England won all the Tests, by nine wickets, seven wickets, and an innings and 187 runs. Fred Trueman, in his final Test, established a new world record with his 307th Test wicket, and New Zealand were really no match for England in what had turned out to be a wet and miserable summer, enjoyed most, perhaps, by John Edrich who took advantage of a weak Kiwi attack at Leeds to score England's first triple century since 1938.

Barry Sinclair, a small but determined batsman from Wellington, topped the averages for this long tour with just over 1,000 runs at 35.23. When England came to New Zealand in 1965-6, Sinclair led the Kiwis in the last two Tests after the appointed skipper, Murray Chapple was injured. Mike Smith's MCC party included Boycott, Parfitt, Edrich, Parks, Cowdrey and Murray, but the weather intervened and the Tests were all drawn, Congdon scoring a century in the First Test at Christchurch, and Sinclair celebrating his elevation to the captiancy with a hundred at Auckland. Games against Australian representative teams were played in New Zealand in 1966-7, and against the states in Australia the following season, before full Tests were resumed with the visit of India in 1967-8 when the Indians won the series 3-1. Despite a second wicket stand of 155 between Dowling (143) and Congdon (58), India's first Test in New Zealand gave them their first win outside the sub-continent. New Zealand fell foul to the off-spin of Prasanna when they batted a second time. The Indian took six for 94 and left his side plenty of time to score 200 which gave them victory by five wickets.

The Dunedin Test was followed by a game at Christchurch which saw New Zealand sweep to what was only their fourth Test victory. The man largely responsible was Graham Dowling, who had assumed the captaincy. Dowling's innings of 239 was then the highest by a New Zealander in Tests and enabled his side to make 502. Six wickets from Dick Motz ensured that the Indians followed-on, and Bev Congdon's 61 not out, when everyone else was failing, saw the New Zealanders to a five-wickets win. But India came back in force, winning the remaining Tests and taking the last by 272 runs after New Zealand failed miserably to the spin of Prassana and Bedi. New Zealand's fifth Test victory came in the Second Test against West Indies in March 1969, when Dick Motz established a new record of eighty-five wickets during the Kiwis' six-wickets win.

By now, New Zealand were becoming accustomed to making truncated tours to England. In 1969 they shared the summer with West Indies, arriving in time to play their first match against Yorkshire at Bradford with the other tourists well underway. The First Test, against an England side skippered by Ray Illingworth, saw the debuts of Dayle Hadlee and Ken Wadsworth. Wadsworth, the safe wicketkeeper and aggressive batsman from Nelson, was embarking on a career as New Zealand's regular wicketkeeper, a career which lasted until 1976 when he died of cancer at the tragically young age of twenty-nine. Hedley Howarth, the slow left-arm spinner from Auckland also made his debut at Lord's, but this young side was soundly beaten by 230 runs after Derek Underwood spun England to victory with seven for 32 and a day to spare (a day, incidentally, when it never stopped raining; if New Zealand could have held out for another thirty minutes on the fourth evening, they would have drawn the Test). A drawn game at Trent Bridge was followed by a resounding England victory at The Oval where Underwood, with twelve for 101, was again the thorn in New Zealand's side. England were then left to score 138 for victory, which they did with eight wickets to spare, though it was a race against the rainclouds which threatened to save New Zealand.

On the way home, New Zealand played Tests in India and Pakistan. Motz, who was injured, returned home and D.G. Trist of Canterbury flew out to replace him, though he did not play in any Tests. Rioting in Ahmedabad prevented that city from staging what would have been its first Test and the initial meeting against India was switched to Bombay where New Zealand lost by 60 runs on an under-prepared pitch, Bedi and Prasanna again doing the damage. This was certainly a historic tour and in the first Test to be played at Nagpur, New Zealand won their first Test in India, Howarth taking nine wickets in the match to spin the Kiwis to memorable victory. The final Test was even more intriguing. The Indian groundman forgot to mow the pitch and although New Zealand had their opponents out for 89, and then struggling at 76 for seven, a combination of rioting crowds, rain, and an indifferent attitude by the Indians to restarting the match, probably robbed New Zealand of their first win in a rubber.

That first win in a rubber for New Zealand was just around the corner, however. They moved on to Pakistan, drew the First Test in Karachi, and won the next at Lahore by five wickets. After dismissing Pakistan for 114 in their first innings, the Kiwis went on to take the game after losing their first three wickets for 29 runs, chasing 82 for victory. Bruce Murray, Wellington's circumspect batsman, scored 90, and Brian Hastings of Canterbury scored 80 in the first innings, to set up a Kiwi win. Bad light and occasional rioting caused the abandonment of the final Test in Dacca with Pakistan, chasing 184 to win, at 51 for four with little more than an hour left. So, with that inconclusive last Test, New Zealand had her first win in a rubber after forty years of trying.

Australia drew three unofficial Tests in New Zealand in March 1969 and New Zealand's next official series was against England in 1970-1 when Illingworth's team gave an England debut to the patient Bob Taylor. Taylor's first England cap in Christchurch was a reward for being a good tourist; happily, Bob, the great gentleman of cricket, was eventually to play many more times in his own right as the world's finest wicketkeeper. England won by eight wickets and yet again Underwood was largely responsible, taking twelve for 97, including his 1,000th first-class wicket, as New Zealand were bowled out for 65 and 254. The Second Test, at Auckland, was drawn after local player Mark Burgess shored up New Zealand with a fine century. Glenn Turner scored 65 in this match. Turner, who made his Test debut against West Indies in 1969, played first for Otago and then elected to learn in the harshest of all schools, the English county championship. The result was that Turner became probably New Zealand's greatest professional cricketer, absorbing the lessons he learnt with Worcestershire and putting them to good use for his own country.

Glenn Turner – the greatest Kiwi batsman? Scorer of a hundred centuries and in 1982 the first man to score 300 in a day in English county cricket since 1949

Just how much Turner had learned was revealed when New Zealand played in West Indies in 1972. Though all the matches were drawn, Turner topped the averages with 1,284 runs at 85.60. On this first New Zealand visit to the Caribbean, Turner scored four double centuries in all games, top-scored with 259 in the Fourth Test where he and Terry Jarvis (who made 182) scored 387 for the first wicket, and that after having already hit a double century in the First Test when he made 223 not out. Though there were plenty of other fine performances, including a brilliant 166 not out by Bev Congdon in the Second Test, Turner completely overshadowed the tour. Even his 259 in the Georgetown Test had been immediately preceded by exactly the same score in the game against Guyana on the same ground! Turner was not in such prolific form when Pakistan won the 1972-3 series, 2-1 in New Zealand. The only New Zealand centuries of the rubber came from Hastings and Rodney Redmond, the tall left-hander, both of whom scored hundreds at Auckland in the drawn final Test. Redmond became the third Kiwi to score a century on his Test debut — it was his only Test — and, strangely, the other two, Mills and Taylor, had also both been left-handed. The best part of the game came, however, when Hastings and Collinge (68) established a Test world record stand at 151 for the last wicket.

Under Congdon's captaincy, New Zealand toured England later in 1973. They lost the First Test by 38 runs, never recovering from being bowled out for 97 in the first innings at Trent Bridge, but then sprang back in surprising fashion at Lord's. In reply to England's 253, New Zealand made 551 for nine declared. Congdon (175), Burgess (105) and Pollard (105 not out) led the way and gave the Kiwis new hope and heart as Illingworth's men spent so long in the field while New Zealand reached their highest total in Tests. Keith Fletcher then scored 178 to make sure of a draw, but New Zealand honour was satisfied. Alas, they failed to improve on that performance at Leeds. When their last second innings

Richard Hadlee, son of the great Walter, who plays with Nottinghamshire

wicket fell at 142 they were still one run short of avoiding an innings defeat, despite Turner's gallant 81.

Though Australia had paid several unofficial Test visits to New Zealand since the war, only one official Test had ever been played between the two countries, that of 1945-6. In 1973-4, all that changed when two three-Test series were held, the first in Australia, the second in New Zealand. The second-ever Test between Australia and New Zealand started at Melbourne on 29 December 1973. It ended on New Year's Day in a comprehensive win for the Australians who scored 462 with a Keith Stackpole century, and then dismissed New Zealand twice to win by an innings and 25 runs. At Sydney, Australia were 425 runs behind with eight second innings wickets in hand when rain prevented any play on the fifth day. John Parker had scored a century in New Zealand's 312 and then Richard Hadlee took four for 33 as Australia dived to 162 all out. It was John Morrison's turn to hit a century in the second New Zealand innings and Congdon declared with nine men out, setting Australia 456 to win. They lost two wickets to Richard Hadlee before the rains came. New Zealand's hopes of squaring the series perished at Adelaide where Australia recorded their third victory by an innings in four meetings with New Zealand. No one could stay long with Bev Congdon whose unbeaten 71 lasted 260 minutes.

Two months later the teams met in New Zealand and this time the Kiwis found success of a fashion. The First Test, at Wellington, produced 1,455 runs — the most in a Test in New Zealand — and the Kiwis scored 484 of them, with centuries from Congdon and Hastings. But the match belonged to Greg Chappell. The brother of Australia's skipper scored 247 in Australia's 511 for six declared; and followed up that with 133 out of 460 for eight. No one had scored as many runs in a Test; and with Ian Chappell scoring 145 and 121, it was only the second time in all first-class cricket that brothers had each scored two separate centuries in the same match. The Chappells dominated this game, adding a record 264 runs at one stage.

If the Basin Reserve match was a historic encounter, then the Second Test at Christchurch was even more so. Congdon sent Australia in when play started after a hold-up for rain. By the end of that first day, Australia had been bowled out for 223 and New Zealand, in reply, were 194 for five with Turner on 99. It took him almost half an hour to reach his century the next morning and New Zealand were all out with a lead of just 32. Now the Hadlee brothers struck. Australia were bowled out a second time for 259, which left New Zealand to score 228 for an epic victory. Thanks to Turner, who became the first New Zealander to score separate centuries in the same Test, they got them with five wickets and most of the last day to spare. New Zealand's first win over Australia now meant that they had beaten every other Test-playing country except England. Though Australia squared the series with a comprehensive victory by 297 runs at Auckland, when Ian Redpath carried his bat for 159, nothing could take away the Kiwis' delight at that important victory at Lancaster Park.

A visit by England in 1974-5 still left New Zealand without a victory over their oldest opponents. Though scoring 326 in their first innings at the Basin Reserve, New Zealand still lost by an innings and 83 runs because a double century from Keith Fletcher and 181 from skipper Mike Denness gave England an unbeatable 593 for six, at which point Denness declared. Though it was Underwood who did most of the damage in New

John Wright, the elegant left-hander who is yet another Kiwi to have made his mark in England. Wright plays with Derbyshire

Zealand's second innings with five for 51, it was a most unfortunate accident to Wellington bowler, Ewen Chatfield, which ended the Test. Last man Chatfield was knocked unconcious by a short-pitched ball from Lancashire's Peter Lever and had the first-aid skills of England masseur, Bernie Thomas, to thank for his life. Rain ruined the last Test at Christchurch and still New Zealand waited for their win. But New Zealand victories over other countries were now becoming more frequent and when India toured in 1975-6, New Zealand won the last of three Tests by an innings and 33 runs to square another series. Richard Hadlee, with seven for 23 as India collapsed to 81 all out, and eleven for 58 in the match, bowled New Zealand to their first win by so big a margin.

The 1976-7 season found New Zealand on another tour to India and Pakistan. In the first two Tests atLahore and Hyderabad, New Zealand were beaten by six wickets and eight wickets respectively; at Karachi, a valiant and critical 152 from Otago wicketkeeper, Warren Lees, saved New Zealand who were 104 for five in reply to Pakistan's 565. In India, New Zealand fared just as badly. Again they lost the series 2-0, with defeats at Bombay — by 162 runs — and at Madras — by 216 runs. Even in the Second Test at Kanpur, an Indian victory looked inevitable until Lees and Gary Troup, the left-arm seamer from Auckland, survived for two hours in adding 59 runs for the eighth wicket.

In February 1977 came another short series against Australia who played two Tests in New Zealand. New Zealand were set to score 350 in 390 minutes at Christchurch, but when the final hour began they were still 90 runs short, while Australia needed to take just two wickets to win. Against the need was for a rearguard action and again it was fought, this time by Congdon and Dayle Hadlee. Bev Congdon was still there at the end, 107 not out in 297 minutes; Hadlee, too, had survived, 8 not out in 52 minutes. This game had been balanced Australia's way since Doug Walters had taken them to 552 with a personal contribution of 250, the highest and last Test century scored by this great Australian batsman. No rearguard action could spare the Kiwis at Auckland where Denis Lillee took eleven wickets for 123 runs, leaving Davis and Turner the simple task of scoring 28 runs for victory with almost two days to spare. In 1977-8, England combined what was then an unusual tour — first Pakistan and then New Zealand. Three Tests were scheduled for each country and in the First Test of the New Zealand tour, the Kiwis at last completed the victory about which they had dreamed for so long. John Wright, the elegant Northern Districts left-hander who continues to thrill English crowds when he plays for Derbyshire, made his debut in the match which started at the Basin Reserve on 10 February 1978.

Wright and Bob Anderson took New Zealand to 42 without loss after Geoff Boycott, captaining England in place of the injured Mike Brearley, had won the toss and put them in to bat. Anderson departed at that score, caught by Bob Taylor off Chris Old for 28. Wright continued, to be the top scorer with 55 in a modest New Zealand total of 228, while Chris Old returned figures of six for 54. When England batted, Richard Hadlee and Richard Collinge broke through to give New Zealand a slender lead of 13 runs; and when New Zealand could muster only 123 in their second innings, a Kiwi victory seemed as remote as ever it had been. But Hadlee and Collinge changed all that. They took wickets at regular intervals as England slumped, first to 38 for six and then to 64 all out. New Zealand had completed her first Test victory over England by 72 runs. Hadlee returned six for 26 and Collinge three for 35. Hadlee, with ten for 100 in the match, was the natural leader of the New Zealand attack and his genuine speed bounce, and ability to make the ball swing dangerously late into the batsman made him virtually unplayable. No wonder Nottinghamshire moved in quickly for him that summer. In the Second Test at Christchurch, Ian Botham began his boy's comic hero feats with a century and five wickets to help England level the rubber with victory by 174 runs. At Auckland, the honours were level and the series halved. Geoff Howarth, younger brother of Hedley, became the second New Zealander after Turner to score separate hundreds in the same Test Match; and Collinge passed Taylor's record of 111 Test wickets for New Zealand. This had certainly been a memorable summer for the Kiwis.

With their first-ever win over England under their belts, the Kiwis went on their 1978 tour looking for their first Test win in England. Mark Burgess's team played three Tests after the Pakistanis had finished their short series, but in all three they were beaten. For a long time in the First Test at The Oval, New Zealand held their own before England pulled away to win in the third of the last twenty overs. At Trent Bridge, the Kiwis had much the worst of the bad weather and lost by an innings and 119 runs. At Lord's their humiliation was complete when, after taking a first innings lead, they were bowled out for 67 in the face of hostile bowling from Willis and Botham who grabbed nine wickets between them. The Kiwis had thrown away their 50-runs advantage and England coasted home by seven wickets. Though needing only 118 to win England were given a nasty jolt by Richard Hadlee who removed Boycott and Radley with successive — and identical — deliveries with the score at 14.

Thus New Zealand were whitewashed; and yet they could rightly complain of some ill-luck on the tour. All their fast bowlers suffered injuries — Dale Hadlee played in only one match — and they were without Glenn Turner who stayed with Worcestershire during his benefit year. The slow bowling fell mostly to the left-armer Stephen Boock but the 'find' of the tour was Bruce Edgar, a twenty-one-year-old left-handed batsman. Eighteen-year-old Brendon Bracewell took a wicket with his third ball in Test cricket, dismissing Gooch lbw at The Oval and almost immediately after that had Mike Brearley caught at the wicket. Geoff Howarth, too, had a good tour, topping the Test batting averages and scoring a brilliant 123 at Lord's. But for skipper Burgess the tour was a disaster. Let down by his side's fielding, plagued by bad luck, hampered by the lack of a specialist wicketkeeper, and dogged by a personal lack of form (his 68 at Lord's apart), Burgess would want to forget this summer as quickly as possible.

The Pakistanis flattered New Zealand when they toured in 1978-9, for after they won the First Test at Christchurch, they became too cautious and allowed the remaining two matches to be drawn. When Bracewell broke down in the First Test, New Zealand's lack of a class pace attack was made even more difficult to overcome and the bulk of the work fell on Richard Hadlee who responded with eighteen wickets at 23 runs each. Lance Cairns tried hard to give Hadlee the support he needed, but the big medium-pacer suffered from dropped catches and took only nine wickets.

When the West Indians came to New Zealand after their tour to Australia in 1979-80, a first-ever win in a series by New Zealand should have given Kiwi cricket much about which to rejoice. Yet the unsportsmanlike behaviour of some West Indian players soured the historic victory. They complained about the umpiring and even suggested that the officials were in league with the New Zealand cricket authority in a bid to ensure that the West Indians could not win a Test! Holding kicked the stumps out of the ground after being refused an appeal in the First Test; Greenidge acted in a similar manner when the match was lost; Croft, after being no-balled in the Second Test, flicked off a bail on his way back; and the same bowler later ran into umpire Goodall. The West Indians then refused to return to the field after tea on the third day of the match unless Goodall was replaced — they finally came out twelve minutes late; and after that Second Test it was distinctly possible that the tour would be cancelled. In the end, through their own behaviour, the West Indians lost the rubber after dropping the First Test and drawing the remaining two. New Zealand won by one wicket and deserved their victory, however narrow. The Kiwis had their stars — the batting of Bruce Edgar and Geoff Howarth; the all-round ability of Richard Hadlee — a batting average of 44.50 and nineteen wickets at 19 runs apiece; and the bowling of Gary Troup, whose left-arm pace took eighteen wickets.

Australia were New Zealand's next Test opponents and they proved to be too strong a challenge. In November 1980, the Kiwis were beaten by ten wickets in the First Test at Brisbane where Lillee's second innings six for 53 compounded the damage done earlier by Wood's century. The match was lost inside three days and in the Second Test at Perth the Kiwis were again beaten in that time, the margin this time being eight wickets. Richard Hadlee bowled magnificently in the series, taking five for 87 at Perth (Cairns had exactly similar figures in the First Test) and in the final match at Melbourne, Hadlee might have bowled New Zealand to victory. His six for 57 in the second innings saw Australia all out for 188 and the Kiwis needing 193 for a win. In the first innings, New Zealand's middle order of Howarth, Parker, Burgess and Coney had given a magnificent display to leave the Kiwis only four runs adrift on first innings. Now they largely failed and were happy, in the end, to draw the Test at 128 for six.

When India came immediately after their Australian tour, Test cricket returned to the Basin Reserve after an interval of three years, during which time much renovation had been done. New Zealand won the First Test by 62 runs, drew the other two, and took their first rubber against India. The turning points of the Wellington victory were the fine century by Geoff Howarth, who scored 137 not out, and the bowling of Hadlee and Cairns who saw to it that India were always adrift. The New Zealanders, so often the whipping boys of international cricket, are beginning to make their presence felt. The blooding of more Kiwis in English county cricket, and the opportunities now afforded to play more Test Matches, means that New Zealand has much to contribute to cricket around the world.

New Zealand's rapid improvement was even more apparent in their 1982 confrontation with Australia. Record crowds saw Australia come from behind to win the Rothman Cup Series in games at Auckland, Dunedin and Wellington. When the First Test got underway at the Basin Reserve in February 1982 there was great excitement which, alas, evaporated with the dreadful weather which allowed precious little play. New Zealand batted first when the match eventually got underway and they made 266. Australia reached 85 for one when play could resume after more interruptions and the game was a complete anti-climax.

In Auckland, the euphoria returned with a New Zealand victory. Troup took four for 82 as Australia were dismissed for 210. New Zealand took a first innings lead of 177, thanks mainly to a dour 161 from the left-handed Bruce Edgar, the highest score by a Kiwi against Australia. It was a winning lead and after the Australians — who bemoaned the umpiring decisions of Messrs Woodward and Bricknall — made 280 in their reply, New Zealand overcame a worsening wicket to win by five wickets. Their saviour was Cairns who blasted his way to 34 runs in twenty-one balls. Richard Hadlee brought about a famous victory by hammering Bruce Yardley for a massive six over long on. The brilliance of Greg Chappell, so out of form before the tour began, earned Australia victory at Christchurch and a share of the rubber. Chappell's 176 took him into second place behind Sir Donald Bradman as Australia's leading Test run getter. New Zealand faced a total of 353 and collapsed to 149 all out against the pace of Thomson, Alderman and Lillee. They followed-on, managed 272 in their second innings, and Australia scored the necessary runs for the loss of two wickets. The spin of Yardley and Border proved New Zealand's undoing the second time around. But although Australia avenged their Auckland defeat, the Kiwis had once again proved their class.

India

Indian Summers

Cricket in India is almost a religion. Though grave doubts were expressed about the tour by England in 1981-2, following the South African connections of Geoff Boycott and Geoff Cook, those who know the Indians best had little doubt that the tour would go ahead. Cricket to the Indians is almost a way of life and it would take a brave government indeed, to call off a tour to the sub-continent which had been eagerly awaited by the populace. But although the Indians took to cricket as the proverbial duck takes to water, it was the British who took the game there. For many years it was only those of European stock who played the game. Records are scarce but it is generally accepted that the earliest cricket on the sub-continent was probably played by sailors of the East India Company at Cambay in the 1720s. In 1784 a team of Old Etonians met the Parsees — the first Indians to become interested in the game — and Calcutta Cricket Club was certainly in operation as long ago as 1792.

The British Army, together with various administrators and workers from the trading companies, kept the game almost totally European, however, and in 1804, Old Etonians played The Rest, which was a team made up solely of civil servants from the East India Company. That game was historic for two reasons. First, it was played on the now world-famous Eden Gardens in Calcutta; second, Old Etonian batsman, R. Vansittart, scored 102 to become the first recorded centurion in Indian cricket. Calcutta Cricket Club was for Europeans only, but in 1848, the Parsees formed Oriental Cricket Club in Bombay and other religions followed suit, the first Hindu club being formed in 1866, and the Mohammedans organising their first club in 1883. Interest in cricket among the Indians now spread like a spark through dry bush. The development of the game was now so great that in 1886, the Parsees undertook the first tour of England by an Indian team, though they enjoyed scant success and won only one of their twenty-eight matches.

Interest was further aroused by the visit of privately-arranged tours from England. These, coupled with the fact that one of India's greatest cricketers, Kumar Shri Ranjitsinhji, later the Jam Sahib of Nawanagar, an aristocratic Indian who had learned the game at Rajkumar College in Kathiawar, was achieving great deeds in the English first-class game, gave Indian cricket the final impetus it needed to become organised on a proper basis. 'Ranji' never played first-class cricket in India so far as we know, though the Indians' major domestic competition, the Ranji Trophy, was named after him. Until he returned to India in 1904, to succeed his father as the ruler of Jamnagar, Ranji played with Cambridge University and Sussex, thrilling the crowds of Victorian and Edwardian England

Prince Ranjitsinhji who played for England but who did much to encourage Indian cricket and after who the domestic Ranji Trophy was named

with his eagle-eye which could send even the fastest bowler crashing to the boundary. He played fifteen times for England and after the major part of his first-class career was over, still found time to play the occasional game for Sussex, though by the time he made his last appearance in 1920, he had lost an eye in a shooting accident and was but a pale shadow of the great cricketer who England best remembered, 'Ranji' did much to further the cause of Indian cricket, though his own cricketing background was essentially English.

In 1889-90, the first English team to visit India was led by George Vernon, the hard-hitting Middlesex batsman who had played one Test with Ivo Bligh's team in Australia in 1882-3. Vernon's side was composed solely of amateurs and played thirteen games, including two in Ceylon, losing one of them to the Parsees, which was another great fillip for Indian cricket. In 1911, India sent her first representative side to England when a party captained by HH the Maharajah of Patiala played fourteen first-class matches — of which two were won — and nine minor matches — four won — and this set the Indian game one further rung along the ladder to being recognised as a proper force in cricket.

Cricket in India, which also, of course, included the areas now known today as Pakistan and Bangladesh, suffered a setback during the period of World War I and immediately afterwards, but in 1926-7 a visit by the first touring party organised by MCC to play on the sub-continent created tremendous interest. The MCC side was captained by the famous Sussex and England captain and all-rounder, Arthur Gilligan, and included such names as R.E.S. Wyatt, Maurice Leyland, Maurice Tate, Andrew

Sandham and George Geary. MCC played thirty first-class matches, winning ten and drawing twenty, and one of the highspots had been the match against a Hindu team in Bombay. MCC had enjoyed an easy run in Northern India and when the first day of this two-day game at the Bombay Gymkhana ground was over, it appeared that even the cricketers of the south would be no match for the English team. On the first morning, Guy Earle, the Somerset amateur, had cleared the boundary eight times; one stroke, a hook off Ramji, had even landed in the Esplanade Road. Earle had powered his way to 130 runs in ninety minutes and MCC had totalled 363, to which the Hindus had replied with 16 for one by the close.

Early the next morning, thousands streamed the ground until there was not a spare place in sight and even the trees had not a single branch left available. The Indian second-wicket pair scored their odd runs carefully against the bowling of Geary and Mercer until Navle, the little wicketkeeper, was out at 56. In came the Hindus' skipper, Vithal, now of advancing years but still carrying his reputation as a great run-getter. Maurice Tate, who had bowled so well in Lahore and Karachi, was bowling just as well here and Vithal could not lay a bat on him. It was G.S. Boyes, the Hampshire off-spinner, who finally accounted for the unhappy Vithal, however, and the Hindus were now 84 for three. The new man was C.K. Nayudu who, in the tourists' previous match at Ajmer, had made 15 and 0 and was found desperately short of the technique required to combat Tate.

Happily for Nayudu, Tate had been removed from the attack and an all-spin attack of Boyes and Ewart Astill of Leicestershire was now operating. Neither held as many terrors as Tate, though Boyes had twenty-five Indian wickets already under his belt and neither man was to be taken lightly. Nayudu played the first two balls he received from Boyes with great caution; to the third he went down the pitch and drove it back over the bowler's head and on to the pavilion roof for 6. L.P. Jai, one of the Hindus' greatest runmakers, played the next over from Astill quietly enough; but when Boyes bowled to Nayudu again, the Indian smashed him into the pavilion for another 6. The crowd erupted and even the umpires joined in the applause! Nayudu had now got the measure of Boyes and turned his attention to Astill who was also hit for 6. By lunch the Hindus had advanced to 154 for six — 138 added in the morning session — and Nayudu had his 50.

The news of this unprecedented assault on the MCC bowlers spread throughout Bombay and when Nayudu and Mahale resumed the afternoon session, every roof top around the ground and way into the distance had been commandeered. Tate managed to quieten matters down, but when Wyatt replaced the Sussex seamer, Nayudu responded with two more 6s, taking 22 runs in Wyatt's first over. MCC now changed their bowlers around with growing alarm, but although Mahale was dismissed, they seemed to have no answer to Nayudu. The Indian passed his century and the Hindus now looked quite capable of overhauling MCC's total. Nayudu reached 150 with a fierce shot off Geary, but then at 153, he stepped out to the same bowler, failed to get hold of the ball properly, and Boyes ran back from mid off to hold a well-judged catch. Nayudu was out, having scored his runs out of 187 in 115 minutes with eleven 6s and thirteen 4s. The fact that the Hindus eventually fell seven runs short of MCC was neither here nor there. C.K. Nayudu was the Indian hero from that moment. Born at Nagpur in 1895, a great schoolboy athlete, 'C.K.' was to become a great figure in Indian cricket, not only as a brilliant batsman, but also as a spin bowler and fine fielder. He was to be India's first skipper in official Tests — and was sixty-two before he made his last first-class appearance in 1958!

The feats of Nayudu in India, those of Ranji's nephew, Duleepsinhji, in England, and visits by great English players like Jack Hobbs and Herbert Sutcliffe, both of whom toured in 1930-1 at the invitation of Maharajah Sir Vijaya Vizianagram, kept interest in Indian cricket at a peak. Even before C.K. Nayudu, India had produced some fine cricketers and yet the illusion persisted that because England was the home of the game, then her cricketers would always be best. Though impromptu cricket games, with no proper stumps or boundaries, could be seen in almost everything that passed for a street in the teeming cities of India in the early part of the century, and though Indian boys everywhere wanted to emulate the feats of great players, there was no real sense that cricket was an *Indian* game, only that it had been borrowed from the Europeans. The change from those knockabout games to cricket played on a basis which would challenge the exclusively European clubs came about when the Indian aristocracy — Nawabs and Maharajahs — began to sponsor clubs, bringing out coaches like the great Middlesex player, J.T. Hearne, and providing the money for proper facilities for the indigenous population. Frank Tarrant, Wilfred Rhodes and George Hirst all played and coached in India around the end of World War I, and with the formation of the domestic competition which became known as the Pentangular Tournament, passing through Triangular and Quadrangular stages as Hindus, Muslims and finally 'The Rest' joined the Parsees and the Europeans in annual competition. There was another important change when part of the military presence began to leave and Indians found themselves taking on more and more of their country's administrative duties, including those in the world of cricket.

It was still the European influence which brought MCC on that visit of 1926-7, however, when the Calcutta Cricket Club led the way in sending their secretary, Murray Robertson, to Lord's to work out the details. It was that tour which put the final seal of approval on Indian cricket at international level. From that moment it was only a matter of time before India played her first full Test. The MCC visit included two 'Tests' against All India, the first just two weeks after C.K. Nayudu had hammered them all around the Bombay Gymkhana ground. The first game was also scheduled for Bombay and the All India team, containing only Indians, had much the better of the match, scoring 437 in reply to MCC's 362, and then having the English team at 97 for five in their second innings when stumps were drawn. Yet incredibly, when the team for the second match at Eden Gardens was announced, only four Indians were in the All India side, the rest being Europeans. MCC balanced the issue somewhat by including the vastly rich Maharajah of Patiala, a man of some eighteen stones in weight who qualified because of his MCC membership. The inclusion of the huge Maharajah had its lighter side when, batting with Maurice Tate, he lost a £10,000 pearl ear-ring. The ear-ring was eventually found in the prince's hair-net, but not before he had cast several suspicious glances at a close fielder who he obviously thought might have pocketed the missing adornment. MCC won the match by four wickets to underline that European cricketers in the Indian eleven were not as successful as the Indians who had played in the earlier game.

The long and arduous tour ended and MCC made for home. Gilligan and his players took with them a lasting impression of Indian cricket and before the party set sail, the MCC captain had suggested to the Indians that the time was now right for them to organise regular visits, both from and to England, and the time was not far distant when they ought to be applying for full Test Match status. Encouraged by such observations from so experienced a cricketer, the Indian cricketers now felt that they could forge ahead with the formation of a Board of Control to administer the game on the sub-continent. That board was duly formed and after much talk between them and MCC, Indian cricket's administrators at last got their wish and in 1932, C.K. Nayudu, doyen of Indian cricket, led the first side to visit England for a full Test Match.

Yet Nayudu became captain only by default. Indian politics crept into cricket as they filtered into almost every other walk of life and the original captain had been the Maharajah of Patiala who was forced to withdraw because he could ill-afford the time away from India, taking into account the delicate political situation. The Nawab of Pataudi, the great Oxford University batsman who was to play for Worcestershire and later appeared in three Tests for England and three for India, had already withdrawn and the new captain was named as the thirty-one-year-old ruler of Kathiawar, the Maharajah of Porbander, who would never have made the side in a million years if the captaincy had been decided on merit, but who had enough aristocratic distinction to make him just the man the selectors were seeking.

The tour got underway with modest success — draws with Sussex and Glamorgan and a win over Oxford University. The MCC match lifted Indian hearts, however, when C.K. Nayudu scored a century as the tourists had the edge in a rain-affected draw. A defeat by Hampshire on a soft Southampton 'turner' was followed by victories over Essex, where Nazir Ali of the Southern Punjab scored a century, over Northants, and over Cambridge University. At Liverpool, another rain-ruined match against Lancashire was enlivened by a rollicking 131 not out from number ten batsman Amar Singh. The last match before the Test was at Worcester where the Nawab of Pataudi was making his first appearance for the county. Although the Indians won by three wickets, having at one time been 13 for three chasing 208, Pataudi made a fine 83 against his fellow countrymen who could not help but reflect on what Pataudi's inclusion might do for their chances at Lord's. On the same day, Duleepsinhji scored 128 off the bowling of Larwood and Voce in an England Test Trial at Old Trafford.

Now came India's captaincy 'crisis' when Porbander, apparently upset by remarks in the press that he was probably the worst cricketer ever to represent a national side and had only been appointed because of his position, announced that he would not be playing again. As his record up to that time had been two runs in three innings, that hardly seemed to matter; but the vice-captain, Limbdi, who was Porbander's brother-in-law, but a much better cricketer, injured his back while making a century against the Eastern Counties at Lincoln. So C.K. Nayudu was pitched into the leadership, although there were many behind-the-scenes rows, and a threat to boycott the Test if Nayudu remained captain was only settled on the morning of the match after the Maharajah of Patiala had personally intervened with a telegram from India.

This was hardly the best preparation for a Test Match against an

England team which fielded Holmes, Sutcliffe, Woolley, Hammond, Jardine, Paynter, Ames, Robins, Brown, Voce and Bowes, all of whom were looking for a place on the tour to Australia that winter. The Indians were not attractive opposition and only a small crowd was present when Holmes and Sutcliffe opened the England innings. England confidently anticipated a total somewhere in the region of 550; India were equally confident of capturing some early wickets and Nissar and Amar Singh began with three slips and three men close in on the leg side. It was England's confidence which was misplaced. The first ball of Nissar's third over removed Sutcliffe's leg bail; the last delivery sent Holmes's off stump cartwheeling; and when Woolley had made 9, he was brilliantly run out by Lall Singh who swooped in from mid on and beat him home to make the score 19 for three. Word swept round the City and by lunch, over 20,000 people packed Lord's. The Indians were to have no further sensations up their sleeves, however, and Hammond, Jardine and Ames steered England to a final score of 259; not a disaster but still far short of the total at which they had aimed. Nissar had five for 93, Amar Singh deserved better than his two for 75, and India had made a tremendous start to their Test career.

India's reply was not good enough to keep them in the match however. Nayudu was the top scorer with 40 and they folded quickly to Bill Bowes, who took four for 49, and Bill Voce, who had three for 23. Perhaps if Nayudu had not been suffering from a badly bruised hand sustained while fielding, then things might have been different for the Indians. As it was, England made 275 for eight in their second innings before Jardine declared, setting the Indians 346 to win. They were never in with a chance. Nazir Ali and Palia were both hampered by leg injuries — Palia was almost dragged out to bat after complaining that his pulled muscle made it impossible to take his rightful place — and Amar Singh had the honour of scoring India's first 50 in a Test Match before falling caught and bowled to Wally Hammond. The match was lost by 158 runs and the tour continued with the county games, India winning nine and losing eight of their twenty-six first-class matches before setting sail for home. Nayudu had enjoyed a personally satisfying tour from the playing point of view, but the strife in the dressing room left a bad taste in the mouths of all the Indian cricketers. Some were openly hostile towards Nayudu and it has to be said that without this continual bickering, Indian cricket might have made an even bigger impact on its first appearance as a Test-playing nation.

India's first four Test series were all against England. In 1933-4, MCC visited the sub-continent with a comparatively strong side and won the three-match rubber 2-0. The Indian captain was again C.K. Nayudu, who had overcome all kinds of objections to his leading the side once more. A match between the 1932 Indian touring team and The Rest of India at Delhi illustrated the point. Captaining The Rest of India was the Maharajah of Vizianagram — 'Vizzy' as he was known. 'Vizzy' had a poor match, making a 'pair' as his side were shot out for 63 and 88 to lose in a day and a half. On the first day, 'Vizzy' led his team in applauding Nayudu on to the field in a gesture which showed appreciation of just how much this man had done for Indian cricket. Meanwhile, Nayudu's own side booed, jeered and yelled obscenities from the pavilion balcony. Against this background Nayudu led India in her first home Test at Bombay Gymkhana in December 1933. The match was England's all the way. They bowled out India for 219, made 438 in reply with a century from the Kent player Brian Valentine who was making his Test debut, and then overcame a century by debutant Lala Amarnath — who thus became his country's first centurion — to win by nine wickets. Amarnath's innings had been a brilliant affair, racing to 83 in seventy-eight minutes and then coasting gently to his target in another forty minutes.

The Second Test at Eden Gardens was drawn after India were forced to follow-on, but at Madras there was to be no such escape. Though Amar Singh took seven for 86 in England's first innings, Hedley Verity was in equally fine form and his seven for 49 saw England to a lead of 190. A century by Cyril Walters helped England to extend that lead to 451 and India, who batted a man short in both innings after Naoomal Jeoomal edged a ball from Nobby Clark on to his head, failed by 202 runs, James Langridge and Verity proving the masters on this occasion. Vijay Merchant was one of the ten Indians to make their Test debuts in the series. Vijay scored one half-century and showed some of the brilliant strokes that were to make this little batsman from Bombay one of India's leading Test players of the next decade. Also making his debut was C.S. Nayudu, brother of 'C.K.' and a great Ranji Trophy all-rounder who was never to reproduce his form in eleven Tests for India.

In 1935-6 Jack Ryder took an Australian team to India which played seventeen first-class matches, winning eleven and drawing three. Yet again the background was of the seething politics of Indian cricket and when the time came to select the captain of the 1936 touring party to England, C.K. Nayudu was challenged by 'Vizzy'. The fact that Bombay had threatened to withdraw all its players if another prince was elected made no difference and it was 'Vizzy' who got the nod ahead of 'C.K.' after Pataudi had again withdrawn. Like Porbander before him, 'Vizzy' was not a first-class cricketer, though he had ploughed much cash into Indian cricket. Unlike Porbander, 'Vizzy' never accepted his shortcomings, played in the first seventeen first-class matches, skippered India in all three Tests where he contrived to score the unprincely total of 33 runs in six innings, and sent home the side's outstanding all-rounder, Lala Amarnath, before one of India's main hopes could appear in a Test.

Five of the first eight matches were lost, three drawn, and after Amarnath had followed up an outburst against his captain in the match against Leicestershire, he really blew his top when pushed down the order to number seven against the Minor Counties at Lord's after scoring a century in each innings against Essex. Amarnath had time to make only a single before the match ended. He returned to the Lord's dressing room, hurled his bat and pads into a corner, and the next day was sent packing back to India. There was little wonder when England won the First Test at Lord's by nine wickets. A lobby to bring Pataudi to the rescue of the side was ignored, though the Nawab was playing brilliantly in London club cricket, and 'Vizzy' and his team were sunk without trace in a low scoring game. Gubby Allen took ten wickets in the match and although England trailed by 13 runs after a six-wicket burst by Amar Singh — at one stage England were a sensational 41 for five — Allen and Verity bowled out India for 93 and India's batting had again let them down badly.

The batsmen did better at Old Trafford where Merchant and Mushtaq Ali, the impetuous opener from Holkar, put on 203 for the first wicket in just 150 minutes. But England had already made 571 to lead India on first innings by 368 and the Indians could only hope for a draw, though the match was enlivened by 588 runs on the second day — the most scored in one day in a Test. A lobby to get 'Vizzy' to stand down for the Second Test achieved nothing and the Indian prince — who had by now been knighted and went to Old Trafford as Sir Gajapatairaj Vijaya Ananda, Maharajkumar of Vizianagram — continued merrily on his way as India dropped catches, got themselves out with some injudicious strokes, and generally went about their business in an undisciplined manner. The final Test at The Oval was lost by nine wickets. Wally Hammond scored 217, Derbyshire's Stan Worthington made 128, and the pair shared a record stand of 266 for the fourth wicket. Gubby Allen declared at 471 for eight and Jim Sims, the Middlesex leg-spinner, took five wickets as India fell 249 runs behind and followed-on.

Their second innings produced better things — 81 from C.K. Nayudu helping them to 312 — but the deficit had been too great and after Allen had seven for 80, England needed only 64 to win. It was C.K. Nayudu's last Test and he had endured a terrible series, coming back to form only in the last innings of the final Test when it was far too late. His first-class career was far from over, however, and at the age of fifty, he made his highest-ever score — 200 for Holkar versus Baroda. His 81 against England had been scored with typical courage after he had been hit in the stomach by a ball from Allen. That was how he lived his life and in later years he became a Test selector and vice-president of the Indian board, passing on his great knowledge. C.K. Nayudu had endured all the bad times and emerged as the elder statesman of Indian cricket.

India's 1936 tour to India had not been as disaster. But it had certainly been a grave disappointment. Only Lancashire and Hampshire had been defeated and the Indian board had suffered a serious financial loss in sending its second touring team to England. There were to be no more Test Matches until after the war, though the Ranji Trophy continued throughout the conflict. The next semblence of international cricket in India came in 1945-6 when Lindsay Hassett brought the Australian Services XI which played nine first-class matches, winning two and drawing five.

Then India became the first team to play official Tests in England since World War II when a side captained by the Nawab of Pataudi, who had already played three times for England, arrived to take part in a three-match series against Wally Hammond's team. Pataudi's team was, once more, selected against a backcloth of discontent, the kind of which had marred Indian cricket for so long. His team included Merchant as vice-captain and the brilliant little batsman had a splendid summer, scoring 2,385 runs (including seven centuries, two of them double centuries) at an average of nearly 75. 'Vinoo' Mankad, destined to become India's greatest all-rounder, was starting out on a career which involved forty-four Tests; Lala Amarnath had survived his sending home in 1936 to return as an all-rounder of international status; Vijay Hazare, the man who had a prolific run-scoring record in Indian domestic cricket with Maharashtra and Baroda was in the party; and so too was Abdul Hafeez, who later, as A.H. Kardar, played so many times in the early Pakistan teams; and there was a link with the earliest Indian Test cricket through C.K. Nayudu's younger brother.

The First Test at Lord's in June 1946 began before a capacity crowd, starved of any serious competitive cricket at this level for seven long years. Pataudi won the toss and India batted first on a damp pitch from which Alec Bedser, twenty years old when war interrupted his career, extracted the maximum amount of life. Bedser celebrated his first Test with seven wickets for only 49 runs and India limped along, thankful in the end to have reached as many as 200. When England batted, however, Amarnath was quick to show that these conditions also suited him. He had Hutton caught, then bowled Compton with the next ball and although Hammond prevented the hat trick, Amarnath had Washbrook caught by Mankad and England were 44 for three. At stumps England had recovered to 135 for four, though wicketkeeper Paul Gibb enjoyed several lives. India went to bed hopeful of a quick breakthrough the next morning but Joe Hardstaff stood firmly in their way. Hardstaff was to score only one big innings in 1946 and this was it. When England's last wicket fell, he was 205 not out and England had a lead of 228. Bedser took four second innings wickets to record the finest debut ever made by an England Test bowler, and Hutton and Washbrook scored 48 for victory.

Bedser took eleven for 145 in the First Test and in the Second Test at Old Trafford, he bettered that with eleven for 93. He could not take a twelfth wicket which would have given England victory. Sohoni and Hindlekar survived the last thirteen minutes of the match to take India to a draw at 152 for nine, still 125 runs behind. Rain had interfered with the Second Test and at The Oval it completely ruined the last match. Merchant scored 128 out of India's 331 before Denis Compton brought in to play the skills which he normally displayed at Arsenal's Highbury and ran out the opener by kicking the ball on to the stumps. England had time to make only 95 for three before the rains returned. The Indians had been popular tourists and with eleven wins and only four defeats in twenty-nine matches, they had achieved the best record by an Indian team in England.

The Australian Services team had brought back promising reports about the standard of, and the interest in, Indian cricket and in 1947-8 India embarked on a tour to Australia for their first Tests against a country other than England. They faced a powerful Australian side which had beaten England 3-0 the previous season, and left India in the wake of Partition which had split the cricketers of All India into India and Pakistan. Amarnath, the elected vice-captain, found himself in charge when Merchant dropped out of the touring party and the all-rounder obviously had a tough task ahead. His side had been further weakened by the withdrawals of Mushtaq, Modi and Fazal Mahmood; and yet again there was dressing room strife. Not surprisingly, India lost the rubber 4-0. Though they had the fillip of a 47-runs win over an Australian XI immediately before the First Test, their luck changed when they were caught on a traditional Brisbane 'sticky' and were bowled out for 58 and 98 after Don Bradman had scored 185 in Australia's 382.

Rain ruined the Second Test at Sydney — where Mankad ran out the non-striker Brown for backing up — and though Mankad made a century at Melbourne, Don Bradman went one better and scored a century in each innings as India went down by 233 runs. At Adelaide, Hazare became the first Indian to score a century in each innings of the same Test — but yet again Bradman denied India. The Don made 201, and with 198 from Hassett and 112 from Barnes, Australia made the record score for a Test in Australia — 674 — to win by an innings after Lindwall had destroyed India with seven for 38. At Melbourne, Australia scored 575 and although India made 331 with a century from Mankad, they still had to follow-on. When they tried a second time there was real disaster. They were all out for 68 to lose again by an innings. Amarnath did little in the Tests and was unlucky to captain a disrupted Indian team against such strong opponents. He was still in charge, however, when India again broke new ground with a visit from the West Indies in 1948-9. In the Fourth Test in Bombay, India needed 361 in 395 minutes to square the series. They fell just six runs short with two wickets in hand (counting the injured Sen) after a series of West Indian time-wasting exploits were compounded by a drinks interval.

India now had visits from Commonwealth XIs before their next Test series against England in 1951-2, and it was against the Commonwealth teams that a young right-handed batsman called Pahlan Umrigar — 'Polly' to everyone in cricket — made some big scores and elevated himself into the side for the First Test against Nigel Howard's team at Delhi in November 1951. MCC, after two hard tours to South Africa and Australia, did not send their strongest side and both the captain Howard, the Lancashire amateur batsman, and the vice-captain Donald Carr, Derbyshire's graceful amateur right-hander, were making their Test debuts, though Carr had played in 'Victory Tests' in 1945 fresh from Repton School. The bespectacled Bengal batsman, Pankaj Roy, and Maharashtra's wicketkeeper-batsman 'Nana' Joshi, made their debuts at Feroz Shah Kotla in a match which India should have won. After Merchant (154) and Hazare (164) had put on 211 for the third wicket before Hazare declared at 418 for six, only a stern rearguard action by Glamorgan's Allan Watkins, who made 137 not out in nine hours, enabled England to avoid an innings defeat after their first innings had been largely destroyed by the leg breaks of Sadu Shinde.

The Second Test in Bombay was drawn after centuries from Roy, Hazare (his second consecutive Test hundred) and Tom Graveney. Here there was an unusual sight when Yorkshire leg-spinner Eddie Leadbeater played in his first Test without having won his county cap. Leadbeater, who later went to Warwickshire and finished his short career still uncapped, had flown out to replace the injured Derbyshire spinner, 'Dusty' Rhodes. At Eden Gardens barely 1,000 runs were scored in an uninterrupted Third Test which ended in a draw. This uninspiring match was hardly a fitting backcloth for Vijay Manjrekar to make his Test debut. Though hardly the most attacking batsman in the world, Manjrekar went on to play in fifty-five Tests for India and not many of them could have been as boring as his debut game.

At Green Park, Kanpur, there was the first definite result of the series. Lancashire's spinners, Roy Tattersall (six for 48) and Malcolm Hilton (four for 32) bowled out India for 121, and although England could only muster 203 in the face of Mankad and Ghulam Ahmed, the left-arm spin of Hilton, and the off breaks of Tattersall were largely responsible for England needing only 76 to win. They went one ahead in the rubber with eight wickets to spare. England needed only to draw the final Test in Madras to win the rubber, but here India scored their first Test victory which came in a most emphatic manner. The left-arm slows of Mankad produced the best bowling figures by an Indian Test player — eight for 55 — as England made 266. India were now intent on capitalising on some fine bowling with some equally fine batting and they found their heroes in Roy and Umrigar. Roy made 111; Umrigar, who before this series had played in one Test against the West Indies, scored 130 not out, and India had a lead of 191. The pitch was now breaking up and England's prospects looked bleak. Against Ghulam Ahmed and Mankad they stood little chance and the Indian spinners captured four wickets apiece to bowl Indian to victory by an innings and 8 runs — their first success in Test cricket.

India thoroughly deserved their first win — at the twenty-fifth attempt — but it has to be said that this was an England 'second eleven' and when they met the full might of England in the summer of 1952, things were very different. Hazare's side lacked Vijay Merchant, who had been forced to retire because of a shoulder injury, Mushtaq Ali, Amarnath, and, most significantly, Mankad, who had accepted a professional engagement in the Lancashire League. The First Test at Leeds saw England appoint a professional captain for the first time, and also saw the Test debut of Fred Trueman. Trueman had a sensational first appearance on his home ground. Len Hutton's England won by seven wickets and in their second innings India made the worst start to an innings by any Test team. They wer 0 for four after fourteen balls, three of them falling to Trueman, and from that they never recovered. The other victim of that incredible collapse was Datta Gaekwad, the debutant from Baroda falling to Alec Bedser.

Mankad was available for the Second Test at Lord's and here he wrote himself into the record books. 'Vinoo' scored 72 and 184 — India's highest in England — and bowled ninety-seven overs in the match with five for 196 in England's first innings. But Mankad still finished on the losing side. Hutton and Evans made hundreds and even Mankad's tremendous effort in the second innings still left England very little to do in recording an eight-wickets win. Hutton's century at Old Trafford was followed by eight for 31 from Trueman, and India were now being humiliated. All out for 58, they were dismissed again for 82 to lose by an innings and 207 runs, and after they were 98 all out in the final Test at The Oval, replying to an England total of 326, only rain saved them from final disgrace.

While India were struggling through this rubber, the ICC announced, on 28 July 1952, that their neighbours Pakistan had been admitted to full Test status. A series between the two countries was already in the pipeline and this meant that the rubber, to be played in India that winter,

Indian and New Zealand players line up before the Fifth Test at Madras in 1956

would now have extra meaning. The series was won by 2-1, thus giving India her second and third Test victories, but three definite results did not set the pattern for later rubbers between the two countries. India's first visit to the Caribbean in 1952-3 was lost by 1-0 with four drawn; and India's first visit to what was now Pakistan yielded five more draws in the twelve-draw sequence which marred Test cricket between these two countries; New Zealand's first visit saw India win the rubber with superior batting and spin bowling. Umrigar recorded India's first double century in the First Test at Hyderabad; Mankad scored their second in the next match at Bombay, equalling Polly's 223. In 1956-7 Australia played their first Tests in India and won the series 2-0, both their victories coming by big margins with India having little success in coping with the bowling of Lindwall, Miller and Benaud. The West Indians won 3-0 in India in 1958-9 and then India made their way to England for a five-match series in one of the hottest British summers for many years.

The conditions in England may have been more to the Indians liking than on previous visits, but they did nothing to take advantage of a batsman's summer. For the first time England won all five Tests in a series, three of them by an innings, and India could not cope with Statham and Trueman. In addition, England's batsmen, Cowdrey, May, Pullar and Barrington, were all in tremendous form. Only at Old Trafford in the Fourth Test did Gaekwad's team show any real fight. They wanted 548 to win and Oxford freshman Abbas Ali Baig, playing in his first Test Match, scored 112 before he was run out. Twenty-year-old Baig had already made a century for Hyderabad against Mysore in the Ranji Trophy while still a teenager. Qualifying for Somerset, he had scored over 1,000 runs for Oxford and came into the Indian side as a convenient replacement for the injured Manjrekar. Baig's century — he became the youngest Indian to score a Test hundred — and 118 from Umrigar gave India the respectable total of 376, but so great was England's batting this summer that the tourists still lost by 171 runs.

Richie Benaud took Australia to India in 1959-60 and straightaway achieved a remarkable analysis of three for none in three overs and four balls, in Delhi, helping to bowl out India for 135. Benaud followed up that with five in the second innings and Australia won by an innings and 127 runs. When the sides moved to Kanpur for the Second Test it was the turn of the Gujerat off-spinner, Jasubhai Patel, to take full advantage of a newly-laid turf pitch. Though India made only 105 in their first innings, Patel came on to return India's best-ever Test analysis of nine for 69 and Australia's lead was kept to a manageable 67. India set the Australians 225 to win and Patel added five more wickets to his haul. Umrigar took four, and India won by 119 runs, their first success over the Australians. It was Australia who took the series, however, scoring an innings victory in the Fourth Test at Madras where Benaud's eight wickets tipped the scales firmly away from India. Star of the Indian side was Nari Contractor, the stylish left-hander from Gujerat who had made his debut against New Zealand in 1956. Contractor scored 438 runs at over 43 per innings to confirm his status as a world-class batsman.

The 1960-1 visit of Pakistan produced another four 'bore-draws', the only highlight of which, so far as India were concerned, being their 539 for nine declared in Madras. Centuries from Borde (177 not out) and Manjrekar (117) steered India to their highest Test total. India were, however, on the threshold of their first victory in a rubber over England.

Ted Dexter's tourists drew the first three Tests of 1961-2, but in the last two India were victorious. Led by Contractor, and including the Nawab of Pataudi's son, now plain Mansur Ali Khan after the Indian Government abolished royal titles, India set England to score 421 in 490 minutes in Calcutta. England failed by 187 runs and India went into the next and final Test at Madras, knowing that they might be about to make history. Pataudi led the way with 103 when India batted first and made 428; then Salim Durani took six for 105 and India were poised on the edge of a historic win with a lead of 147. Tony Lock fired back with six wickets to restrict India to 190 in their second innings, but England once more found Durani in fine form. The slow bowler took four wickets, Borde had three victims, and England were bowled out 128 runs short of levelling the scores. India had done it and with names like Engineer, Prasanna and Nadkarni making their way in the side, the prospects looked rosy.

Yet within a month of defeating England, India were at the start of a Caribbean tour which saw them lose all five Tests and Nari Contractor, felled by a ball from Charlie Griffith — a typical Griffith bouncer — was seriously injured and never played Test cricket again. India recovered from all this to draw their five Tests against England in 1963-4, though England did well to get within 52 runs of victory in the First Test at Madras when Mike Smith's men were set 292 in 265 minutes on a dusty pitch. Pataudi led his side well and after that England — who were troubled with illness and injury and had to call out Cowdrey and Parfitt — were never given another chance to win. Australia called on India en route from their 1964 tour to England and won the First Test in Madras by 139 runs; India won with two wickets and half an hour to spare at Bombay; and rain ruined the last match at Eden Gardens. New Zealand, going the other way for their 1965 tour of England, played three Tests and after three drawn games an Indian victory in the final match gave them the rubber.

The man who did most of the damage in that final Test against the Kiwis was the Tamil Nadu off-spinner Venkataraghavan. Venkat, who later played with Derbyshire, took eight for 72 and four for 80. He was one of a fine breed of spinners produced by India around this time. Bhagwat Chandrasekhar had already made his debut. Chandra bowled right-arm leg-spinners but threw left-handed, the legacy of a childhood attack of polio which left him with a withered right arm. Chandra and Venkat were joined by another great spinner when India played a three-match series against West Indies in India in 1966-7. Bishen Bedi, left-arm spinning Sikh who delighted crowds with a succession of coloured patkas, made his debut in the series which the West Indians won 2-1. Ajit Wadekar, a tall left-hander from Bombay, also made his debut at the start of a Test career which would see him score over 2,000 runs for India in thirty-seven Tests.

India now have to share English summers with other tourists and their 1967 three-match tour saw them lose the first two Tests heavily, despite making 510 in the second innings of the First Test. Bad weather and a crop of injuries ruined the summer for Pataudi's team and England, captained by Brian Close, were never stretched, although Geoff Boycott was disciplined and dropped after scoring 246 at Leeds. The problem was that his first hundred had taken 341 minutes! The Indian tour to Australia in 1967-8 was a disaster and all four Tests were lost, though India did make a gallant attempt to score 395 to win at Brisbane and lost by only 40 runs.

The visit to New Zealand brought better fortunes, India winning their first Tests outside the sub-continent and subsequently, their first series away from home, by 3-1. Graham Dowling's team underlined the improvement in New Zealand cricket by drawing the series in India in 1969-70; and Bill Lawry's Australians followed the Kiwis and won 3-1 after India had levelled the series at Delhi, thanks to some fine bowling from Prasanna and Bedi.

Wadekar's 1970-1 Caribbean tourists, though not fancied to do so, won the rubber 1-0 with four games drawn. Little Sunil Gavaskar, standing less than 5ft 5in tall, made his debut at Port-of-Spain and scored 65 and 67 not out as India beat West Indies for the first time. Gavaskar was already showing the form that would make him the most consistent opening batsman in the world. In his second match for India he scored 116; in his third he totalled 117; and in his fourth — the last Test at Port of Spain, he became the second batsman after Doug Walters to score a double century and a century in the same Test. His aggregate was 774 at an average of over 154, and that was a record for any batsman playing in his first rubber, and a record for any Indian, even though Gavaskar had missed the First Test.

Dilip Sardesai is brilliantly caught by Alan Knott on the final day of the Third Test at The Oval in 1971. India won the match by four wickets – their first win over England in England in twenty-two Tests. It ended England's record run by any country of twenty-six matches without defeat and gave India the rubber

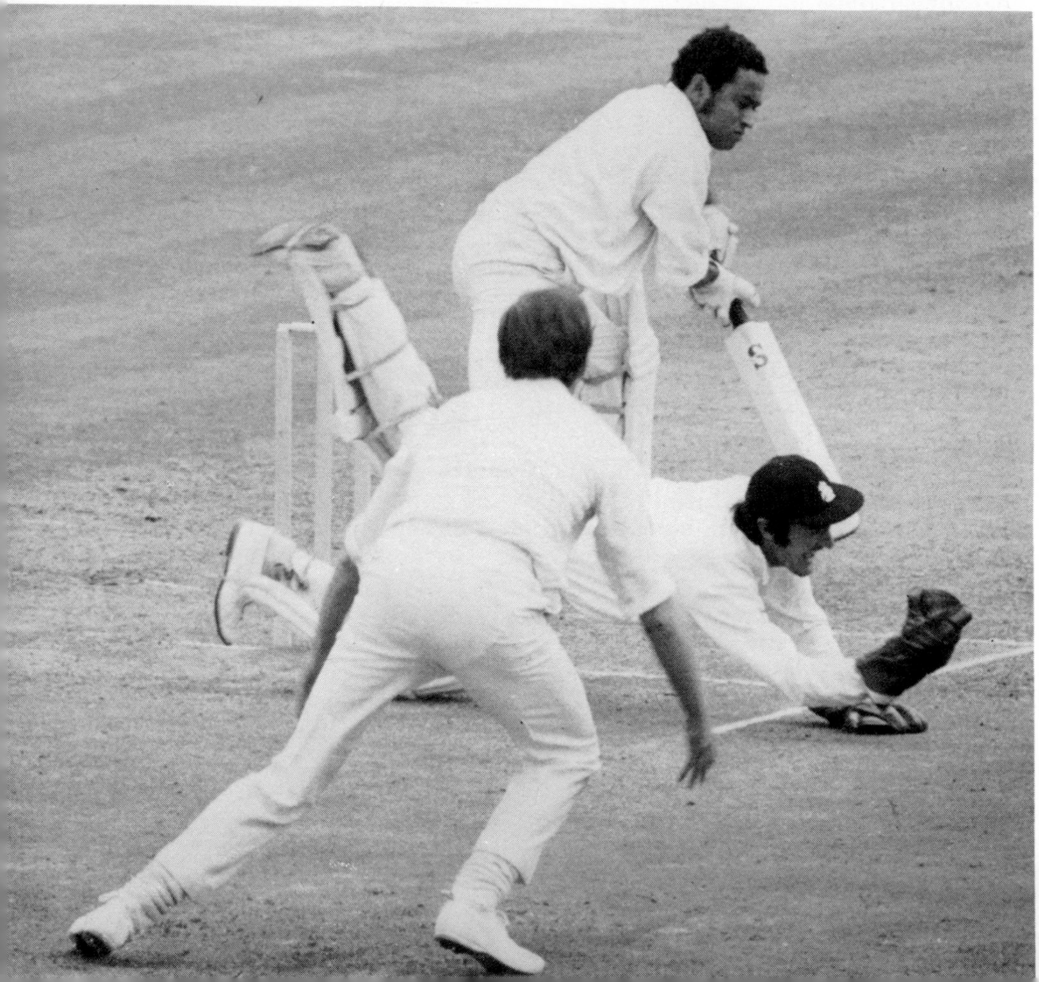

Ironically, Gavaskar failed to reproduce this form in the 1967 series against England — ironic because India won her first rubber in England. Indeed, only rain had saved England in the First Test when India, with two wickets in hand, were denied the chance to make 38 for victory in a Test in which John Snow was disciplined for apparently deliberately colliding with Gavaskar as the little Indian went for a quick single. Snow was omitted from the next Test when rain this time probably rescued India from defeat when they were 65 for three chasing 420 for victory. At The Oval, it was Chandra who bowled India to their first win in England. He took six for 38 as England were skittled for 101, leaving India to score 172 for victory. Gavaskar was out without scoring but the middle order took India almost there and when Abid Ali, the stocky all-rounder from Hyderabad, stroked Luckhurst to the boundary soon after lunch on the last day, Indian cricket was cockahoop. One of the batsmen who saw India close to their target was Gundappa Viswanath — 'Vishy' — who is the brother-in-law of Gavaskar. 'Vishy' had scored a century in his first Test, at Kanpur in November 1969 against Australia. He was to play in well over fifty Tests for India and yet this must have been his proudest moment. The thrilling, stylish little batsman from Mysore had taken part in one of India's greatest cricketing moments.

In 1972-3, India proved that their victory over England was no lucky accident. After England won the First Test in Delhi, India took the next two. Chandra, who had eight for 79 in England's first innings at Delhi, took nine in the Calcutta Test and when he bowled Bob Cottam in the first over after lunch on the fifth day at Eden Gardens, India levelled the series with victory by 28 runs. Six wickets from Chandra at Madras set up a second Indian win, this time by four wickets. Chandra took his 100th Test wicket in this match and he continued to torment England in the last two Tests, both of which were drawn. Chandra finished the rubber with thirty-five wickets, an Indian record, and there was no doubt that England had no answer to his wiles, nor indeed, to those of Bedi. Neither player could reproduce such consistent form in England in 1974; though Bedi did manage six wickets at Lord's they cost him 226 runs. England won the three-match rubber easily, thanks to some big scores from Keith Fletcher, John Edrich, Dennis Amiss, Mike Denness, and David Lloyd. England won the First Test by 113 runs, and the last two each by an innings.

In 1974-5, India fought back to 2-2 in the rubber with West Indies at home. All rested on the final match at Bombay where Farokh Engineer, that great Indian wicketkeeper-batsman from Bombay, was playing the last of his forty-six Tests which had seen him score 2,611 runs and take eighty-two dismissals behind the stumps. An aggressive late-order batsman who scored thirteen centuries in his first-class career, Engineer was a great favourite with Lancashire. Sadly, his last Test was not to be on the winning side as West Indies, with a double century from Clive Lloyd, trounced India by 201 runs to win the rubber. A series in New Zealand in 1975-6 was drawn; and so was a series in the West Indies which started a month later; and when New Zealand returned to India in 1976-7, India this time won 2-0.

Tony Greig's side which toured India in 1976-7 found things very different from their predecessors who had led tours to the sub-continent. Up until then England had won only four Tests in India, but Greig's side took the first three of this rubber to establish an unbeatable lead. The

Street cricket in Calcutta

route of India started in Delhi where Dennis Amiss reached his century with a 6 and went on to score 179, England's highest individual score in a Test in India. John Lever, the Essex left-arm seamer, made a splendid debut appearance with seven for 46 and three for 24 as England stormed to victory by an innings and 25 runs. For Sunil Gavaskar there was the consolation that during the match he became the first Indian to score 1,000 Test runs in a calendar year. At Calcutta it was Willis's turn to break down the Indian batting, and Greig's turn to write a new record. His 103 in England's ten-wickets win made him the first player to score 3,000 runs and take 100 wickets in Tests for England. At Madras England won their first rubber in India since 1933-4 and although Bedi had the satisfaction of becoming the first Indian to take 200 wickets in Tests for India, he was on the losing side when Underwood and Willis took the lion's share of the glory as India were dismissed for 83 in their second innings to lose by 200 runs. Bedi had more reason to smile at Bangalore where England's first four second-innings wickets fell for only 8 runs — two of them to Bedi — and India restored some pride by taking the match by 140 runs. Little Bedi had six for 71. With the last Test in Bombay drawn, India had stemmed the flow of England supremacy. They had still failed miserably overall, however, and never has an England team returned from India with such a comprehensive victory under their belts.

India's visit to Australia in 1977-8 also ended in a defeat — by 3-2 — but the important thing was that the Australian public, though tempted by Packer's World Series Cricket which had taken all Australia's Test team, still preferred the 'real thing'. Bobby Simpson, called out of retirement to lead his country's 'second eleven' steered them to a narrow 16-run win at Brisbane; a tight two-wicket victory at Perth; and a win by just 47 runs at Adelaide. India's wins, meanwhile, were of much bigger proportions —

by 222 runs at Melbourne, and by an innings and 2 runs at Sydney. Chandra took twelve wickets in the Melbourne game which included his 200th in Tests. When India fell short in the last Test, they did so only after scoring 445, the second-highest fourth innings total in Test cricket.

India had not met Pakistan for almost eighteen years, though the two countries had met twice on the battlefield since then. In 1978 relations had been restored to the point where another Test series could be arranged and India undertook an eight-week tour. They were met with a warmth which underlined that the renewal of Tests between India and Pakistan was long overdue, although the First Test at Faisalabad in October carried on where the others had left off, the drawn match being the thirteenth such result in consecutive Tests between the two sides. It was the pitch, not the players, which was to blame, however. The over-prepared state of the ground meant that there was no chance of a definite result in this, the first Test to be played at the Iqbal Stadium. Thereafter, the stronger Pakistan team took control and won the last two Tests. Gavaskar and Viswanath apart, India did not have the batsmen to compete with Pakistan's magnificent array of run makers. Against the young and inexperienced West Indians who came in 1978-9 minus many of the players who had opted for World Series Cricket it was a different story. India won the Third Test at Madras with three wickets and a day to spare. The other Tests were drawn and so India took the rubber, though their inability to beat the raw tourists more than once, served only to underline that India was not the power of previous days. The bowling of Ghavri and Venkat, the batting of Amarnath, Gavaskar and Viswanath, and the emergence of Kapil Dev as a fine all-rounder, were the bonuses of an otherwise uninspiring series.

It was Kapil Dev who dominated the first day of the Indians 1979 tour to England, scoring a brilliant century in seventy-four minutes at Northampton But the twenty-year-old from Haryana failed to come to terms with the England seam attack and it was his bowling which caught the eye in Tests. His fast-medium pacers captured sixteen wickets to leave him top

In the foreground a club match takes place on Bombay Gymkhana, where the first-ever Test between India and England in India was played. In background, other club cricketers perform on the Maidan

of the Indian bowling averages. It was a poor tour from India's viewpoint. In the Prudential Cup they even managed to lose to Sri Lanka, and won only one first-class match, against Glamorgan who failed to win a championship match that season. They lost the First Test after David Gower (200) and Boycott (155) gave England the impetus to reach 633 for five declared and Willis, Botham and Hendrick bowled the hosts to an innings win. With the last three Tests all drawn, India lost the rubber and again, only the batting of Gavaskar, Viswanath, and Vengsarker and Chauhan gave the Indians hope. For a variety of reasons their usual spin challenge was non-existent.

Australia's visit to India in 1979-80 was Australia's last rubber before settlement was reached between the authorities and World Series Cricket; and with it came India's first win in a series against the Australians. Six Tests brought two Indian victories and four draws against an Australian team short of touring experience and totally unused to Indian conditions. Kapil Dev continued his fine progress with twenty-eight wickets and Doshi, new to Test cricket but at the age of thirty-one having tremendous experience with Nottinghamshire and Warwickshire, took twenty-seven. For the first time in eleven years India took the field without any of their celebrated spinners Bedi, Chandra and Prasanna, while Venkat fell from favour after the first two Tests. Viswanath, Kirmani, Gavaskar, Yashpal Sharma, Chauhan and Vengsarker were all among the runs — all but Chauhan scored centuries in the Tests — and against a lethargic Australian pace attack in which even Hogg, after a record forty-one wickets against England could find no rhythm, India were never in difficulty.

After being together for the rubbers against England and Australia, the morale of the Indian players was high when Pakistan toured in the period immediately following the Australian visit. In contrast, Pakistan's morale was low with behind-the-scenes strife affecting them. They left their leading wicket-taker, Sarfraz, behind while India's Kapil Dev once more signalled his class with thirty-two victims in the rubber. Keeping a settled side throughout the series, India won 2-0 with four drawn; and that might have been 3-0, for they came close to winning the Second Test as well. This was a different Indian team to the one which was defeated by Pakistan twelve months earlier, and the penetration of Kapil Dev was perhaps the deciding factor.

At Bombay, in February 1980, India met England in a Test to mark the Golden Jubilee of the Board of Control for Cricket in India. England left India with little to celebrate in this particular match, however, winning by ten wickets with a day to spare. After their three-match defeat in Australia, England bounced right back and Bob Taylor, the brilliant Derbyshire wicketkeeper who has so often been cold-shouldered by the selectors, held ten catches in the match to set a new world record (which was promptly repaid by England dropping him). The Indians struggled to find any zest after sixteen Tests in the previous seven months, and collapsed to 149 all out in their second innings, Ian Botham following up a first innings six for 58 with seven for 48, and only Kapil Dev, with an unbeaten 45, stayed overlong. Indian showed little resolve in a match designed to celebrate so much fine Indian cricket that had gone before.

But overall, Indian cricket was riding relatively highly and the success was maintained in Australia in 1981 where they drew a series there for the first time. Australia won the First Test by an innings and 4 runs, and drew

Indian police show scant regard for spectators who came on to mob Sunil Gavaskar after he reached 150 against England at Bangalore in December 1981

the next at Adelaide where Sandip patel responded to being knocked out by a bouncer in the Sydney match by scoring a magnificent 174 at Adelaide Oval. At Melbourne, India needed a victory tosquare the rubber — and they achieved it in dramatic style. Australia took a first innings lead of 182 and when Lillee took another four wickets, they needed only 143 to secure what looked like being a comfortable victory. But the pitch was totally unreliable and after Doshi had broken through with two vital wickets — and did so bowling with a fractured instep — Kapil Dev, who had been unable to bowl in the early part of the innings, shook off the effects of a muscle strain in fire back with five wickets. Australia were bowled out for just 83 — their lowest since England dismissed them for 78 in the 1968 Lord's Test, and India were home by 59 runs for a historic win.

India went on to New Zealand where they lost a fascinating First Test at Wellington by 62 runs. The Kiwis margin of victory looked likely to be greater after they gained a first innings lead of 152, but the teenage left-arm spinner Ravi Shastri, playing in his first Test, followed up his first innings four for 54 with an extraordinary spell of three for 9. His three wickets came in four balls — all caught by Vengsarker, and New Zealand went from 100 for seven to 100 all out. Rain spoiled the Second Test at Christchurch, and the final match at Auckland was also drawn to give New Zealand their first series win over India.

England's visit to India in 1981-2 was threatened by the South African connections of Boycott and Cook. The tour finally got underway — and at its end there were many who wondered if it was worth all the fuss. Only in the opening Test in Bombay was there a definite result where India won by 138 runs at Bombay on the only pitch likely to achieve that. England felt that they were heading for victory on the fourth day; but Kapil Dev's five for 72 put the skids under them and India shot their visitors out for 102. After that, the pitches, the weather and some strange umpiring

India's 'Ian Botham' - Kapil Dev, the brilliant all-rounder who so excited English crowds in 1982

decisions ruled out any chance that England might have had of pulling back. In Madras, Viswanath (222) and Yashpal Sharma (140) battled throughout a whole day's play. Had England won the First Test, then perhaps the pitches would have been less docile than they eventually turned out.

England had a thoroughly adruous programme throughout in which there seems to have been hardly a day when they were not either playing or travelling. But, though it was obvious that Gavaskar would not let go his one-match lead, no matter what, it should be said that India were slightly the better side. They could look towards England later in the year with some confidence; as for England, shorn of their South African rebels, including Boycott who came home early from India once he had passed Gary Sobers's world record, they could only ponder their future, especially with a defence of the Ashes in 1982-3 to come. They could also reflect that Indian cricket had come a long way since the Parsees.

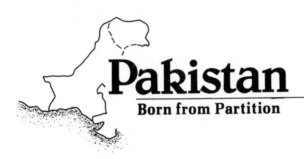

Pakistan

Born from Partition

Since World War II it seems that politics has interfered with cricket so often that in the 1980s we have seen the real prospect of Test match cricket being polarised into black and white camps. Happily, that danger is, for the moment, not so acute as it at one time seemed. But just as politics threatened the game over South Africa, so in 1947, another political act actually created a new Test-playing country. The partitioning of India and the birth of the state of Pakistan in August of that year gave us a new Test team. Left with Baluchistan, N.W. Frontier Province, the Sind, some fifty per cent of the Punjab and Eastern Bengal, an area which included two of India's former Test match grounds in Dacca and Karachi, the cricket fanatics of Pakistan set about building up the game in their new country.

When East Bengal became Bangladesh in 1971, Pakistan lost Dacca as a major centre of cricket. Karachi thus became the main centre and this was perhaps fitting since it was in that city that Pakistan enjoyed their first major triumph when they beat MCC in 1951-2. The heroes of that win were led by Abdul Kardar, the aggressive left-hander who had already played three Tests for India before partition and who would go on to captain Pakistan in her first twenty-three official Tests. A.H. Kardar played the innings which won the match for Pakistan while Khan Mohammad, the fast-medium opening bowler from Bahawalpur who later played with Somerset, took eight wickets in the match. It was a tremendously encouraging start for the infant nation and less than twelve months later they were getting ready to play their first official Test Match in Delhi at the start of a five-match rubber against India.

In October 1952, A.H. Kardar took to India a side which included just two players who had previously played Test cricket, himself and Amir Elahi, the bowler who had first toured with India in 1936; though his one appearance in a Test for India had not come about until their visit to Australia after the war. It was a side which relied upon fast-medium bowling. Pakistan's main strike bowlers were Fazal Mahmood and Mahmood Hussain, both of whom found plenty of work to do when Khan Mohammad, the third seamer, was injured early in the tour. Fazal was the Pakistani's great seamer of those early years. Before Partition he had played Ranji Trophy cricket with Northern India, making his first-class debut in 1943; afterwards he moved on to Punjab where he continued his long first-class career. Fazal, equally effective on matting or turf, kept up a steady length which batsmen found hard to get off the square, moved the ball through the air, and with an ability to cut the ball both ways, was the mainstay of Pakistan's opening attack. Mahmood Hussain of Karachi

Whites was faster than his opening partner, swinging the ball into the batsman but lacking Fazal's great consistency. The other players in the First Test at Delhi making their international debuts, included Hanif Mohammad, then just seventeen years old and yet to become the great cricket hero of Pakistan. From Bahawalpur, Hanif, one of four brothers, all of whom played cricket in brilliant style, was the baby of the side in 1952, a small, boyish opening batsman who was to one day score the highest innings in all first-class cricket. In the very first match of this tour, Hanif showed the way. Against North Zone he scored 121 and 109 not out; in the sixth match, against Bombay, he scorched to a brilliant unbeaten double century. A legend had been born. Hanif kept wicket in these historic Tests. Imtiaz Ahmed, who had played for Northern India in the Ranji Trophy at the age of sixteen, would take the gloves later. But he was foremost an aggressive batsman who delighted in pulling and hooking the fast bowlers. He and Hanif would be two of the rocks on which Pakistani Test cricket was built.

The First Test was staged at the Feroz Shah Kotla ground in Delhi, and for Pakistan it proved to be a tough baptism. India took all the honours, staging their first century partnership for the last wicket between Adhikari and Ghulam Ahmed, and totalling 372. It was a target well beyond the capabilities of Pakistan. Only Hanif, with 51 in the first innings, came to terms with the Indian attack and Mankad, with eight for 52 and five for 79, established new innings and match figures for India as they cruised to an innings win. Yet Pakistan had not long to wait for their first Test victory, for it came in the very next match on the jute matting of Lucknow which was staging its first Test. This time it was India's turn to struggle against the debutant Mahmood Hussain who, with Fazal, ripped through the Indian batting to shoot them out for 106. Fazal was in tremendous form with five wickets, Mahmood Hussain took three, and Pakistan began their reply with renewed confidence after their fall at Delhi. They passed the Indian score for the loss of only one wicket and when the last man fell, Pakistan had reached 331 and Nazar Mohammad had carried his bat for 124, scored in eight and a half hours.

Nazar's innings had been a supreme model of concentration from the man who began his first-class career with Northern India as a nineteen-year-old in 1940-1. The maker of Pakistan's first Test century, Nazar was now about to create another record. As India were bowled out for 182 in their second innings, leaving Pakistan with their first Test victory, by an innings and 43 runs, Nazar became the first man to have been on the field for an entire uninterrupted Test. It was Fazal who wrecked the Indians again. This time he had seven for 42, showing his immense liking for the matting pitch. It was a fine victory, even if India had been without Hazare and Mankad. But at Bombay in the Third Test, the rubber was decided. Pakiston had no answer to the veteran Amarnath. At one stage they were 60 for six and Amarnath had four of the victims. India's reply was 387 for four delcared, with centuries from Hazare and Umriger, and although Hanif scored 96 in Pakistan's second innings, India coasted to an easy ten-wickets victory. Mankad completed the fastest double of 1,000 runs and 100 wickets in Tests and India, now 2-1 ahead, drew the last two Tests to take the rubber, Kardar setting them a total of 97 runs in fifteen minutes to win the last game at Calcutta, a target not unnaturally declined. In the previous Test in Madras, which was affected by rain, Zulfiqar Ahmed and Amir Elahi added 104 for the last Pakistan wicket.

Pakistan may have lost their first Test rubber but, apart from England and Australia, they were still to make a better start in international cricket than any other country. They already had a victory over India; in 1954 they would beat England; and within seven years of playing their first Test would win rubbers against Australia, West Indies and New Zealand. Of course, they had one great advantage over other infant Test-playing nations. Many of their team had been playing first-class cricket for many seasons in the Ranji Trophy. West Indies had played them within two years of the state of Pakistan coming into being, pulling in some games during their official Test series in India; and Pakistan had toured Ceylon, after which they recorded that victory over MCC in Karachi.

All this experience, together with the rubber in India, meant that the Pakistani team to visit England for the first Tests between the two countries, was as strong a side as any which about to engage in only its second rubber. A.H. Kardar's side was a fine one and many think it is still the best to have visited England. Besides Kardar, two other former Indian Test players were Gul Mahomed and Amir Elahi. Fazal Mahmood, 'Pakistan's Alec Bedser', was still an outstanding bowler and he was backed up by Khan Mohammad. The brilliant Hanif, still barely a man, led the batting and Pakistan looked forward to a successful tour. Yet Hanif, who would go on to hold the records for the longest innings in first-class cricket — 970 minutes in scoring 337 against West Indies in 1957-8; the biggest first-class innings — 499 for Karachi against Bahawalpur in 1958-9 (he was run out going for his 500th run); and the world's slowest first-class century — in 525 minutes against MCC in 1955-6, did very little in the 1954 Tests. This little man with the amazing powers of concentration found himself out of place in the rain-interrupted rubber which started off in dismal fashion for Pakistan, though it was to end in a blaze of glory.

It was not until midway through the fourth afternoon that play could begin at Lord's in Pakistan's first Test against England. With the rain-affected pitch it was obvious that what little remained of the match would belong to the bowlers. Hutton won the toss, elected to field, and Brian Statham and Johnny Wardle had four wickets each as Pakistan slumped to 87 all out. When England batted, they fared only marginally better in the face of some hostile bowling from Khan Mohammad who clean bowled Hutton with his first ball. A gritty stand between Reg Simpson and Peter May eased things for England, but their lead was only 30 runs. Khan's five victims had all been clean bowled, and Fazal had four wickets. After Simpson and May had gone, only Evans and Laker reached double figures. Time was running out and when Pakistan began their reply, Hanif was obviously intent on survival rather than run-scoring. At the close, Pakistan had reached 121 for three with Hanif making 39 before Laker trapped him leg before. Hanif's 59 runs in this drawn Test had taken him 340 minutes.

At Trent Bridge England won with ease after Bob Appleyard broke down Pakistan's early order. They made only 157 and the match was won by an exhilarating stand between Compton and Simpson, and another between Compton and Bailey. Simpson made 101 in staying until 185 for three. Compton reached 200 in 245 minutes, 278 in 290 minutes, and with Trevor Bailey added 192 in 105 minutes. At 558 for six, Hutton declared and Pakistan, though reaching 272, still lost by an innings. It had been a memorable match for two bowlers making their Test debuts. Bob

Appleyard took the wicket of Hanif with his second ball in Test cricket and had seven in the match; Khalid Hassan, the little leg-spinner from the Punjab, became the youngest Test cricketer when at the age of sixteen years and 352 days he played in his only game for Pakistan. He took two for 116, including the wicket of Denis Compton, who he bowled when the Middlesex man was looking for quick runs for his third century, and was never selected again.

The Third Test at Old Trafford was drawn after rain prevented any play on three days, though there was time for the Glamorgan off-spinner, Jim McConnon, to take three for 19 on his Test debut as Pakistan slumped to 90 all out and were forced to follow-on in the face of England's 359 for eight declared. The tourists were in real trouble at 25 for four in their second innings when they were saved by the bell. Let off the hook at Old Trafford, Pakistan now went to The Oval needing victory to square the rubber. For the match at Surrey's HQ, England brought in two pace bowlers for their Test debuts, Peter Loader, the local hero, and Frank Tyson, the man from Northants who was to earn the nickname, 'Typhoon'. It was a thrilling match with Pakistan, having won the toss, losing wickets with regularity until they were dismissed for 133, Tyson claiming four victims, and Loader three, to give themselves more than satisfactory debuts. But when England batted, Fazal and Mahmood Hussain were also in destructive mood. Only Compton, who reached a deserved half-century, and May got to grips with these two, though Fazal eventually claimed both their wickets. England were three runs short of Pakistan's first innings total with Fazal (six for 53) and Mahmood (four for 58) in charge.

England's second innings bowling hero was Johnny Wardle. The Yorkshire spinner charmed out seven Pakistanis for 56 and England now needed 168 to win. At 109 for two they seemed well set. But there then followed a quite dramatic collapse. Fazal led the way with his second six-wickets analysis of the match and the last eight wickets fell for only 34 runs. Pakistan had beaten England by 24 runs to become the first side to win a Test in their first rubber in England. Fazal's match analysis was twelve for 99, his figure for the four Tests were twenty wickets at around 25 runs apiece, and in sixteen first-class games he had seventy-seven at just over 17 runs each. It was this 'Pakistani Bedser' who had done so much to lift the newcomers' fortunes and with a famous victory under their belts and the rubber drawn, Pakistan could look forward to their five-match rubber at home to India, starting in the New Year, with every confidence.

Pakistan's victory over an England side containing such illustrious names as Hutton, Simpson, May, Compton, Graveney, Evans, Wardle and Statham, and the up-and-coming Tyson and Loader, was a considerable achievement. But the 1954-5 series againstIndia proved to be a great anti-climax. The last two Tests between the countries had been drawn and there now followed a further ten drawn Tests before the series was allowed to lapse, the outbreak of war between the two countries in 1965 serving only to widen the gulf between the two combatants. The Tests of 1954-5 were of four days each, but one felt that if the sides had been allowed double that time, then they would still have failed to achieve a positive result. Pakistan's first official home Test, starting at Dacca on New Year's Day 1955, set the tone for what was to follow and only 710 runs were scored in four days, the run rate being something under two runs per over. At Bahawalpur, Lahore, Peshawar — where the run rate dropped to nearly one and a half per over — and in Karachi, the big yawn continued. These were two evenly-matched sides, Pakistan with their three pace bowlers, India with their spinners led by Fergie Gupte who took twenty-one wickets in the rubber, and both teams seemed fearful of chasing victory, lest it should end instead in defeat.

Later that year, Pakistan entertained New Zealand when the Kiwis visited the sub-continent. The tourists came to play three Tests in Pakistan and five in India. In the first of these matches, at Karachi in October 1955, Pakistan enjoyed their second win in a Test Match and breathed a welcome whiff of fresh air after the stale drawn series against the Indians. Pakistan won by an innings and one run and the deciding factor between these two sides meeting for the first time, was the spin of Zulfiqar Ahmed who took eleven wickets on the matting with his stock of off-breaks and the occasional leg-spinner. At Lahore Imtiaz scored Pakistan's first double century in what was their highest Test score so far — 561 — and Waqar Hassan aided him with 189. Pakistan took the series by four wickets with less than twenty minutes to play.

On the turf of Lahore's Bagh-i-Jinnah ground, New Zealand had fared much better with two scores in excess of 300, though Pakistan's massive total meant that they still had the whip-hand. Imtiaz, who had taken eighty wicketkeeping victims on the England tour the previous year, had the highest score ever made by a wicketkeeper in Tests and with Waqar he raised Pakistan from 111 for six to 419 for seven and an unassailable position. At Dacca, persistent fine rain found the matting pitch in an impossible condition for the New Zealanders who had first use of it and were bowled out for only 70. Khan Mohammad claimed six Kiwis, though the humid atmosphere was as much to blame as the pitch for New Zealand's dramatic fall. With only three out of five days fit for play, New Zealand were able to hang on at 69 for six in their second innings, needing 56 more runs to avoid an innings defeat. They moved on to India while Pakistan rejoiced at their first overall win in a rubber.

Pakistan cricket was growing in stature and in October 1956, Ian Johnson's Australia played the first official Test between the two countries en route for a three-Test rubber in India. Australia were on their way home after an unsuccessful tour of England where they had been baffled and bemused by Jim Laker. The only Test of their visit to Pakistan was scheduled for Karachi and on the first day, when Australia were bowled out for 80 on matting, the two sides contrived to establish a new record for Test cricket — only 95 runs scored in a day. Yet it was a fascinating day's play. Fazal was in tremendous form with six for 26 to completely bemuse the Australians. Before the close Pakistan had lost two wickets for 15 with Hanif falling to Miller for a duck. Wazir Mohammad and Kardar, both with 60s, lifted them to 199 and then Fazal struck again, this time with seven wickets, so that Pakistan needed only 69 to win. Yet though they had 160 minutes of the fourth day to get them, they fell six runs short. Hanif had fallen to Davidson and Alimuddin and Gul Mohomed scratched painfully towards the total. With the following day one of mourning on the anniversary of the death of a former Pakistan Prime Minister, the final runs were not struck until two days later.

After beating England, India, Australia and New Zealand, Pakistan now had only to meet the West Indies, although of course apartheid ruled out any meeting with South Africa. The West Indies were finally challenged in 1957-8 and although Pakistan lost the series in the Caribbean by 3-1, it was a rubber full of incident and which ended with a Pakistani victory. The first meeting between Pakistan and West Indies took place in Bridgetown in January 1958. For the match, Pakistan, still captained by A.H. Kardar, brought in Nasim-ul-Ghani, the left-handed batsman and slow left-arm bowler from Karachi who, at sixteen years and 248 days old, became the youngest Test cricketer. Nasim was in for a baptism of fire, though he had been used to bowling long spells, having bowled seventy-nine overs and taken three for 184 on his first-class debut for Karachi Blues against Karachi Whites at the age of fifteen. This time he was restricted to just fourteen overs (and took none for 51) in the face of a fierce onslaught from West Indies who totalled 579 for nine before Alexander declared. Weekes (197) and Hunte (142) had sent the Pakistani bowling crashing to all parts of the Kensington Oval. Then Gilchrist led the way with four wickets and Pakistani were soon following on 473 runs behind. If ever they had needed the immense powers of concentration shown by Hanif, it was now, and how splendidly he responded. Hanif stayed for sixteen hours and ten minutes in making 337 and steering Pakistan out of troubled waters.

The next three Tests went to West Indies, and at Sabina Park, Sobers created a new world Test record with 365 (see the West Indian chapter of this book). But Pakistan had managed to beat all their other opponents during their initial rubbers, and this trip was no exception. At Port of Spain they triumphed by an innings and one run. The pace of Fazal (six for 83) in the first innings, and the spin of Nasim (six for 67) in the second, did the damage while Wazir Mohammad led the batsmen to a total of 496, his own contribution being 189. Wazir, eldest of the Test-playing Mohammad brothers, had enjoyed a fine tour with 850 runs (average 70.83) in all first-class matches. Though beaten in the rubber, Pakistan had once again shown that they were a match for anyone.

The West Indians first visit to Pakistan ended in defeat for the tourists by 2-1 after a cock-a-hoop Caribbean side had won 3-0 in India. They found the brilliant Fazal too much for them and in the first innings of the Second Test at Dacca, the last six West Indian batsmen failed to score in falling to the combined skills of Fazal and Nasim. In three Tests Fazal took twenty-one wickets. How different from the Kingston Test of 1958 when his two wickets had cost 247 runs off eighty-five overs!

Pakistan cricket was still moving along very nicely at the top level and after the 1958-9 visit by the West Indians, they faced a stern Test when Australia returned for their second visit. The only Test played between the sides up until then had resulted in a Pakistan victory against a tired and largely demoralised Australian eleven. Now they came fresh at the start of their tour of the sub-continent. It showed from the first ball that was bowled and although rain prevented the grass pitch from being used in the First Test at Dacca, Australia had no fears of the matting this time. Fazal failed to trouble them in the way in which he had in 1956-7. Even though he took five wickets in the Australians' first innings, they were well in charge and won their first Test against Pakistan by eight wickets.

The Second Test was the first to be staged on grass at the new Lahore Stadium and Australia went 2-0 ahead in the series, scoring 122 runs to win at more than a run a minute. The final Test at Karachi was drawn after Pakistan managed only 104 for five on the fourth day — on the same ground where the two sides had conducted the slowest day's play in Test

India's Contractor tosses the coin while Fazal Mahmood awaits the outcome. The result of this match - and all the others in this 1960-1 series - was a draw, thus extending the indecisions which littered Pakistan-India cricket

cricket three years earlier. This was the second-slowest and it came in a match which marked the start of a distinguished Pakistan Test career. Intikhab Alam, leg-spin and googly bowler and aggressive middle order batsman from Karachi, took a wicket with his first ball in Test cricket. Aged barely nineteen 'Inti' already showed much of the skill which would earn him nearly fifty Pakistan Test caps and a fine career with Surrey in the County Championship.

In 1960-1 Pakistan went to play another boring rubber in India and extended the run of drawn Tests between the two unhappy neighbours to twelve matches. Kardar's reign as skipper had ended after the visit to the West Indies in 1957-8 and Fazal had taken over. In India, however, Fazal, despite taking five for 26 in the Third Test when India were shot out for 180 — the only time in the series when they failed to reach at least 400 — he was but a pale shadow of his former self. But with Hanif in such good form — and batting which also boasted Javed Burki, the Oxford Blue from Karchi, and Saeed Ahmed, Lahore's attractive stroke-maker — as soon as Pakistan had won the toss, which they did in four of the five Tests, the result was always going to be a draw. Hanif and Saeed put on a Pakistan record second-wicket score of 246 in the First Test in Bombay before India replied with 449 for nine declared; at Kanpur, India did not complete their first innings until just before lunch on the fifth day; in Calcutta, rain interfered with play; and in Madras, after Hanif and Imtiaz had opened with a record 161, India responded to Pakistan's declaration of 448 for eight, with 539 for nine.

Only in the last Test in Delhi did a result look remotely possible. Here, Pakistan had to follow-on and only a last-wicket stand between Mamhood Hussain and Mohammad Farooq, which raised 38, saved the day. If they had lost the last wicket without addition to the score of 212 for nine, then India would have needed only 36 to win. Instead they needed 74 and had time to make only 16 without loss. This thrilling finish was in direct contrast to what had gone before and no one in cricket shed any tears when the series was allowed to lapse for almost two decades. The sort of matches which had been served up by Pakistan and India had done cricket no good at all.

Pakistan's dour battled against the Indians had brought little positive cricket, but when England came to play a three-match rubber in 1961-2, the first meeting between the two sides since 1954 brought a result in England's first Test in Pakistan since Partition. Imtiaz won the toss at Lahore Stadium and batted first when the historic game started on 21 October 1961. The England side was led by Ted Dexter and during the early stages, all the success seemed to swing England's way. Dexter's side included three players making their Test debuts — Middlesex batsman Eric Russell, and two seamers, 'Butch' White of Hampshire and Alan Brown of Kent. It was White who triumphed most and in his second over he had Imtiaz caught behind. In White's next over, Hanif was clean bowled and Pakistan were 24 for two. White's immediate reign of terror was not to last, however, and Saeed Ahmed and Javed Burki steered Pakistan to 162 before Saeed fell to Bob Barber. Burki went on to 138 and with Mushtaq Mohammad, another of the famous brothers, joining Saeed in the 70s, Pakistan could declare at 387 for nine.

England's reply was fashioned in similar vein — two wickets down for 21 before Ken Barrington took charge to score a fine 139 and, with Mike Smith run out one run short of his century, England were all out just seven runs behind. Pakistan could manage only 200 in their second innings and though England again had shocks at 17 for two, sound batting by Richardson, Smith, Dexter and Barber saw them through to a five-wickets win. The first official Test between England and Pakistan in Pakistan had been an entertaining match and England now moved on to a five-Test rubber against India before picking up the rest of this inaugural series in Pakistan. When they returned for the Second Test at Dacca three months later, England had lost their first rubber to India. They were in no mood to surrender the series to Pakistan, however, and two dull draws ensured their overall victory. In the first of these Hanif batted for nearly

Mushtaq Mohammad became the first Pakistani player to score more than 25,000 first-class runs. The most versatile of the famous brotherhood, his fluent batting and leg spin bowling was a mainstay of the Test team

900 minutes in the match in becoming the first Pakistani to score centuries in each innings of the same Test, Burki and England's Geoff Pullar joining him with centuries. At Karachi, the game was even duller. Ted Dexter's double century in England's 507 ensured no slips and the safety-first match ground to another stalemate.

After drawing their first series in England and losing the first in their own country by 1-0, Pakistan returned to England in 1962, hopeful of doing well. But their side was now a young combination, inexperienced in foreign conditions and their batsman had been used to playing only on the lifeless turf pitches of their homeland which had taken the place of matting. Under new conditions, and facing seamers like Trueman, Statham and Len Coldwell of Worcestershire, Pakistan's batting was no match for England. They lost four Tests — and would have lost them all had the weather not saved them in the Fourth Test at Trent Bridge. England started the rubber in tremendous style, scoring 544 for five declared at Edgbaston where Cowdrey and Parfitt both hammered centuries. The Pakistanis had no answer and lost by an innings and 24 runs; at Lord's, Coldwell made his debut and took six second innings wickets — Trueman had six in the first innings and took his 200th Test wicket — and with Graveney in century-making form, even brave innings from Burki and Nasim-ul-Ghani, who both scored hundreds in Pakistan's second innings, could not save them from a nine-wickets England win.

At Headingley the pattern was the same — England making over 400 with Parfitt hitting a century, and then bowling out Pakistan twice to win by an innings. Graveney and Parfitt made centuries when the Nottingham match finally got underway, and again Pakistan found themselves following-on before the game was ended with them only 13 runs ahead with six wickets down. At The Oval, England's batsmen were again in match-winning form. Cowdrey (182) and Dexter (172) piled up most of the 480 runs they scored before Dexter declared with five wickets down; then Northants' giant pace bowler, David Larter, took nine wickets as Pakistan went down again. This time a brave 98 from Imitiaz, and 72 from Mushtaq, saved their faces a little, though England still won by ten wickets. In every department of the game they had been outplayed on this tour. While Parfitt and Graveney both averaged over 100, and Dexter and Cowdrey 80s, there was not one Pakistan batsman who could boast an average anywhere near them; and the tourists bowlers all averaged over 30 runs per wicket in the Tests. From the triumphs of earlier matches, this transitional Pakistan side was now tasting the bitter end of Test cricket.

There was now a period of readjustment in Pakistan international cricket and when the time came to play another series of Tests, against Australia and New Zealand in four separate 'mini' series over 1964-5, new players had come into the side. Australia, on their way home from England, played one Test at Karachi following their three-Test rubber in India, and it was this match which re-established Pakistan as a growing force in the game. Though this solitary Test was drawn, it did not find Pakistan wanting. Khalid Ibadulla, known to all Warwickshire fans as 'Billy', had toured India in 1952-3 without playing in a Test. When he eventually made his debut against Australia in October 1964, he did so with a record-equalling score. Ibadulla, who played with Lahore, became the first Pakistani to score a century on his Test debut, his 166 equalling the highest scored then made by a Pakistani against Australia. With his partner Abdul Kadir, the Karachi wicketkeeper, he put on 249 for the first wicket before Kadir was run out for 95. It was a record for any Pakistani wicket and set them well on the way to a 400-plus score. Australia were eventually set 342 in 290 minutes and Bobby Simpson led the way with his second century of the match before stumps were drawn at 227 for two. Though a Pakistan win was never on the cards, they had done more than enough to show the world that they were on their way back. Within five weeks, Pakistan met the Australians again, this time in Melbourne. Again the match was drawn with Hanif, who skippered Pakistan in their first Test in Australia, top-scoring in both innings with 104 and 93.

This was the only Test of a short visit to Australia, and Pakistan now moved on to New Zealand where they were to stay for eight weeks. Three Tests were played but they were all drawn. The cricket was dull to say the least and in the face of three excellent pace bowlers, Dick Motz, Richard Collinge and Frank Cameron, Pakistan were in no mood to take chances with Hanif particularly disappointing. Six weeks later, however, New Zealand paid their second visit to Pakistan after a tour of India and found the home country in more positive mood. Pakistan won the First Test at Rawalpindi by an innings after some fine bowling from Pervez Sajjad, the left-arm unorthodox spinner from Pakistan International Airways who had taken twelve wickets in New Zealand. Hanif made 203 in the drawn Second Test at Lahore; and in the final match at Karachi, Mohammad Ilyas, also of PIA, scored 126 as Pakistan scored 205 at a run-a-minute to win the Test and the rubber with eight wickets to spare.

This Pakistani side had a more positive look about it. Hanif was still there, now firmly in charge of the team, and Burki, Saeed Ahmed and Mushtaq were international-class all-rounders as were Asif Iqbal and Majid Khan. Asif, fleet-footed and stylish batsman and solid seam bowler, and Majid, aggressive batsmen and a man who was a natural enough bowler to both open the Pakistan attack and, later in his career, bowl off-spinners, were, with Saeed and Mushtaq, ensuring that Pakistan had plenty of variety in both batting and bowling without either department in favour of the other. These gifted players, along with Ibadulla, Intikhab and new wicketkeeper, Wasim Bari of PIA, came to England for a three-match rubber in 1967, following a visit of similar length by the Indians. Yet until the last Test we had little sight of the exciting cricket which we knew they could play. At Lord's, Hanif, scored 187 in 542 minutes, and when Pakistan were set 257 runs for victory in 210 minutes, they scored only 88 before play was given up after 165 minutes.

At Trent Bridge, Pakistan had the misfortune to be caught on a pitch made difficult by a thunderstorm which broke over Nottingham on the first day. They made 140 and although Ken Barrington found things much easier when England batted, scoring an unbeaten 109 in 409 minutes, Pakistan found Underwood in deadly form. He took five for 52 and Boycott and Cowdrey had no difficulty in scoring three runs for an England win. At The Oval, matters got even worse for Pakistan. Geoff Arnold led the way to bowl them out for 216, and after Barrington's third successive Test century helped England to 440, Ken Higgs and Derek Underwood struck to leave Pakistan reeling at 65 for eight with an innings defeat staring them in the face. A result on this third day seemed imminent but that was not accounting for Asif Iqbal. With Intikhab he added a world Test record of 190 for the ninth wicket, reaching his century in 139 minutes and finally falling for 146. Though England's win
 had only been delayed — they took the game by eight wickets on the

following evening, we had at last had a glimpse of the exhilarating cricket of which the Pakistanis were capable.

Politics, it seems, are never very far away from international cricket and England's team to Pakistan in 1968-9 faced a series played against a backcloth of political upheaval. It was apparent in the First Test at Lahore where England set Pakistan to get 323 runs in 295 minutes. They made 203 for five and the match was drawn, Tom Graveney handling the bowlers for the final innings after Cowdrey, who had earlier equalled Wally Hammond's England record of twenty-two Test centuries, was injured and unable to field. The match had been interrupted throughout by crowd invasions and although the dull Second Test at Dacca was incident-free — both on and off the field with only Basil D'Oliveira's brilliant unbeaten 114 standing out — the Third Test at Karachi was abandoned with England at 502 for seven in the first innings of the match. Poor Alan Knott needed only four runs for his first Test hundred when rioting spilled on to the playing area and the match was stopped there and then, thus marking a sad last Test for Colin Milburn. The rollicking Northants batsman who had flown in from Western Australia, scored a century. A few weeks later he lost his left eye as the result of a car smash near Northampton. A fine and entertaining career had ended in the shameful scenes of Karchi, but not before Milburn had marked what was to be his last Test with an innings of characteristic fire.

The future of Test cricket in Pakistan was now in doubt in the shadow of that country's political turmoil. Against all that, however, they managed to stage the series against Graham Dowling's up-and-coming New Zealanders who called on the sub-continent en route from England. It was six months since England's tour had been curtailed and in the same Karachi Stadium, Hanif played his last Test for Pakistan. He had missed only two of their first fifty-seven official Tests and with him would go part of cricket history. Hanif's last appearance saw him score 22 and 35 and New Zealand were set to score 230 runs in 195 minutes. They reached 112 for five on a pitch which had taken spin since the start. At Lahore, Pakistan lost to New Zealand for the first time, going down by five wickets in spite of Pervez's match analysis of nine for 112; at Dacca, New Zealand sealed their first victory in a Test rubber after forty years when rioting reared its ugly head again. Pakistan needed 184 in 150 minutes. They were 51 for four when bad light stopped play and when the crowds spilled on once more, the match was left drawn with more than an hour to play.

Pakistan, racked with internal problems and having lost their previous rubber to New Zealand, came to England in 1971 looking hardly likely to test England to any great degree. Yet in the First Test at Edgbaston, they kept their opponents on the field for more than two days as they piled up 608 runs before Intikhab declared with seven wickets down. England had enjoyed an early success when they took a wicket at 68, Aftab already having retired hurt after the third ball of the innings from Derbyshire's Alan Ward struck him on the head. Yet after the fall of Sadiq's wicket at 68, England were not to taste success again until Pakistan had ground to 359. The men who piled on those runs were Zaheer Abbas and Mushtaq Mohammad. Zaheer, bespectacled genius of a batsman who made his first-class debut with Karachi Whites, marched on to 274 in nine hours and ten minutes of what was only his second Test. Mushtaq scored 100, Asif an unbeaten 104, and Pakistan eventually delcared with the match beyond England's recall. England followed-on, over 250 behind, and were 229 for five at the close of the match, the last day of which had lost almost all to bad light and rain. Asif Masood, the right-arm medium-pacer from Lahore who did a 'double shuffle' before starting his run proper, swung the ball about to take nine wickets in the match and underline that the sub-continent can still produce seamers to trouble the world's best.

Rain ensured that the Lord's match was also a draw and the sides moved to Leeds for the deciding match. Here there was an exciting match in prospect after Geoff Boycott, with 112, led England to 316. Pakistan took a lead of 34 runs and then Asif Masood, Saleem Altaf, another medium-pace seamer, and Intikhab bowled out England, leaving their side to score 231 for victory with more than a day to play. The target proved too much for them. Ray Illingworth's off-spinners did the early damage and when John Lever took the last three wickets in four balls, England were home by 25 runs. Pakistan had lost the rubber and yet they had played enough attractive cricket to justify at least a share of the spoils.

Pakistan's cricket was never smooth for long and when they visited Australia and New Zealand in 1972-3, they found further problems. In Australia they lost the rubber 3-0 and two players were sent home in a dressing-room conflict which threatened to rock the whole team. Ashley Mallett's eight for 59 at Adelaide sent them plunging to an innings defeat after Australia had totalled 585 with Ian Chappell falling just a boundary short of 200. At Melbourne, Pakistan scored their highest score in this series — 574 for eight declared — but still lost by 92 runs. Majid Khan, the fine all-rounder from Punjab, scored 158, and Sadiq made 137. But Australia also had their century-makers in Ian Redpath, Greg Chappell, Paul Sheahan and John Benaud. Two Australians made their debuts in the match — Jeff Thomson and Max Walker, and although Walker had five victims, Thomson would have to wait a little longer for his first wicket. At Sydney, Thomson did not play, but Walker more than justified his reselection. Pakistan needed only 159 to win — Walker took six for 15 and

Asif Iqbal, thrilling batsman, excellent seamer and brilliant fielder. A cavalier figure in Pakistan cricket

Wasim Raja, left-handed batsman and right-arm leg-spinner who topped the batting and bowling averages in West Indies in 1976-7

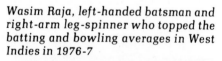

Pakistan fell 53 runs short of victory to be whitewashed in the rubber. They did better in the three-Test rubber in New Zealand where they won 1-0, taking the Second Test at Dunedin by an innings and 166 runs. Mustaq scored 201, Asif Iqbal 175, and against the spin of Intikhab (eleven wickets) and Mushtaq (seven) New Zealand collapsed to a humiliating defeat. There was consolation for the Kiwis at Auckland however where they faced 402 in the first innings and equalled it after the world record score for the last wicket was broken. Richard Collinge and Brian Hastings added 151 runs to take the record which had stood for almost seventy years.

Pakistan's tour of Australasia had been a gruelling affair, and so had England's five-match rubber in India. It showed when England went on to Pakistan and drew three Tests there. None of the matches produced any real excitement. Hyderabad staged its first Test — a boring draw which saw Pakistan score their highest total in a home Test against England — and at Karachi, various riots meant that some play was lost. Play was finally abandoned during a dust storm and with it disappeared another Test rubber on the sub-continent now seemingly renowned for long and tedious drawn matches, though England's visit to India had yielded three clear-cut decisions.

Pakistan's team to England in 1974 contained some familiar names in what was now a fairly settled side. Sadiq, Majid Khan, Mushtaq, Zaheer, Asif Iqbal, Intikhab, Imrån Khan, Wasim Bari, and Sarfraz Nawaz, the big fast-medium bowler whose career has been marked by several controversial incidents. Sarfraz has had his ups and downs with both Northamptonshire and Pakistan over the years, being released by the county for a spell in 1972, but he has always fired back and in the First Test of 1974, at Leeds, he not only took seven wickets in the match, but also shared in a tenth-wicket stand of 62 with Asif Masood. The match was evenly balanced with England needing 44 more runs to win with four

Sadiq Mohammad is the youngest of the brothers and a left-hander whose brilliance lived up to the family name

wickets in hand when rain ruled out any play on what should have been a fascinating last day. Rain again foiled England at Lord's where they needed 60 to win with all wickets in hand when the weather intervened. This time, perhaps justice was done, for Pakistan had been caught out by Derek Underwood (who took eight for 51) only after water had seeped through the covers. The final Test was again drawn, though this time it was the massive Pakistan total of 600 for seven declared, followed by England's 545, which ruled out a definite result. Zaheer was again in brilliant form, his incredible powers of concentration taking him to 240 in 545 minutes. England had Amiss, with 183, and Fletcher (122) to thank for their survival.

Pakistan's sequence of draws continued when West Indies, after their tour to India, made their first visit to Pakistan for sixteen years to play the first Test between the two countries since 1959. In the Second Test at Karachi, rioting again spoiled the match with so much time lost that West Indies had only twenty-five minutes in which to score the 175 they needed for victory. Though each side had its centurions, the greatest innings was surely that of Sadiq who scored 98 not out, despite being unable to turn his head because of injury. Again, however, Pakistan had taken part in a Test Match which had failed to produce a definite result.

Pakistan's very next Test brought them victory, however. New Zealand's tour of the sub-continent in 1976-7 began in Lahore and the home side won by six wickets after Javed Miandad (163) and Asif Iqbal (166) added 281 for the fifth wicket following a near sensational collapse to 55 for four. The partnership between Asif and Javed Miandad, the young man who was making his Test debut and who was embarking on a career as one of the most brilliant young batsmen of recent times, turned the scales. Miandad was finally out, caught by Richard Hadlee off the bowling of the young off-spinner from Otago, Peter Petherick, who went on to remove Wasim Raja and Intikhab in successive balls to become only the second man to the hat trick on his Test debut. But by the time Petherick achieved his remarkable feat, the damage was done and Pakistan coasted to a six-wickets win. The Second Test, at Hyderabad, was also won comfortably, so comfortably in fact that the runs which gave Pakistan a ten-wickets win were scored off the bowling of wicketkeeper Warren Lees with over a day to spare. Two wins gave Pakistan the rubber, but New Zealand were not to be defeated in all three Tests. At Karachi, the Third Test produced 1,585 runs, the most for any Test on the sub-continent. Javed Miandad continued his brilliant start to a Test career with a quite stunning 206 which included a century before lunch on the first day. With Mushtaq also in century form, Pakistan made 565 and, with New Zealand at 104 for five, looked set for another big win until Lees came in to score 152 and add 186 with Hadlee for the seventh wicket.

A win in this rubber gave Pakistan great confidence for their visit to Australia towards the end of the year. It was not misplaced and though Australia went 1-0 ahead in the Second Test at Melbourne, winning by a massive 348 runs after Pakistan's batting collapsed against Lillee (ten wickets in the match) and O'Keeffe (five), the tourists did not have to wait long for their first victory in Australia. It came at Sydney where fine bowling by Imran Khan, who had twelve for 165, and a century from Asif Iqbal gained them victory by eight wickets. Admittedly, Jeff Thomson had missed the last two Tests through injury, but Pakistan had still squared the rubber in fine style.

This was a busy time for Pakistan cricket. The following month they found themselves in the West Indies where, in the First Test, they came near to inflicting West Indies' first defeat at Bridgetown since 1934-5. At one Test each and one to play at Sabina Park, Pakistan lost the rubber. Indeed, throughout this series they had never come to terms with the West Indians' fearsome pace battery. They had rather less trouble in coping with England's attack on their visit to Pakistan in 1977-8. England played three Tests and in the first of them at Lahore, Mudassar Nazar, son of the former Test player Nazar Mohammad Mudassar, crawled to the slowest century in all first-class cricket. Mudassar took not the slightest chance against Willis, Old, Lever and company in making his hundred in 557 minutes. He was finally out eighteen minutes later for 114. Haroon Rashid also made a century and once Pakistan had made 407 for nine, at which point Wasim Bari declared, they were in no danger of losing. Wasim Bari, Pakistan's record-breaking wicketkeeper, leading his country for the first time, was in no mood to take chances and the game was naturally drawn. So was the Test at Hyderabad, although the scoring was a little better here and Haroon reached his century with his sixth hit for 6. The leg-spin and googlies of Abdul Qadir took six for 44 as England trailed by 84 runs, though Boycott's fifteenth hundred in Test cricket eased them to safety when they batted again. At Karachi, Pakistan and England achieved their eleventh successive draw in Pakistan. This time there were no big individual scores, just a succession of batsmen making useful totals on a pitch not at all helpful to any of the bowlers on show.

After almost eighteen years, hostilities on the cricket field were resumed with India when the Indians came to Pakistan in 1978. After a long run of draws, it was pleasing to see that positive cricket on the part of both skippers, helped by a fragile Indian batting side, led to two decisive results in the three Tests played. The over-prepared wicket at Faisalabad — the first Test to be played at the Iqbal Stadium — defeated everyone with scores of 503 for eight declared and 264 for four declared from Pakistan, and 462 for nine declared from India. But then Pakistan took the lead and never let go of their advantage. They bowled out India for 199 at Lahore to win by eight wickets, and completed a similar victory at Karachi by scoring 164 runs in less than 100 minutes, striking the winning run with seven balls to spare. The Pakistani batsmen had been magnificent throughout. Zaheer averaged 194.33 and scored an unbeaten 235 at Lahore; and Javed Miandad, with an average of 119 and a fine 154 not out in the First Test supported him well, while Sarfraz (seventeen wickets at 25) and Imran Khan (fourteen at 31.50) bowled exceptionally well. Not once in the series were Pakistan bowled out and they stood, at this point, far ahead of their oldest foes.

Earlier in the year, Pakistan played three Tests in England, losing two and drawing one. A few months earlier, on the lifeless wickets of their homeland, Pakistan had drawn three Tests with England. But in England they were dogged by rain and never played to their full potential. In the first two Tests they were beaten by an innings each time, though in the final Test they were in charge for much of the match which was again ruined by rain. The absence of their Packer men — Zaheer, Majid, Mushtaq, Asif Iqbal and Imran — made their problems worse in England than in Pakistan where the quintet were also missing. The Pakistanis' lack of match practice was largely to blame for such resounding defeats. Of the bowlers, Sarfraz finished top of the averages with five wickets at

10.20. The highest wicket-taker was Sikander Bakht with just seven. Of the batsmen, only Sadiq managed to score a half-century. As Old, Botham, Willis and Edmonds ripped through them, Pakistan's fortunes dipped starkly.

Pakistan's Australasian tour of 1978-9 began in New Zealand where they won the First Test at Christchurch by 128 runs. Thereafter, thanks to over-cautious tactics by Pakistan, the remaining Tests were drawn and the Test series duly won, though New Zealand could blame themselves for at least one expensive dropped catch in the rubber. Mushtaq proved to be a popular captain as far as his treatment of the small boys who followed the Test team about went — they were often allowed to join in practice — but his slow-scoring tactics and even slower over rates — less than ten runs an hour at one stage — left much to be desired. Javed Miandad, Majid, Wasim Bari, Asif and Zaheer were the leading batsmen; Wasim Raja, Mushtaq, Sikander Bakht and Imran the main bowlers with Sarfraz taking only eight wickets at 37 each. Nevertheless, he formed part of Pakistan's best pace attack for many years and the party flew to Australia for a short end-of-season tour involving two Tests. One Test was lost, one ended victoriously for Pakistan, and the form of all the players on the New Zealand part of the tour was maintained with Sarfraz firing back to take thirteen wickets at 24.76 each. In the First Test at Melbourne, Sarfraz took nine for 86 including a sensational seven for 1 spell, as Australia were bowled out for 310, leaving Pakistan the victors by 71 runs; at Perth, Pakistan lost by seven wickets, Hurst taking five for 94 in their second innings.

The Tests had been entertaining, but too often they were marred by bad sportsmanship. From the moment Asif Iqbal made derogatory comments about Australia — and England — on the eve of the First Test, bad-feeling overshadowed the cricket. At Melbourne, Miandad ran out Hogg after he had gone down to inspect the wicket; at Perth, Hurst ran out Sikander who was backing up; and in the same match, the non-striker, Hilditch, picked up the ball and helpfully tossed it back to Sarfraz, to be given out on appeal 'handled the ball'. Pakistan's sensational victory at Melbourne, and Australia's fine win at Perth were thus each spoiled by some petty behaviour which one would like to think is the perogative of infant school cricketers and not men representing their country at the highest level.

Bad temper by the Pakistanis continued in their tour to India which started in November 1979. This time they toured without Sarfraz and the whole trip was undertaken against a background of strife. This time it was India's morale which was high and they won the series 2-0 with four matches drawn. Umpiring was called into question by the Pakistanis — not without some justification let it be said — and during the Third Test in Bombay they accused the grounds authorities of 'doctoring' the pitch. An ill-tempered Fourth Test saw Sikander Bakht kick down the stumps after having an appeal turned down, and had it not been for the serious political implications of such a move, the tour might have been abandoned there and then. Twelve months earlier, India had been unable to bowl out Pakistan in three Tests; now they did so seven times in eleven innings and the tourists found themselves demoralised, bitter, and struggling for survival.

Amazingly, that was all to change when Australia started their tour the following February. Asif Iqbal announced his retirement from Test cricket and his place was taken by Javed Miandad who led Pakistan to victory in the First Test at Karadu by seven wickets in a match dominated by spinners. Greg Chappell elected to have first use of a turning pitch and Tauseef Ahmed (on his Test debut) and Iqbal Qasim bowled them out for 225. Pakistan managed 292 as Ray Bright took seven wickets; and then Qasim took seven for 49, Australia were all out for 140, and Pakistan scored 76 for three and victory. Rain washed out the first day of the Faisalabad Test and delayed the start of the second day by over an hour. With double centuries from Greg Chappell and Taslim Arif, an innings of 172 from Yallop, and a century from Javed Miandad, the game was not unnaturally drawn with Pakistan scoring 382 for two in reply to Australia's 617. The final Test realised 1,218 runs for the loss of only twenty-four wickets and Pakistan took the series. Majid had a Test average of 199, the sum total of his runs for once out in two innings, and more realistically, Taslim Arif averaged 102.23. In a series dominated by batsmen, Pakistan won the sole victory through the off-spin of Iqbal Qasim who finished with sixteen wickets, the largest haul of any Pakistani bowler.

When the West Indians came to Pakistan in 1980-1 they inflicted the Pakistanis' first defeat in a home Test since the New Zealanders in November 1969. The setback, the only definite result of the four-Test rubber, came in the second match played at Faisalabad where the Pakistan batsmen found the West Indians' pace attack too much for them. The West Indies themselves made only 235 and 242, falling largely to Nazir, Abdul Qadir and Iqbal Qasim (who took six for 89 in the second innings) but those relatively modest totals were enough. Clarke, Croft and Marshall shot the home side out for 176 and 145 to win by 156 runs. Only Javed Miandad, with a fine half-century, looked anything like comfortable against the hostile West Indies attack.

The First Test at Lahore lost one day and a draw there was inevitable, although Imran Khan, on his twenty-eighth birthday, scored his maiden Test hundred and became the second Pakistani, after Intikhab Alam, to do the double of 1,000 runs and 100 wickets in Tests. The Third Test at Karachi began sensationally when Pakistan lost two wickets for no runs and at one time were 14 for four before Javed Miandad came to their rescue with 60. Facing 128, West Indians were also struggling at 44 for five, but their saviour was Larry Gomes with 61. He added 99 with Murray. A low-scoring Test should have produced a result, but the combination of another day completely lost and some appallingly slow scoring destined this match to another draw. The final Test saw a new Test ground — Multan — and another drawn match. The only highlights worth recalling are a splendid 120 not out by Viv Richards, and some fine bowling by Imran who took five for 62. The fact that Sylvester Clarke responded to some oranges being thrown at him, by hurling a brick into the crowd and sending a spectator to hospital is best forgotten.

Australia beckoned the Pakistanis once more towards the end of 1981 for a three-match series which was to produce two heavy defeats for the tourists, one sensational victory, and yet another unsavoury incident. Javed Miandad's team were humiliated in the First Test at Perth in a match overshadowed by the disgraceful behaviour of Dennis Lillee. The details of the match are simple enough. On an over-watered WACA pitch, Javed put Australia in, no doubt in fear of Lillee as much as wanting his own bowlers to have first use of the pitch. His decision was justified on both counts. First, Imran, Sarfraz and Sikander bowled tremendously on the opening day, at the end of which Australia were 159 for seven, and an all out Australian total of 180 more than justified the decision. But when Pakistan batted there was total mayhem. In under twenty-two overs they were all out for 62, their lowest Test score. Lillee took five for 18, Alderman four for 36, and at one stage an appalling batting display left Pakistan at 25 for seven before Sarfraz got behind the line of the ball and showed his batsmen how to combat the threat. With the pitch now dried out, Australia began again with a lead of 118 and built that up with another 424 with a century from Hughes. When Pakistan batted again it was Jim Yardley's turn to create havoc. He took six for 84 and Pakistan were beaten by 286 runs.

The Lillee incident involved Pakistan's captain. Javed played Lillee wide of mid on and set off for what looked like an easy single. Lillee was in the middle of the pitch after following through and he quite deliberately stepped into Javed's path. The Pakistani not unnaturally barged 'through' him, for the ball was now in the fielder's hands, and made his ground. When the run was completed there followed some angry words and millions of television viewers saw Lillee lash out with his left foot and kick Javed on the back of the left knee as the Pakistani walked away from the argument. Javed turned, raised his bat as if to strike Lillee, and only the timely intervention of umpire Crafter and Greg Chappell prevented the incident from developing into a full-scale brawl. The resultant enquiry and 'sentences' are detailed in the Australian chapter of this book. The fact that Javed refused afterwards to shake Lillee's hand, or accept his apology, is a measure of how strongly the Pakistanis felt about this lamentable incident.

Pakistan made three changes from the side which lost at Perth for the Second Test at Melbourne, bringing in Zaheer Abbas, Ejaz Faqih, and Mohsin Khan to replace Iqbal Qasim, Mansoor and Riswan. But yet again

Zaheer Abbas made his name with an innings of 274 against England in 1971. Since then he has delighted English crowds playing both for Pakistan and for Gloucestershire. The vice-captain for Pakistan's 1982 England tour

their batting let them down disastrously. The pitch bore no resemblence to the quite awful track at Perth, but Pakistan wasted a golden opportunity to build up a commanding start. Only Zaheer passed 50, his 80 taking 157 minutes and belying his great feats for Gloucestershire in 1981, though in this match it was still a fine innings. Pakistan made 291, and then Greg Chappell took over. Dropped by Sarfraz off his bowling when on 87, Chappell went on to an otherwise chanceless double-hundred. He closed Australia's innings at 512 for nine to give his side a lead of 221. Mudasser and Mohsin took Pakistan to 64 before a storm broke and the ground was flooded, though the match resumed on time the following day. Within four hours, Pakistan were bowled out for 223 in an appalling display of batting. The conditions were not to blame, simply Pakistan's lack of application; Australia coasted to a ten-wickets win.

The final Test at Melbourne was altogether different. On a slow, dead pitch, Pakistan, now happily unbothered by Lillee who could work up no pace, ground on towards 500 before declaring with eight wickets down. There were no centurions but, Mohsin Khan apart, everyone got into the runs and Mudasser and Zaheer both scored 90s. Australia had a good start with Wood — who went on to 100 — and Laird putting on 75. But after Laird departed for 35, the wickets began to fall and an all out total of 293 meant that Australia followed-on. This time they made only 125, again the wickets were shared around, and Pakistan won the match by an innings and 82 runs, their biggest win over Australia. Both captains blamed the pitch — at the time of writing it is to be dug up — and to some extent the match was a lottery. But Australia had largely got themselves out. Pakistan found no devils lurking and their victory was a welcome fillip for the tour of England in 1982. Since its birth as a cricketing nation some thirty-five years ago, Pakistan has added immeasurably to the Test Match arena.

Sri Lanka

New Boys from the Resplendent Isle

The historic first-ever Test played by Sri Lanka at Colombo in February 1982. Sri Lanka and England line up for the camera

Cricket was first introduced into Ceylon, as Sri Lanka was then called, by British troops in the 1820s, to be further established by the tea and coffee planters of the Empire. The first recorded club was Colombo CC, founded in 1832, and, just as the Marylebone and Melbourne clubs became the leading authorities in England and Australia respectively, so the Colombo Club took on much of the early work in organising cricket in this lovely country. The Hon Ivo Bligh took the first English touring party there in 1882 and almost every Test team plying its way, before air journeys, between England and Australia called there. First-class cricketers like Gamini Goonesena (Notts and New South Wales), Laddie Outschoorn (Worcestershire), Clive Inman and Stanley Jayasinghe (Leicestershire) and J.D. Piachaud (Hampshire) have come out of Sri Lankan cricket to make their names. For many years the cricketers of Ceylon, or Sri Lanka, have campaigned to be admitted to full Test status and in the 1980s they had their wish.

On 17 February 1982 a Sri Lanka team met England at Colombo in the first full Test Match played by this island some half the size of England and home to 14 million people. The preamble to this great Sri Lankan occasion was a match between England and the Board President's XI where Geoff Cook, an uncomplaining tourist who spent weeks of inactivity in India, scored his second successive century to press hard for a Test appearance. The match was drawn and England moved from Kandy to the Sinhalese Sports Club in Colombo and two one-day internationals. The first, which Sri Lanka should have won, was taken by England who squeezed home five runs to spare; the second, which England should have won, was a triumph for Sri Lanka who won an even narrower victory by three runs, and then it was on to the P. Saravanamuttu Stadium and the real thing.

Geoff Cook duly won his first Test cap, along with eleven Sri Lankans, and after Bandula Warnapura won the first Test Match toss for his country, Sri Lanka batted on a pitch which had been over-watered the previous day. Before lunch, Sri Lanka slumped to 34 for four and wise heads nodded. This side was really not a Test standard combination. But then Arjuna Ranatunga, an eighteen-year-old schoolboy left-hander came to the wicket and proceeded to score 54 with a confidence which belied both his years and his extremely limited experience of any kind of first-class cricket. Ranatunga helped Rankan Madugalle to add 99 priceless runs for Sri Lanka's sixth wicket. The Test babes ended the day at 183 for eight and were all out the following morning for 218, of which Madugalle had scored 65. Underwood had five for 28 and England began their reply with Gooch and Cook. The pitch now drying out and taking varying degrees of spin, England found the going only marginally easier. It took a restrained 89 from David Gower, who added 80 with Keith Fletcher (45) after England were struggling at 40 for three, to bring England round and give them a slender first innings lead of just five runs.

Sri Lanka's second innings found them nicely poised at 152 for three by the end of the fourth day. Only two late wickets had given England even that indentation on the Sri Lankan innings and there were thoughts of a sensational win among some of the more optimistic Sri Lanka supporters whose pride had received a great boost. So far, their team had proved itself at least equal to England at full Test level. Dias made 77 before he was caught by Taylor off Underwood — Taylor also stumped him for good measure — and Warnapura stayed 185 minutes for 38. Even Wettimuny, though he made only 9, served Sri Lanka's cause well by staying at his crease for over an hour in the face of a fierce assault by Willis and Botham. But that was as far as Sri Lanka's glory went. The pitch was now taking spin at right angles and the following morning they crashed to 175 all out. John Emburery was the destroyer. Bowling round the wicket he had a spell of five for 5. The last seven Sri Lankan wickets fell for eight runs in forty-seven minutes and Emburey ended with six for 33. It was one of the most sensational batting collapses in Test cricket. England survived the early scare of losing Cook at 3 and Gooch, Tavare and Gower negotiated the pitch to take England to victory by seven wickets.

In March 1982 Sri Lanka played three more Test matches and registered her first Test century. The opponents were Pakistan and while several Pakistanis refused to play under the captaincy of Javed Miandad, Sri Lanka's fortunes were pleasing enough. At Karachi, as in their inaugural

'Percy', Sri Lanka's famous supporter, salutes Chris Tavare with the Sri Lanka national flag

Test, Sri Lanka stayed in contention for the first half of the match, scoring 344 in reply to Pakistan's 396 with almost all the batsmen contributing good scores, notably Sidath Wettimuny with 71. But when Pakistan set them 354 to win, Sri Lanka folded to defeat by 204 runs. At Faisalabad, Sri Lanka reached two milestones. First Wettimuny scored their first Test hundred — 157 — and Dias and Madagalle reached 90s to give Sri Lanka a first innings total of 454; then D.S. de Silva became the first Sri Lankan Test bowler to take five wickets in an innings. De Silva had four wickets in the first innings as Pakistan managed only 270 and did not pass the follow-on target until their last pair were at the wicket. Then Sri Lanka collapsed.

Their second innings wobbled dangerously and only a gutsy 56 from Goonatillake took them to a point where Mendis could declare at 154 for eight to set Pakistan 339 in 270 minutes plus twenty overs. At 137 for six Pakistan looked a beaten side until Ashraf, who made 58 in the first innings, again batted with great good sense and the match was drawn at 186 for seven. D.S. de Silva's match analysis was nine for 162. For the last Test at Lahore, Pakistan had their stars Zaheer, Majid Khan, Mudassar Nazar and Imran Khan back after Miandad agreed to step down as skipper of the party to tour England that summer. All four made significent contributions — Zaheer 134, Imran fourteen wickets, Majid 63, Mudasser 37 — and Sri Lanka were put firmly in their place, defeat by an innings and 102 runs coming by lunch on the fifth day after they mustered 158 runs in answer to Pakistan's first innings lead of 260. Test cricket's newest recruits now knew that they had much ground yet to cover.